Fiberglass Boat Repairs Illustrated

INTERNATIONAL MARINE / McGRAW-HILL
Camden, Maine · New York · Chicago ·
San Francisco · Lisbon · London · Madrid ·
Mexico City · Milan · New Delhi · San Juan ·
Seoul · Singapore · Sydney · Toronto

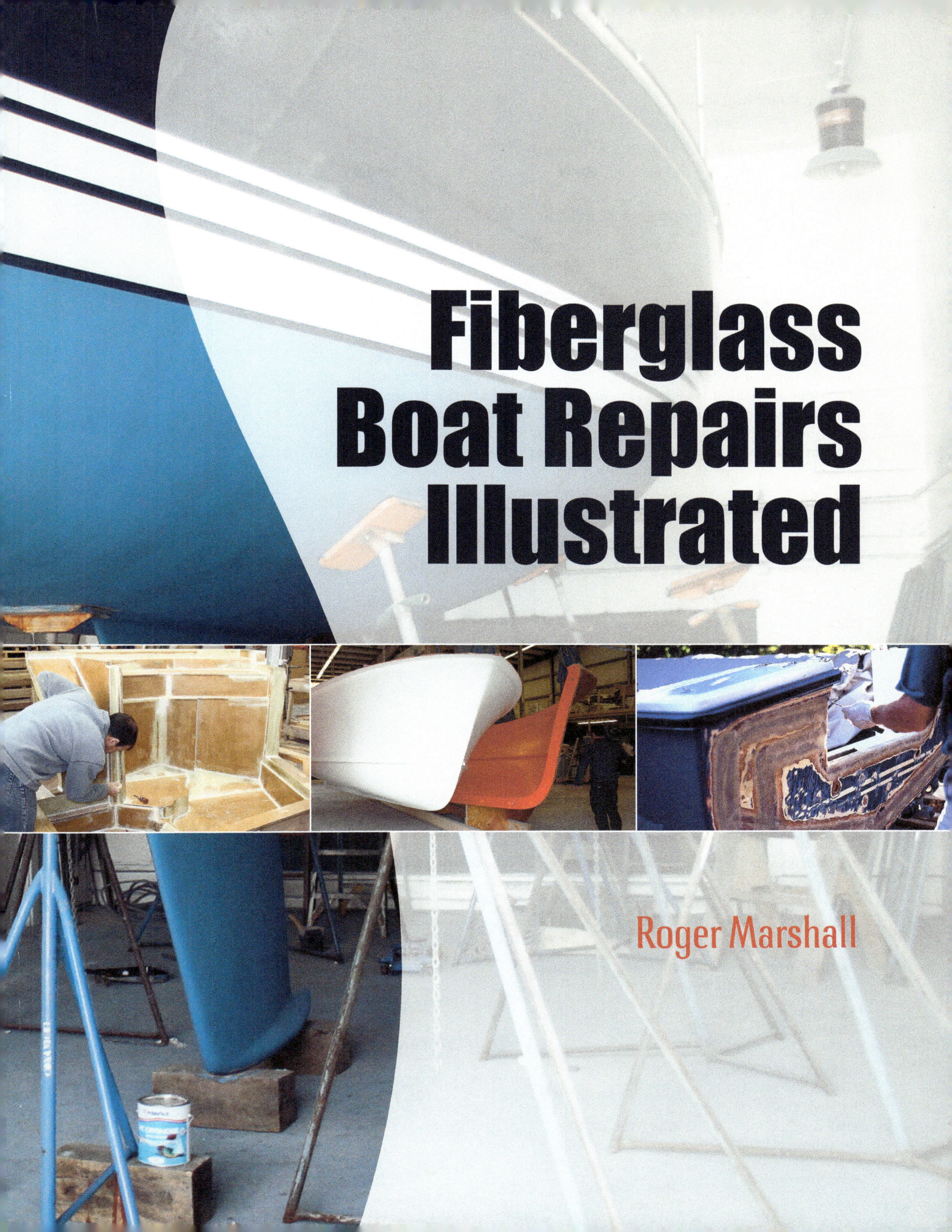

Also by Roger Marshall
All About Powerboats
The Complete Guide to Choosing a Cruising Sailboat
Designed to Cruise
Designed to Win
Rough Weather Seamanship for Sail and Power
Sail Better
Yacht Design Details

© 2010 by Roger Marshall
All rights reserved. The publisher takes no responsibility for the use of any of the materials or methods described in this book, nor for the products thereof. The name "International Marine" and the International Marine logo are trademarks of McGraw-Hill Education. Printed in the United States of America. Except as permitted under the United States Copyright Act of 1976, no part of this publication may be reproduced or distributed in any form or by any means, or stored in a database or retrieval system, without the prior written permission of the publisher.

12 13 14 15 16 17   QVS/QVS   22 21 20 19 18

ISBN 978-0-07-154992-9
MHID 0-07-154992-7
e-ISBN 0-07-154993-5

Library of Congress Cataloging-in-Publication Data

Marshall, Roger.
  Fiberglass boat repairs illustrated / Roger Marshall.
      viii, 184 p. : col. Ill. ; 28 cm.
Includes index.

ISBN 0-07-154992-7
e-ISBN 0-07-154993-5

Contents: How fiberglass boats are build—Identifying damage to a boat—Materials, tools, and basic techniques—Gelcoat restoration and cosmetic repairs—Minor structural repairs—Hull, keel and rudder fairing—Major repairs—Osmosis and blister—Finishing your repair work—Building a shelter.

  1. Fiberglass boats—Maintenance and repair—Handbooks, manuals, etc.

VM321 .M285 2010
623.8'458'0288
                                                            2010007022

Questions regarding the content of this book should
be addressed to www.internationalmarine.com

Questions regarding the ordering of this book should
be addressed to
McGraw-Hill Education
Customer Service Department
P.O. Box 547
Blacklick, OH 43004
Retail customers: 1-800-262-4729
Bookstores: 1-800-722-4726

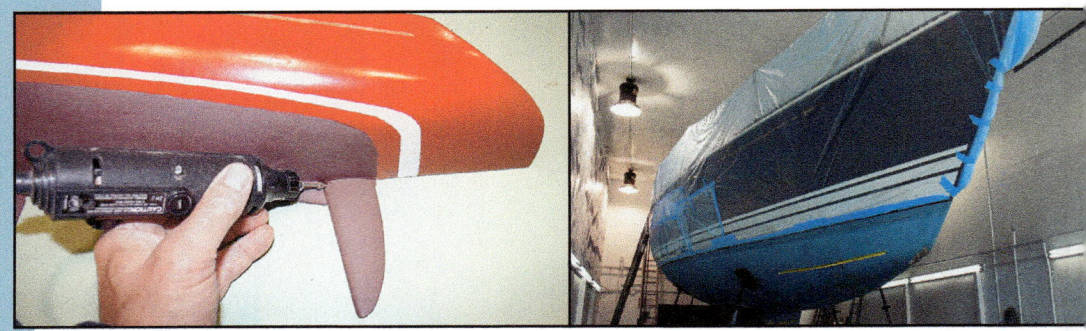

CONTENTS

Acknowledgments.. viii

Chapter 1   HOW FIBERGLASS BOATS ARE BUILT..1
Fiberglass Hulls.. 1
Hull Reinforcements.. 20
Hull Liners.. 22
Interior Furniture... 23
Deck Construction.. 25
Hull-to-Deck Joints... 27

Chapter 2   IDENTIFYING DAMAGE TO A BOAT.. 29
Hull Damage... 30
Deck Damage... 40
Rudder Damage... 43
Other Damage.. 44

Chapter 3   MATERIALS, TOOLS, AND BASIC TECHNIQUES........................ 46
Materials... 46
Tools.. 53
Basic Techniques... 62

Chapter 4   GELCOAT RESTORATION AND COSMETIC REPAIRS...................... 67
Gelcoat Restoration... 68
Gelcoat Repairs... 74

Chapter 5   MINOR STRUCTURAL REPAIRS.. 85
Before You Start Any Repair Work............................ 85
Repairs to a Single-Skin Laminate............................ 87
Repairs to a Cored Laminate................................. 93

	Repairing or Installing a Bulkhead.	97
	Reinforcing a Flat Panel	100
	Replacing Missing Parts	102
Chapter 6	**HULL, KEEL, AND RUDDER FAIRING**	**107**
	Fairing a Hull	107
	Fairing a Keel	112
	Fairing a Rudder	115
Chapter 7	**MAJOR REPAIRS**	**116**
	Project #1: Making an Engine-Well Guard to Keep Water Out	117
	Project #2: Replacing Rotten Floors.	119
	Project #3: Replacing a Water-Damaged Deck Core	123
	Project #4: Repairing a Rotten Transom	125
	Project #5: Repairing Major Grounding Damage	134
	Project #6: Replacing a Foredeck Hatch	140
	Project #7: Repairing Damage to a Cored Hull.	143
Chapter 8	**OSMOSIS AND BLISTER REPAIR**	**150**
	DIY Blister Repair.	150
	Professional Blister Repair	151
	Blistering Caused by Valiant's Fire-Retardant Resin	157
	Protecting against Osmosis	158
Chapter 9	**FINISHING YOUR REPAIR WORK**	**159**
	Safety	159
	Sanding.	160
	Painting	165
Appendix	**BUILDING A SHELTER**	**177**
	Index.	180

Acknowledgments

As usual with any technical book, many people have provided expertise on specific materials and projects, as well as ideas and thoughts. These folks deserve many thanks for their help, advice, and patience. One constant source of aid and advice is my wife Mary who patiently edited my disorganized paragraphs and made sure that the words meant exactly what they said. She also tolerated fiberglass parts, solvents, boats, paints, and other gear on the deck, the driveway, the garage, and wherever else I was working at the time. My sons, David and Michael, made a big contribution by finding boat projects for me to help with—no matter how overloaded I was with other work! Some of the boats shown in these pictures belong to them.

Outside my immediate family, Jan Mundy, Editor of *DIY-Boat Owner*, read the manuscript and not only offered many words of advice, but also enclosed articles and stories from her magazine to illustrate points that I may have missed or erred on. Besides Jan, Mo Mancinni and Mike Irving of Connanicut Marine Service, Jim Archibald and Xavier Martinez of Jamestown Boat Yard, and Steve Anderson of J & J Marine offered advice and technical help whenever I asked. And as you can see from the pictures, Jim Archibald offered more than just help, providing many of the images that illustrate Chapters 6 and 7.

Bob Donat and Jim Seidel of Interlux offered information on finishes and paints that produced stellar results on many of the projects. Thanks too to Jock West of JWI, and to Scot West of Ronstan for parts, images, and information that improved this book and upgraded several of the book's projects.

Finally, thanks to the many folks who have helped me judge the NMMA's Innovation Awards and the METS DAME awards in Holland over the years. Their questions and answers have improved this book immeasurably. In addition, seeing new products, fabrics, and fiberglass techniques, especially at the IBEX show where they are often on display, has helped formulate some of the background to this book. To all of you, thanks.

Chapter 1: HOW FIBERGLASS BOATS ARE BUILT

Before you can begin repairing or rebuilding a fiberglass boat, you need to understand how it is put together. Such knowledge will also tell you when a contemplated repair job is worth the time and money, and when it is likely to be so difficult or costly that you'd be better served to give up on the boat.

Consider, for example, a boat with a foam-cored hull that has been holed in a collision. You need to determine how to get to the back of the hole. This usually means cutting away the damaged section of the outer fiberglass skin, or *laminate*, pulling out the core around the hole, repairing or replacing the inner fiberglass skin, filling the area with new core material, and finally replacing the outer laminate. If you are not familiar with fiberglass composite construction, you could spend more time than the boat is worth just trying to get it apart.

This chapter's aim is to avoid such problems by familiarizing you with the materials and methods of fiberglass boat construction. Entire books have been written on this subject. Though this chapter is only an overview, it will provide sufficient background for the repairs a boatowner or small shop is likely to do.

FIBERGLASS HULLS

Just as a cotton sheet drapes over a mattress, a sheet of fiberglass material conforms to the shape of any object into which or over which it is draped. Only when resin is added to the fiberglass and allowed to cure does the fiberglass shape become fixed. But what does fiberglass get draped over or into to create the shape of a hull or any of the other parts that go into the construction of a boat? The answer, of course, is a mold.

A *mold* can be either female or male. The finished part fits inside a female mold or over the outside of a male mold, the choice depending upon whether the inside or outside surface of the part is intended to be the smooth, finished surface. Since the outside surface of a hull is the one we present to the world and want to have mirror-smooth, a fiberglass hull is usually laminated in a female mold. Most boats built today also have a smooth interior *liner*, which fits into the hull somewhat like a garbage bag fits inside a kitchen trash can, and into which the cabin or cockpit furniture is molded. This part, also known as a *pan* (see the Hull Liners section on page 22), is made in a separate fiberglass mold.

1

Fiberglass revolutionized boating in the postwar years by enabling multiple copies of a hull to be produced one after the other from a single mold. Since the mold has a highly polished interior surface, the hull comes out of the mold with smooth topsides that are then polished mirror-smooth. While the hull is still in the mold, its interior reinforcements and structures are installed. Its deck and its furniture and fittings are added as the boat moves down the production line. A successful fiberglass boat enjoys a production run of dozens, hundreds, or in a few cases even thousands of copies, depending on the boat's size and popularity.

Building a Mold

Clearly the hull mold is critical to the appearance and integrity of the finished hull. The method of building a hull mold has evolved over the decades of fiberglass boatbuilding, but the fundamentals have remained unchanged. The builder must first create a male *plug* of the same size and shape as the finished hull and then shape the female mold over that plug. The mold is then reinforced on the outside, removed from the plug, and polished on the inside to prepare it for the production run. Building a plug and a mold and all the other smaller parts for a production run may cost as much as or more than building a single boat. The builder hopes to amortize the cost of the plug and mold over the production run of the model.

When a fiberglass boat is built on a custom, or *one-off*, basis, the plug and mold represent costly items that are used once only to be thrown away. To avoid the need for a mold, custom fiberglass builders almost always laminate the hull over a male plug or forms. This necessitates laborious fairing and polishing of the hull's exterior surface, however. Alternatively, a one-off large powerboat may be made in a female mold that is built from plywood and does not require building a plug. Fiberglass is laid up inside the mold and polished to a high sheen, and the boat's hull is then laminated in this.

Almost all production runs begin with both a plug and a mold, however. The photos that follow show the building of the plug and mold for one of my designs, the 24-foot Avid powerboat. Construction details vary from one mold to the next, but this one is representative.

(1) *The plug for the 24-foot Avid under construction. The first step in making the plug is to set up the station frames. These frames are cut to the shape of the hull but are smaller than the full-sized boat by the thickness of the plug's longitudinal framing and skin laminate. (The Avid 24 was designed by the author.)*

Building a Mold

(2) Once the frames are covered with longitudinals, the shape of the hull is clearly defined. Notice how the framing is altered around the bow area to suit the pronounced changes in curvature there.

(3) Strips of wood laminate are laid down over the longitudinals with irregular gaps between the strips. A router is then used to make each gap a consistent 2 inches (50 mm) wide. Then 2-inch-wide strips (the lighter-colored strips) are laid into each gap to make the surface fair.

(4) The plug is epoxied to stabilize the wood and prepare it for a finish coat of high-build primer. The epoxy brightens the wood, highlighting the striping effect.

(5) A first coat of high-build primer is applied to the plug, turning it gray. This and successive coats will be sanded smooth to get a good finish.

4 • HOW FIBERGLASS BOATS ARE BUILT

Building a Mold

(6) When the hull plug is completely smooth, the spray rail, quarter rails, and a cove stripe are added. The flange at the bottom of the image (i.e., what will be the hull's sheerline) is for the deck mold to be fitted to the boat. The joint will be covered with a rubrail when the boat is built.

(8) This is a two-part mold because of the boat's tumblehome. The mold has been split apart, and the boat will be craned out ready to be fitted out with the cockpit and interior. A bow-to-stern flange is set up along the plug's fore-and-aft centerline to divide the two halves of what will be a two-part hull mold. This permits the two mold halves to be pulled sideways off the plug (rather than having to be lifted vertically off the plug, as would need to be done with a one-part mold) and then be mated along the flange. This is useful when overhead space is limited, and also when a boat has tumblehome in its topsides (as this boat does in its stern sections), which would prevent the hull from being removed from a single-piece mold.

(7) The hull plug after it has been turned upright and removed from the mold. Here the flange along the top is being worked on to ensure a tight hull/deck joint.

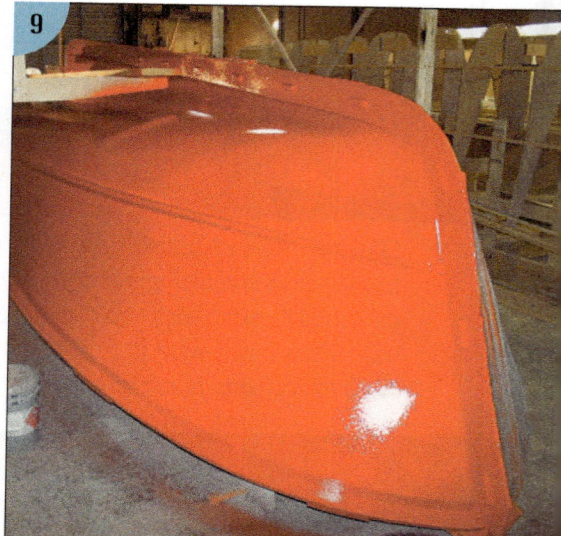

(9) The plug has been sprayed with red tooling gelcoat. This layer will be coated with mold release wax to allow the mold to peel away easily from the plug. The coats of resin and wax are thin enough not to change the shape of the plug. The plug will then be ready for constructing the hull mold.

Building a Mold • 5

(10) Here the hull mold is being formed over the plug. A layer of gelcoat thick enough to prevent print-through of the fiberglass cloth that will follow is first applied over the plug's mold release wax. The interior surface of the mold must be mirror-smooth, and the gelcoat ensures this. After the gelcoat sets, a thick layer of laminate is gradually built up. The mottled color visible here is a balsa core that is being added to the mold laminate to give it more stiffness.

(11) Still more stiffness is imparted to the mold by the cradle built over its exterior. Here the finished hull mold is standing upright in its cradle after the two halves of the mold have been joined along the centerline flange. The curved cradle rockers permit access to the mold interior from either side simply by tipping the mold over. This allows a hull to be laid up in the mold without workers having to walk around inside it. (All courtesy JWI)

6 • HOW FIBERGLASS BOATS ARE BUILT

A hull mold for a bigger boat, showing how it is reinforced on the outside to stiffen it so that it can be used many times.

Multiple coats of mold release wax are applied to a hull mold and buffed out, creating a highly polished surface for laminating the hull. (Courtesy Ranger Boats)

Molds for decks, cockpit tubs, and smaller parts are made in the same way, although usually most of the inside of a mold is reachable without having to use a ladder or staging as is needed with a hull mold. Complex shapes, such as a steering console, may be constructed in two- or three-part molds designed to allow the piece to be removed easily when formed.

Forming a Hull in a Mold

Having made a plug and a female mold, a boatbuilder's next step is to laminate the first hull in the mold—hull #1 of what the builder hopes will be a long and successful production run. We'll discuss solid-fiberglass hulls first, and then look at how the laminate schedule is modified to build a hull cored with balsa, foam, or some other material.

Making a Plug Using a Five-Axis Router

Making a plug as described in the accompanying text can be a laborious job of hand labor. A faster, more recently developed method is to carve the plug from a large foam-covered frame, or **armature**, using a computer-controlled five-axis router. Such plugs are built off-site by specialized facilities, then shipped to the boatbuilder.

The armature is usually a steel grid, since wooden armatures have been known to break into pieces when the finished plug is transported by road. This steel frame is then covered with wood and foam to form a structure that approximates the shape of the finished plug. The outer layer of foam is sprayed in place and allowed to cure.

(1) *The steel armature for a portion of a large yacht's upperworks is welded together.*

(2) *Foam blocks are glued to the armature. Filler foam has been sprayed between the blocks to help glue them together.*

(3) *Here you can see the parts of the finished plug. The steel armature is in the middle of the yellow foam section made of foam blocks. Pink fairing compound covers the layer of sprayed-on foam, but a little of it shows as a darker yellow than the foam blocks. This sprayed-on foam is cut by the five-axis router, and the fairing compound is applied over the newly cut surface. The router then goes back over the job to make a finish cut, which then receives a final handfairing.*

(continued)

8 • HOW FIBERGLASS BOATS ARE BUILT

Making a Plug Using a Five-Axis Router *(continued)*

While this part of the process is underway, a computer drawing of the finished plug is adapted to program the router. Allowances are made for the thickness of the plug's fiberglass outer layer and its final fairing to ensure that the finished plug is exactly the dimensions shown on the drawings.

(4) Here a router bit is cutting foam. To the right you can see a stream of chips coming off the bit.

(5, 6, 7) The router at the D. L. Blount Associates production facility in Norfolk, Virginia, runs for two shifts a day to keep up with the workload. These parts for a large fiberglass yacht show some of the complex shapes that can be molded with a computer-controlled router. Note how the steps in photo 6 are cut into the bulkhead. (Courtesy D. L. Blount Associates)

Solid, Single-Skin Fiberglass Construction

Solid, single-skin fiberglass construction is the original method of fiberglass boat construction, and it's still in use. First, gelcoat is sprayed to a more-or-less uniform thickness against the mold's mirror-smooth polished interior surface and allowed to set up. The gelcoat might be anywhere from 5 to 20 mils thick (a mil is a thousandth of an inch) but is usually at least 10 mils thick and more often 15 to 20, making it an order of magnitude thicker than a coat of paint. Unlike a coat of paint, it is also chemically cross-linked (not just mechanically adhered) to the fiberglass laminate that follows it into the mold. When the hull is later lifted out of its mold, the gelcoat becomes the laminate's outer coating and serves to protect the hull from UV degradation, scratches, and minor dings. It is not only beautiful but also highly durable.

(1) Spraying gelcoat into a mold to form the polished exterior surface of a hull. (2) Rolling resin over fiberglass. (Courtesy Ranger Boats)

Through the first three decades of fiberglass boatbuilding, gelcoats were almost universally a pigmented polyester resin. But polyester has the drawback of allowing moisture to penetrate the gelcoat via osmosis and attack the structural laminate beneath it. This can cause blistering (see Chapters 2 and 8), and after blistering began to show up in boat hulls beginning in the late 1980s, most production builders began using a *vinylester* (a vinyl-based polyester) gelcoat in lieu of the traditional polyester gelcoat—or an epoxy barrier coat *over* a traditional polyester gelcoat—thus curtailing moisture penetration. Some builders—generally those building high-performance boats—now use vinylester or epoxy throughout the hull laminate, not just in the gelcoat, but this is rare in production boatbuilding.

The gelcoat is usually followed by one or more commonly two layers of *chopped strand mat* (CSM). *Mat* consists of short strands that are packed together in random orientations to form a flat sheet, then held together with a binder that is resin-soluble. CSM is more easily molded than any other fiberglass material. For this reason— and because it prevents the pattern of the woven fiberglass materials beneath it from *printing through*, or showing on the hull surface—it is the obvious choice to comprise the first one or two layers of laminate behind the gelcoat. The common weights of CSM are ¾ ounce and 1½ ounces per square foot.

In production boatbuilding, some manufacturers apply CSM not in sheets but with a *chopper gun*, a tool that chops continuous strands of fiberglass into predetermined lengths and fires them into the mold along with a fine spray of resin. The idea is that the fiberglass is coated with resin on its way into the mold. Chopper guns were commonly used ten years ago because they make the initial laminating go faster, but they are less commonly used now because they emit large quantities of volatile organic carbons (VOCs) and can produce uneven results in the hands of an unskilled operator. You should not need a chopper gun for repair work.

On top of the CSM (i.e., beneath it in the finished hull), builders usually place the first layer of woven fiberglass reinforcement. The usual choice for this among commercial builders is *woven roving*, which consists of thick bundles, or *rovings*, of parallel strands, with the warp and weft rovings crossing each other at 90 degrees. The result is a heavy, coarse weave that builds up laminate thickness fast, which is why builders favor it. The most common weights are 18 and 24 ounces per square yard. (Note that all fiberglass materials except CSM are weighed by the square yard, not the square foot.)

Woven roving provides great strength in the warp and weft directions but is not as strong along the bias. To address this, successive layers of roving in a laminate can be oriented at 45 degrees from one another. Also, adjacent layers of woven roving do not bond well enough for boatbuilding purposes, so a typical laminate schedule alternates layers of roving with layers of CSM, which provides superior interlaminar bonding. Early fiberglass builders aimed for a laminate comprising about 30% fiberglass reinforcement and 70% resin, but builders today can get more than 40% glass in a hand-laid laminate, and even more if using vacuum bagging or resin-infusion techniques. (For more on vacuum bagging and resin infusion, see the sidebar on pages 15–17.)

In *fiberglass cloth*, as in woven roving, the warp and weft fibers cross each other at 90 degrees, but cloth is woven from yarns (each yarn comprising two or more strands of glass twisted together) rather than stout rovings, and the material is therefore neater, easier to work, and more finely woven. Cloth is available in weights from 2 to 20 ounces per square yard, with weights between 6 and 11

(1) CSM is the most common fiberglass material. To make it, short lengths of fiberglass about 2 to 3 inches (50 to 75 mm) long are lightly glued into a scrim. The glue, or binder, dissolves in the laminating resin, leaving the fibers frozen in the cured resin. CSM is used beneath the gelcoat and also between layers of heavier woven roving to absorb resin and to fill voids within and between the layers of roving. **(2)** Using a chopper gun to spray a stream of glass fibers and catalyzed resin. Though no longer commonly used to build hulls, the guns are still used to lay up small parts quickly. (Photo 2 reprinted with permission from The Modern Cruising Sailboat *by Charles J. Doane*)

Forming a Hull in a Mold • 11

(1) *Because it takes time to lay down a layer of CSM and then a separate and distinct layer of woven roving, glass manufacturers have combined the two as a single composite with woven roving on one side and CSM on the other. The result is named after the weight of the material on each side, such as 1808 for 18-ounce woven roving combined with ⅞-ounce CSM (which weighs 8 ounces per square yard).* **(2)** *When rovings are woven, the weft and warp rovings tend to crimp slightly where they cross. Under load these crimps straighten, and this can lead to elongation and fracturing of the laminate. To eliminate crimping and the potential for stretching, builders sometimes substitute unidirectional unwoven roving, in which parallel rovings are lightly glued or stitched together (see the thin lines crossing the material) with no crossings. This gives great strength in the roving direction but not at right angles to it; to rectify this, two layers of unwoven roving can be stitched together at right-angle orientations to form a biaxial roving (not shown here). If additional strength is required along the bias, an additional layer can be added at ±45 degrees, forming a triaxial roving. Adding a fourth layer on the other bias forms a quadraxial roving without the stretch inherent in weaving.*

ounces being most common and most versatile. Cloth is stronger for its weight than woven roving and makes a neater repair, so although boatbuilders don't use it much in their laminate schedules, it serves well for repairs. In fact, 1½-ounce mat and some 6- to 10-ounce cloth may be all you'll ever need for fiberglass repairs, though 18- to 24-ounce woven roving is also good to have on hand. (Remember, mat is weighed by the square foot, so 1½-ounce mat weighs the same per given coverage as 13½-ounce cloth.)

The thickness of a 30-foot solid fiberglass hull (i.e., one without a core) might range from ⅛ inch (3 mm) at the toerail to ½ inch (12 mm) or more at the keel. Three layers of woven roving separated and sandwiched by five layers of CSM might

(continued on page 14)

(1) *Fiberglass cloth. (Reprinted with permission from* The Modern Cruising Sailboat *by Charles J. Doane)*

(2) *From left, mat, woven roving, and cloth. (Reprinted with permission from* Maintain and Improve Your Powerboat *by Paul Esterle)*

Exotic Skin Materials

E glass is the most basic of the fiberglass family of materials. Developed as electrical insulation (the E stands for electrical-grade), it was first used to build boats in the late 1950s and is still used today by most production boatbuilders. Its strength is lower than that of the latest materials, but so is its cost. It is perfectly adequate for most production boatbuilding purposes, but lighter, stronger reinforcement materials are sometimes substituted for specialized building, and especially for high-performance boats.

S glass. As the use of E glass spread, aircraft builders began demanding more strength and lighter weight in a fiberglass material, and S glass was developed to meet these needs. But S glass may be several times more expensive than E glass, and that's a showstopper for production boatbuilding, a low-volume, low-margin business. So the slightly less expensive but still high-strength S-2 glass was developed for boat construction. E glass is all you're ever likely to need for repairs on a standard fiberglass boat, however.

Graphite. Graphite fiber, more commonly known as carbon fiber, is probably the best-known high-strength fiber. It has a much higher tensile strength than fiberglass. Developed for high-speed turbine blades, carbon fiber is becoming the material of choice for high-performance hulls and decks. A carbon fiber laminate is twice as strong and five times as stiff as a conventional fiberglass laminate of the same thickness, and as a result, a carbon hull might weigh a third as much as a conventional hull of the same strength. Sometimes carbon fiber is used to reinforce critical areas in boats of otherwise conventional construction.

When a carbon fiber hull is laminated, it is often vacuum bagged and cured in an autoclave to enhance the high-performance characteristics of the material even more

(1) Rolls of unidirectional carbon fiber.

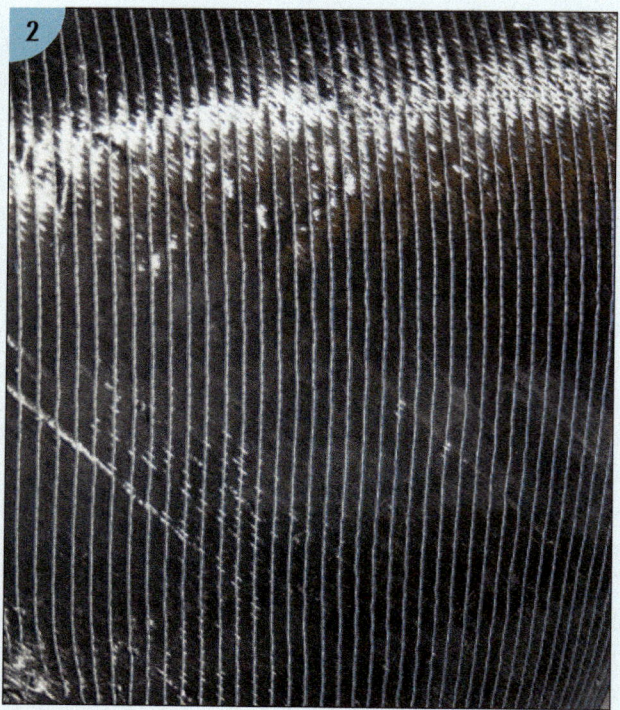

(2) A laminate of fiberglass and polyester resin has a tensile strength of about 27,000 psi (pounds per square inch), whereas a laminate of carbon fiber and epoxy resin has a tensile strength of about 61,500 psi.

(for more on vacuum bagging and autoclaving, see the sidebar on pages 15–17). If you are ever faced with a repair to a carbon fiber hull, you will need to find out how the original laminate was made in order to make a repair of comparable strength. The techniques of carbon fiber repair, however, are nearly identical to the techniques for fiberglass repair as outlined in this book.

Kevlar. Kevlar is an aramid fiber made by DuPont. It is very strong in tension but not as strong as graphite or fiberglass in compression. Kevlar is used in high-performance boat hulls to absorb impacts in the same way that Kevlar bulletproof vests absorb bullet impacts. Repairs to a Kevlar laminate are difficult, as the material is hard to cut and difficult to laminate, but the techniques are, again, pretty much the same as outlined in this book.

Boron fibers. Boron is the very latest in high-strength fibers and has yet to appear in boats, although it is used in aircraft. Boron fibers are made of tungsten and coated with boron vapor to give them strength and stiffness.

The state of the art for racing boat hulls (both power and sail) has become graphite (carbon fiber) with epoxy resin, while cruising sailboats still use fiberglass and vinylester or polyester resin. More esoteric boats might incorporate a laminate of graphite, Kevlar, and S glass laid down as *prepregs* (see page 14) and cooked in an autoclave at elevated temperature and pressure.

(3) *A carbon fiber hull under construction. This entire hull and deck weighs under 600 pounds. With a hull this light, you can use smaller engines, carry less fuel, and achieve a much higher performance.*

(4) *Unidirectional Kevlar combined with S glass makes this high-strength, impact-absorbent material. The Kevlar is light brown, and the S glass is silvery. The thin lines crossing the material are the glue lines that hold the scrim together.*

14 • HOW FIBERGLASS BOATS ARE BUILT

(1) *WEST System epoxy resin together with hardener and metering pumps. (Courtesy WEST System)* **(2)** *Epiglass epoxy resin and hardener from Interlux. This epoxy is mixed in a ratio of 4 parts resin to 1 part hardener. Other epoxies are mixed in a 3:1 ratio of resin to hardener. In contrast, it takes just a few drops of MEKP (a catalyst) to cure a polyester resin. (Courtesy Interlux)*

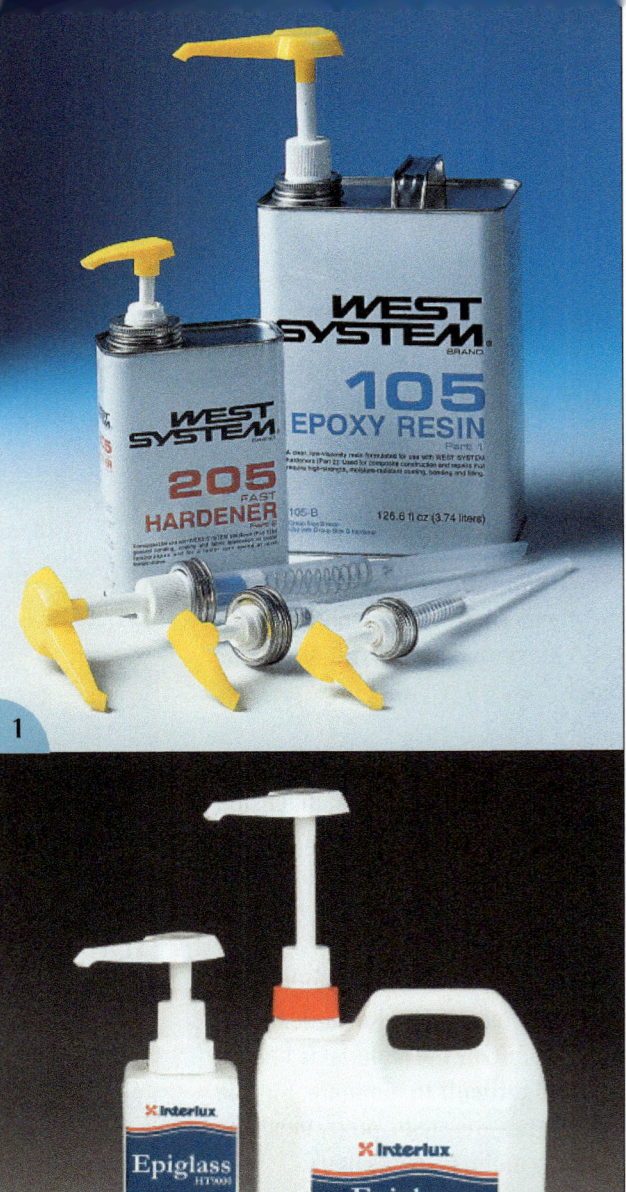

yield a finished thickness of ⁵⁄₁₆ inch (8 mm). The builder typically lays dry sheets of woven roving into the mold, then wets it with resin in place, working the resin into the weave with squeegees and rollers. (These tools are described in Chapter 3.) This *hand layup* of roving layers may be alternated with chopper-gun layers of CSM.

As an alternative to hand layup, sheets of resin-impregnated roving or mat—chilled to prevent the premature completion of curing—can be laid into the mold without additional resin. After being laid down, these *prepregs* are cured by heating, vacuum bagging, or autoclaving. (For more on vacuum bagging and autoclaving, see the sidebar on pages 15–17.)

The resin used in fiberglass building was invariably polyester until the late 1980s, and polyester remains the predominant choice today. As mentioned, however, since osmotic blisters were found to be a problem on older boats, most builders have switched from polyester to vinylester gelcoat or an epoxy external barrier coat. Some use vinylester throughout the laminate, but vinylester is more expensive than polyester, so others switch to polyester after the gelcoat is in place.

Polyester products are comprised of the resin, a catalyst, and an accelerator. Usually the accelerator comes premixed with the resin (which has the consistency of maple syrup), and a few drops of the catalyst are added as needed. (The catalyst is methyl ethyl ketone peroxide, or MEKP, which is nasty stuff and not something you want in contact with your skin.) Mixing the two components initiates an exothermic reaction, and heat is given off as the catalyzed resin sets up into a solid, never to be liquefied again. Because heat is emitted in curing, polyester resins are known as *thermosetting resins*, and the laminating process must proceed a couple of layers at a time, since the simultaneous curing of more layers than that might produce enough heat to damage or warp the mold and, in a worst case, even start a fire.

Like polyester resins, *epoxy laminating resins* come in two parts—the resin and a hardener—that need to be mixed before they will cure. Performance craft are built almost exclusively with epoxy resins because the resulting laminate is stronger and stiffer. Few production boats are built with epoxy resin—which is much more expensive than polyester—but that doesn't mean you can't use epoxy for repairs. I prefer epoxy for many repairs, in fact, as discussed in Chapter 3 and elsewhere in this book.

Laminating Methods Other Than Hand Layup

Hand layup is still the standard laminating method used by many boatbuilders, but emissions controls and the ongoing search for lighter, stronger laminates are inducing more and more builders to adopt closed-mold and other high-tech processes. These range from using prepregs (as described in the accompanying text) or vacuum bagging to employing resin-transfer molding as described here, but one objective they all share is reducing hazardous VOC emissions. Unless you're attempting to repair a high-performance boat, however, you're unlikely to encounter the more exotic laminates.

Autoclaving. An autoclave is an industrial machine that delivers elevated temperature (up to 240°F) and pressure. After a mast or boat part has been laid up and partially cured, it might be placed in an autoclave, where exposure to pressure and heat forces air and VOCs out of the laminate. A laminate cured this way is stronger for its weight and contains fewer voids, so using autoclaves has become standard for manufacturers of high-tech boat parts.

Closed or resin-transfer molding. Resin-transfer molding (RTM) is a relatively recent laminating technique developed to reduce the quantity of VOCs released into the air. It is becoming mandatory in some places, and the consensus is that this type of boatbuilding will become standard in the future. Several variations exist, the most popular of which is known by its trade name, SCRIMP (Seemann Composites Resin Infusion Molding Process). In all the variations, the fiberglass is laid up "dry" (without resin) in the mold and lightly tacked in place. Structural parts, such as frames and floors, can also be laid up dry along with the hull skin. This means that all parts are infused with resin at the same time, which eliminates secondary bonds and potentially weak joints. When the dry fiberglass is in place, it is covered with a molded plastic bag (rather like a vacuum bag) or by a second part of the mold (like a cap or lid). A
(continued)

(1) After a carbon fiber mast is laminated, it is pressurized and heated in an autoclave such as the one in the background that shows as a black hole. (2) This oven has the capacity to cure an entire yacht hull up to 100 feet long. The door opens to a second area to allow a larger hull to be fitted.

16 • HOW FIBERGLASS BOATS ARE BUILT

Laminating Methods Other Than Hand Layup (continued)

vacuum is generated by a siphon, and the resin valves are opened, sucking resin into the dry laminate. When resin begins to flow out the vacuum tubes, the resin flow is cut off and the entire laminate is cured under pressure, or it might be cured in an autoclave under both heat and pressure.

RTM reduces the need for many layers of precisely aligned cloths. The builder can instead use one or two heavier layers of quadraxial roving precisely cut and aligned on the mold before injecting the resin. Using fewer, heavier layers and injecting the resin cuts laminating costs while preserving laminate thickness and achieving a higher glass-to-resin ratio for greater strength. VOCs, which are emitted in copious quantities during open-air molding, are contained in the vacuum lines and can be filtered out and captured. RTM is therefore healthier for workers.

Vacuum bagging. After a laminate has been laid up wet in the conventional way, it can be cured under an airtight plastic sheet, or vacuum bag, that is sucked tightly onto the laminate via suction tubes inserted through one or

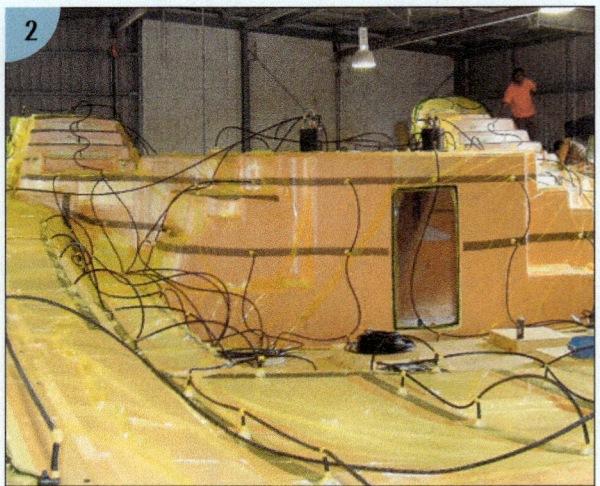

(1) In resin-transfer molding (RTM), the fiberglass is laid up dry and covered with a plastic sheet. A vacuum then sucks all the air from under the sheet. When the vacuuming is completed, resin valves are opened, and the resin is sucked into the laminate. **(2)** Another view of this catamaran deck about to be infused with resin.

The infusion lines are in place, and as soon as the vacuuming is completed, the valves will be opened and resin will pass through the larger-diameter lines into the laminate. (Courtesy Perry Catamarans, Queensland Composites, and High Modulus)

Cored Construction

Single-skin, solid fiberglass hulls were universal among early fiberglass boats, but balsa-cored decks and a lesser number of balsa-cored hulls were being built by the 1970s, and other core materials followed. Cored, or sandwich, construction is in most respects the same as single-skin construction, except that the builder inserts a layer of lighter material midway through the layup, separating the laminate into inner and outer skins. This makes the hull or deck thicker, and therefore much stiffer, without adding much weight. It also insulates against heat and sound and reduces condensation in the boat's interior.

The builder must ensure a good bond of the core material to the outer and inner skins. This is critical. Delamination of a core-skin bond is difficult for a do-it-yourselfer to repair.

Forming a Hull in a Mold • 17

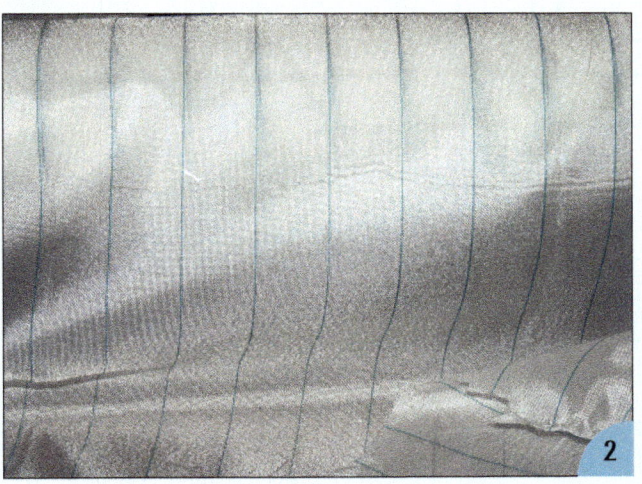

more holes in the bag. The vacuum isn't total, but the resulting pressure can amount to several pounds per square inch—not as high as in an autoclave, but still substantial. Vacuum bagging reduces the number of voids in a laminate and compacts the laminate (increasing the glass-to-resin ratio) for better strength.

A layer of release fabric (the brand name Peel Ply has become more or less generic) can be placed under the vacuum bag to absorb excess resin and allow it to wick out of the job. A bleeder cloth (usually a polyester blanket) placed on top of the release fabric ensures an even distribution of vacuum and also absorbs excess resin. The Peel Ply is later pulled off the cured laminate.

Unlike autoclaving and RTM, vacuum bagging is feasible for a small shop or for do-it-yourself repairs, as described in the sidebar on page 138.

(1) *A vacuum bag in place. Air is sucked from under the green plastic and then the spar is inserted into the autoclave. The whole mast is cured at a higher temperature and pressure than normal to give it additional strength.* **(2)** *Peel Ply ready for use.*

Through-hulls, deck hardware, and other laminate-penetrating items should not be mounted on or through a cored laminate without proper precautions. To ignore this warning is to invite moisture through the outer skin and into the core along hardware fasteners, and this will sooner or later cause a balsa core to rot and a foam core to become waterlogged and spongy. Further, even when hardware is through-bolted with adequate backing plates, cinching up on the nuts can crush a balsa or foam core and form an indent in the deck, perhaps cracking the laminate. A good builder will make a transition from a cored deck to a solid laminate for a hardware installation, at a deck edge, or for the tightly radiused curve from deck to cabin side. Most experts now agree that the core taper through the transition to solid laminate should be about 3:1—i.e., if the core is

18 • HOW FIBERGLASS BOATS ARE BUILT

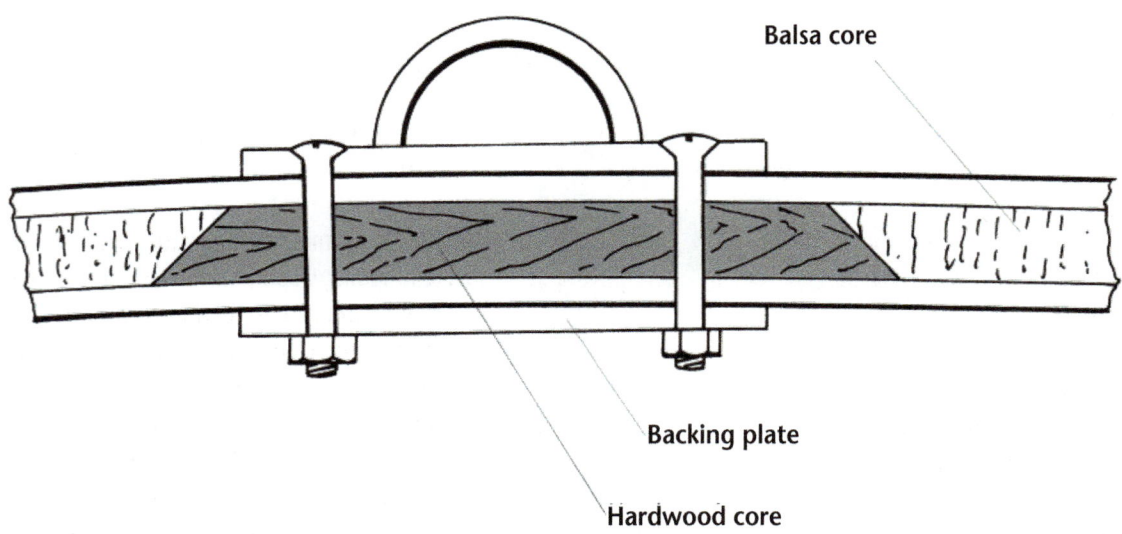

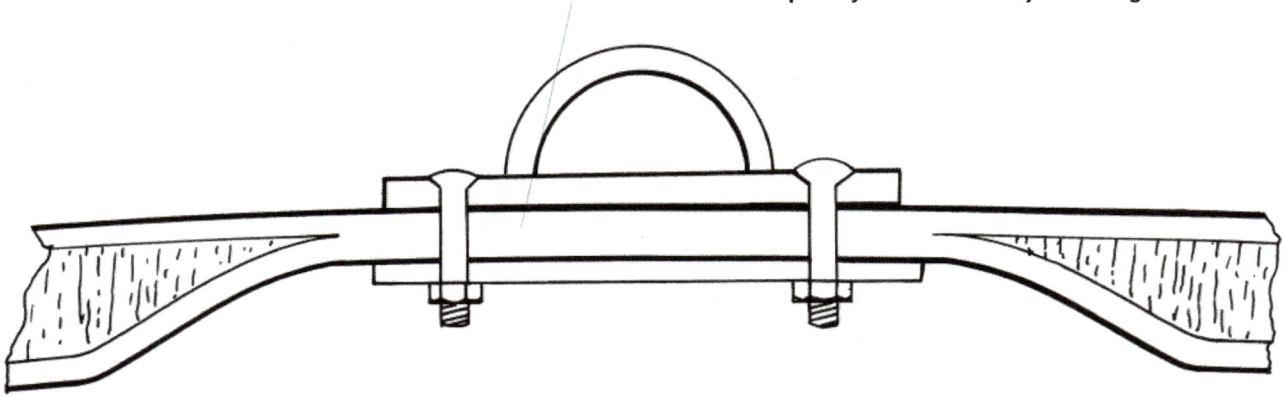

Installing hardware over a foam or balsa core is asking for trouble. Water might reach and attack the core through the fastener holes, and tightening the fasteners might crush the core, which could damage the outer skin and, again, admit water into the core. A better solution is to replace the balsa or foam with a noncrushable core material (such as plywood or hardwood) beneath the hardware, or to transition from cored to solid-fiberglass construction under the hardware. Both solutions are shown here. When this isn't feasible— for example, when you retrofit hardware on a balsa- or foam-cored deck—you should at least ream out the fastener holes oversize, plug them with thickened epoxy, and drill the fastener holes through the epoxy plugs. The plugs not only keep moisture away from the core but also serve as compression struts. (This procedure is illustrated in Chapter 5 on page 96.) All hardware installations should be backed by load-distributing backing plates as illustrated here.

1 inch (25 mm) thick, the taper to a single skin should be 3 inches (75 mm) long. This allows the single skin to flex slightly and transition the load to the cored section, whereas an abrupt change in material stiffness might fracture under load.

If you install a through-hull (for a transducer, a toilet outlet, etc.) in a cored hull, you should cut the hole oversize, remove the core, replace the core with thickened epoxy, and cut a hole of the proper size through the epoxy. Use the same approach for fastener holes in a cored deck. This is covered in detail in Chapter 5 on page 95.

Core Materials

Builders use core materials to increase the thickness of a laminate and thus the distance between its outer and inner skins, which are the laminate's strongest part. A cored laminate acts like an I-beam. The core itself absorbs very little load but greatly increases the structure's stiffness.

Balsa. End-grain balsa is one of the most popular core materials, especially for decks and cabintops. It is light and will not rot as long as it is totally encapsulated in the laminate. The styrene present in polyester resin inhibits rot. Wet or even damp balsa should be dried thoroughly before it is laid up, however. Also, if water gets into the core through laminate cracks or fastener holes, balsa may rot, although the rot does not often spread across the grain unless the leakage is severe.

Foam. There are a number of foam cores on the market, exhibiting varying degrees of density and flexibility. Most builders use Divinycell or Klegecell from Diab Group (www.diabgroup.com). Diab Group also produces ProBalsa core, and Corecell is available from SP, the marine business of Gurit (www.gurit.com). Builders also use Penske board (now called Airex PXc), a urethane foam board with fiberglass laminate on either side, where a high-density foam is needed, such as in a transom repair. Airex PXc is made by Baltek (www.baltek.com) and is available from Jamestown Distributors (www.jamestowndistributors.com).

Sharply curved laminates may use a scored foam core to allow the material to bend. Curved cored laminates tend to be heavy, however, because resin fills the voids between the core materials unless a special lightweight filler is used for this purpose.

When a builder must fill a larger void, such as the space between an interior pan and the hull, he may use a special cavity-filling foam such as Kwik Foam from DAP (www.dap.com), a single-part, spray-in, closed-cell polyurethane foam that expands to fill any void. Evercoat Marine (www.evercoat.com) supplies an equivalent two-part foam that can be used to fill buoyancy

(continued)

(1) *Balsa core material shown close up so that the grain is visible.* (2) *A balsa core laminated into a panel with upper and lower skins. This is what a cored deck or hull looks like in cross section. (Courtesy Nida-Core)*

The interior of a hand-laid boat I designed. The Penske board structure has been bonded in place before the installation of the interior pan.

Core Materials (continued)

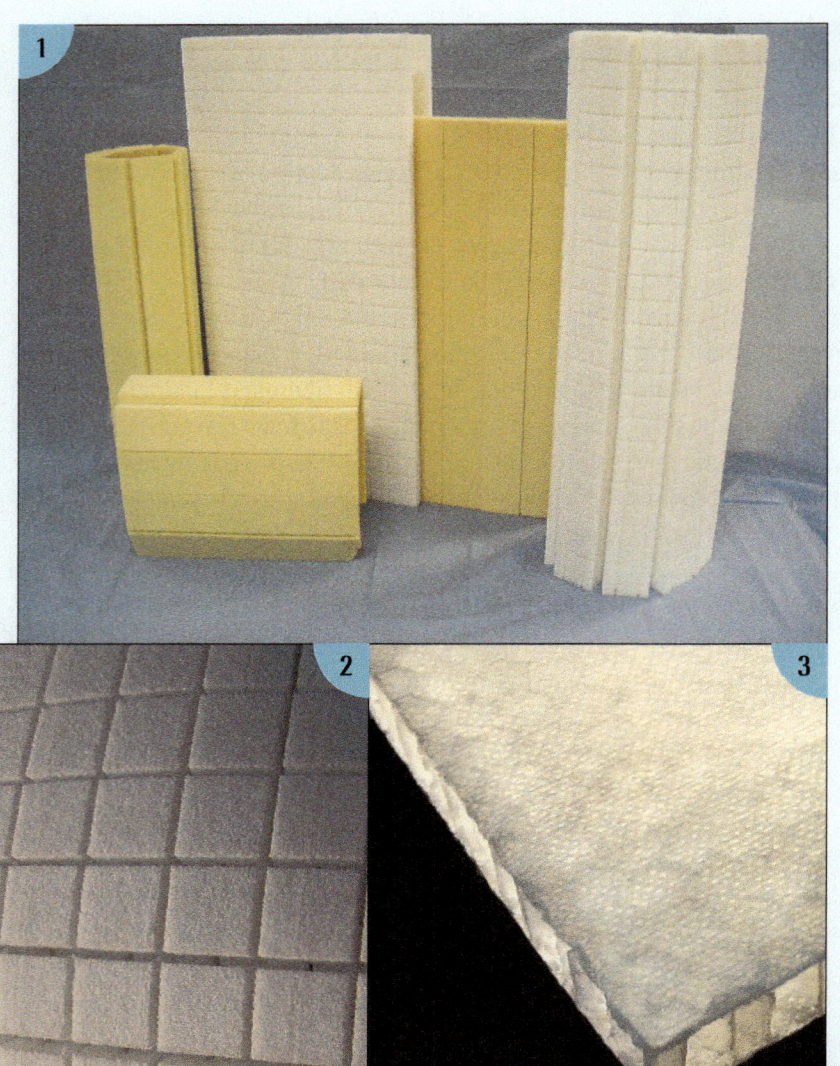

chambers and any other voids that need to be watertight. Both types of foam can be fiberglassed, but it is more usual to put the fiberglass shell together first, then spray the foam into the void.

Hexcel core. Hexcel (often known as HexWeb honeycomb) is an aramid honeycomb core material that is mostly air. It is very light but requires special laminating techniques. A repair to a hexcell-cored laminate in a high-performance boat is a highly specialized job requiring the use of prepregs and a good understanding of how to get a strong laminate.

(1) Foam core materials of various densities. (2) This foam core sheet is scored to allow it to conform to the curvature of a boat's hull. Scored balsa core is also available. (3) Nida-Core honeycomb is an ultralight honeycomb material similar to HexWeb honeycomb. It usually comes with a laminate prebonded to either side, as shown here, because bonding laminate to the core is difficult. (Courtesy Nida-Core)

HULL REINFORCEMENTS

Once a hull is laminated, the builder customarily adds interior reinforcements—floors, longitudinals, and bulkheads—to stiffen the hull before removing it from the mold. The common practice prior to the early 1970s was to bond wooden floors, stringers (i.e., longitudinals), and bulkheads to the hull using fiberglass tabbing, fillet joints of thickened resin, or both. *Tabbing* consists of laying strips of fiberglass cloth over the joint between the hull and covering the reinforcing member with polyester resin. *Fillet joints* dispense with the fiberglass cloth and instead use thickened resin to accomplish the same thing. (Fillet joints today use thickened epoxy rather than thickened polyester, as covered in Chapter 5 on page 97.) These wooden parts were prone to rot after a few years, and their removal and replace-

Hull Reinforcements • 21

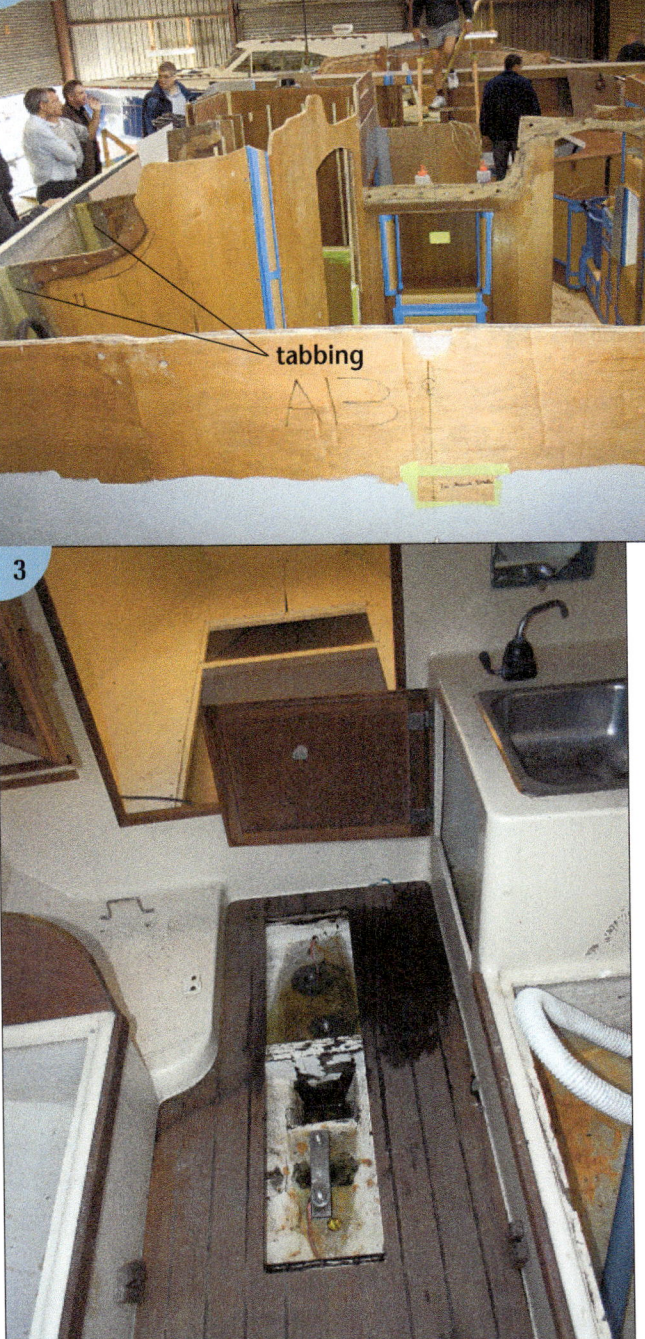

(1) *Setting interior framing into a hull and levelling (with light blue shims) before lifting the hull out of the mold. This wood framing helps stiffen the hull, but the modern practice is to use fiberglass rather than wood floors and stringers.* **(2)** *Fitting and tabbing bulkheads (see green tabbing on left) into a hull before removing the hull from the mold.* **(3)** *These plywood floors in an older J/24 sailboat have delaminated and need to be replaced. The replacement project is described in Project #2 in Chapter 7.*

ment with foam-cored fiberglass floors is Project #2 in Chapter 7.

Today a boat's floors (transverse reinforcing members) and stringers (longitudinal reinforcing members) are more likely to be constructed of foam-cored fiberglass than of wood. The foam core gives a member the hat-shaped cross section it needs for stiffness, while the necessary strength comes from the fiberglass laid over the foam. The floors and stringers may be laminated as a single-piece waffle-like grid and then glued into place in the waiting hull, or they may be formed individually in place. Such modern methods have decreased the time required to build a fiberglass boat from thousands of hours to hundreds, if not fewer.

Once the hull is sufficiently stiffened with interior reinforcements, it can be removed from the mold, which is then rewaxed and prepared for the next hull layup.

22 • HOW FIBERGLASS BOATS ARE BUILT

The stringer system of a modern small powerboat shows a completely encapsulated wood or foam structure. The rearmost portion of this hull (in the foreground) is visible when the hatches are opened and has therefore been painted white. This boat has a two-piece hull liner, the forward section of which is already in place. A transverse bulkhead will be installed next and will separate this forward section of the hull liner from the main piece.

HULL LINERS

In contemporary boatbuilding practice, an *interior pan*, also called a *hull liner* or *hull pan*, is customarily set in place over the reinforcing grid, or the grid may be part of the liner. This liner, which is formed over a male mold in one, two, or even ten or more pieces, depending on the boat's size, provides the polished gelcoat surface of the cabin sides and floor (or of the inner hull sides and cockpit sole in an open powerboat), hiding the raw fiberglass of the hull laminate and reinforcing members. It also provides a foundation

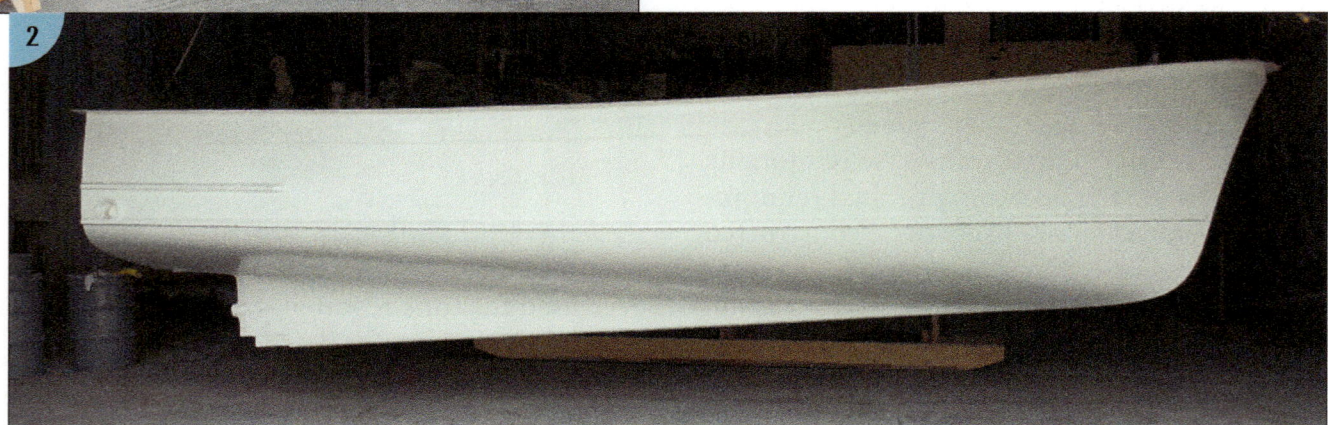

(1) *The first 24-foot Avid emerging from its mold. Because this boat has tumblehome in its topsides aft, a split mold is necessary to enable the finished hull to be removed from the mold.* **(2)** *Having been pulled from the mold, the Avid is suspended from a chain hoist waiting for a cradle to be wheeled under it.*

Interior Furniture • 23

(1) A partial hull pan ready to be fitted with equipment. This is part of the forward head unit and will be fitted with drains and other parts before it is installed. **(2)** A craftsman making a mock-up of the forward part of a cabin before tooling is made. Building a mold of this complexity is difficult and requires a thorough knowledge of the parts that will be fitted in order to allow sufficient space behind the unit for wiring, piping, and even bolt heads. **(3)** An interior pan before it is installed in the hull. On this pan the locker liners (pale blue) have been installed. Other parts are in the process of being installed.

for furniture and for the engine and generator (if fitted), while at the same time serving as the shower pan in the head (if a shower is fitted).

The use of hull liners dates back to the early 1970s. On some smaller craft the bunk flats and countertops may in fact be molded into the hull pan. The tooling to create an elaborate hull pan can be incredibly complex.

A hull pan frequently poses the most difficult challenge in a fiberglass boat repair. When a pan is installed, it is often bonded to the hull structure with a nonremovable glue. If you can't get behind a hull pan to reach a damaged area, you will need to cut into or through it in order to access the problem. Often this means also cutting away wiring, plumbing, and other parts that were fitted before the pan was bonded to the hull. Sometimes access to the back of the pan is virtually impossible, and even if access can be obtained, the whole structure will have to be rebuilt after the repair is made.

INTERIOR FURNITURE

The furniture in older fiberglass boats was often "stick-built"—that is, carried into the boat's interior piece by piece and built in place. Alternatively, it was built in small sections outside the hull and taken into the boat to be assembled and fitted. In production factories today, however, the furniture is simply dropped into place before the deck is installed. On smaller boats, the furniture might be part of a module that is fitted into the pan be-

24 • HOW FIBERGLASS BOATS ARE BUILT

Interior Furniture

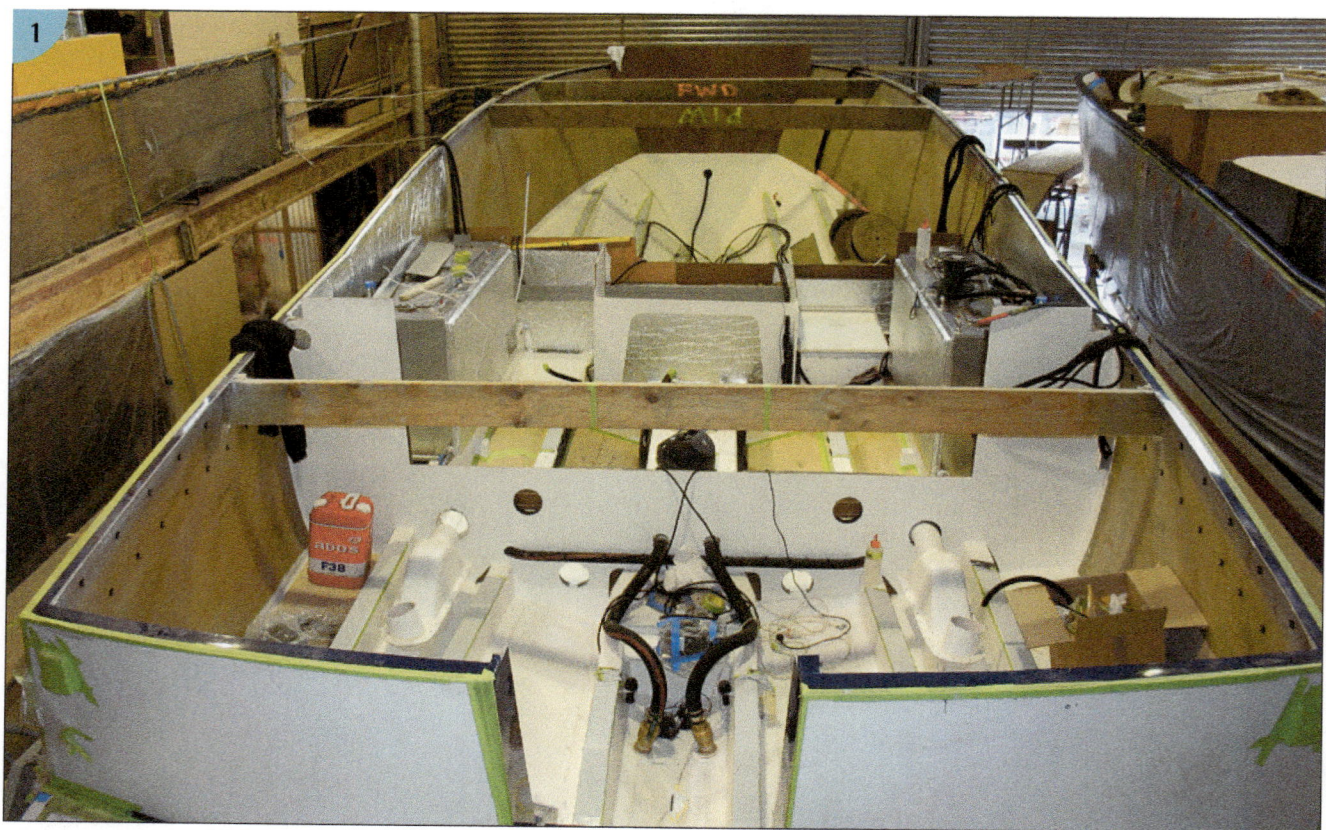

(1) *The interior of this boat is being fitted out before installing the deck. This procedure cuts down on the time needed to build the boat, but it also makes some components hard to reach for later repairs or rebuilding.*

(2) *On larger boats the interior may be made in a furniture shop and fitted to the boat while the deck is still being made. Here the components of the cabin spaces can be easily seen.*

fore the pan is installed on the yacht. On some boats the entire lighting harness—including the lights—is installed before the deck and hull are mated. On larger yachts, the furniture might be built in a cabinet shop and then installed aboard the yacht before the deck is placed.

These contemporary building practices may make it difficult or even impossible to remove parts of a hull pan in order to change an interior layout. To tell how an interior has been constructed and how difficult making changes to it will be, simply look at a bulkhead-to-hull joint. If the wooden bulkhead is carefully fiberglassed to the hull with a fillet, tabbing, or both, it is likely that the furniture is simply glued and screwed to bulkheads and glassed in a few places. This makes the renovator's job much simpler. Parts can be removed in small enough sections that they can be taken out through the companionway hatch. In contrast, restoring a boat whose furniture is built into the pan may be extremely difficult, because

(3, 4) *Furniture for a yacht being built off-site. These joinery pieces will be carried to the vessel and installed after the boat is built.* (5) *The SMI plant in New Zealand*

many of the connections were likely made before the pan was installed in the hull, and these connections may be inaccessible.

DECK CONSTRUCTION

Like the hull, the deck of a production fiberglass boat is usually built in a mold. Typically the gelcoat is sprayed on, the outer laminate is installed, and then a core is set in place. For most yachts this core is lightweight balsa, which can lead to problems of waterlogging and rot later in the boat's life. After the core is in place, the inner skin of fiberglass laminate is laid down. If the job is done in one shot, it might be vacuum bagged to reduce weight.

If a production builder is constructing a number of boats, the deck might be given its own interior liner to ensure that the overhead (the ceiling) in the cabin is smooth and shiny. This provides

(6) *A cabin interior of a large luxury yacht under construction. This furniture was assembled in the SMI Group plant in New Zealand and trial-fitted in a mock-up cabin before being shipped to Italy for fitting into the yacht.*

a nice finish for the boat's interior, but it can be a nightmare for later repairs. In many cases, wiring for cabin lighting is installed on the underside of the deck, and an interior liner covers that wiring. To facilitate future repairs, the wiring should be installed in conduits so that it can be removed or replaced easily. In fact, all wiring should be installed in conduits to protect it from damage and make it easier to work on.

26 • HOW FIBERGLASS BOATS ARE BUILT

(1) *A deck is almost ready to be bonded to its hull.* **(2)** *This view of the bottom surface of a deck shows wiring already in place. A headliner (i.e., an interior liner) may be fitted to this bottom surface before the deck is lowered onto the hull and bolted in place. This construction restricts access for later repairs.* **(3)** *The deck of the boat shown in photo 2 with a molded-in cockpit and pilothouse, ready for installation.*

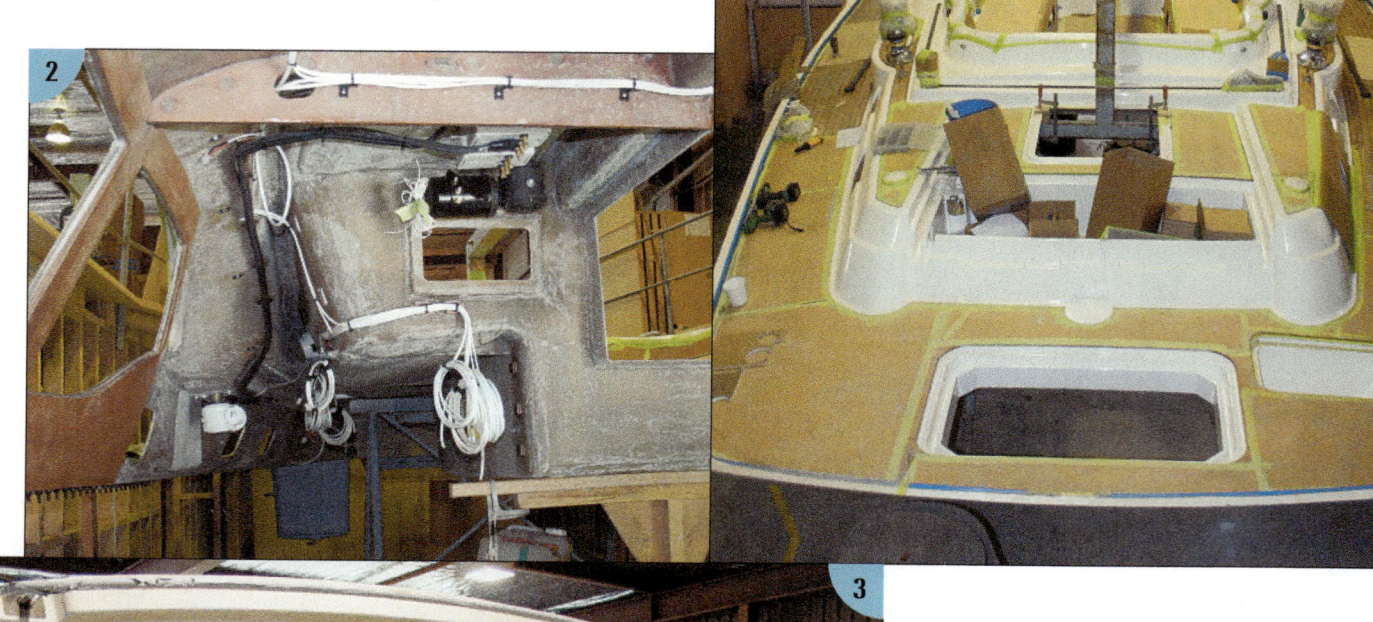

As mentioned, deck hardware and fittings should not be installed over a cored deck surface. In original construction, the builder will (hopefully) taper the deck core to solid fiberglass wherever hardware is fastened. When hardware is later relocated to cored deck sections, the core under the hardware fasteners should be removed and replaced with thickened epoxy as described in Chapter 5 on page 96.

Similarly, when hardware and fittings are removed from a cored deck—whether to reconfigure the deck layout or to repair or refinish the deck—the holes left in the deck must be filled so that water can't permeate the core. This is true even if the gear removal is only temporary, especially if you're working outdoors. If you find filled holes in the deck of an older boat, try to determine what material was used as a filler. Silicone sealer is popular for this job but also ineffective.

Hatch and window replacement is another common abovedeck renovation task. Although it can take many hours to replace these fittings (see, for example, Project #6, Replacing a Foredeck Hatch, in Chapter 7), the cost of a new hatch or window and the caulking to seal it is relatively low. Again, when stripping out an old hatch or window, you must take care not to let water into the core.

HULL-TO-DECK JOINTS

On rare occasions a repair will require tearing apart the hull-to-deck joint to get at parts of the boat under the deck. Should you be so unlucky, it

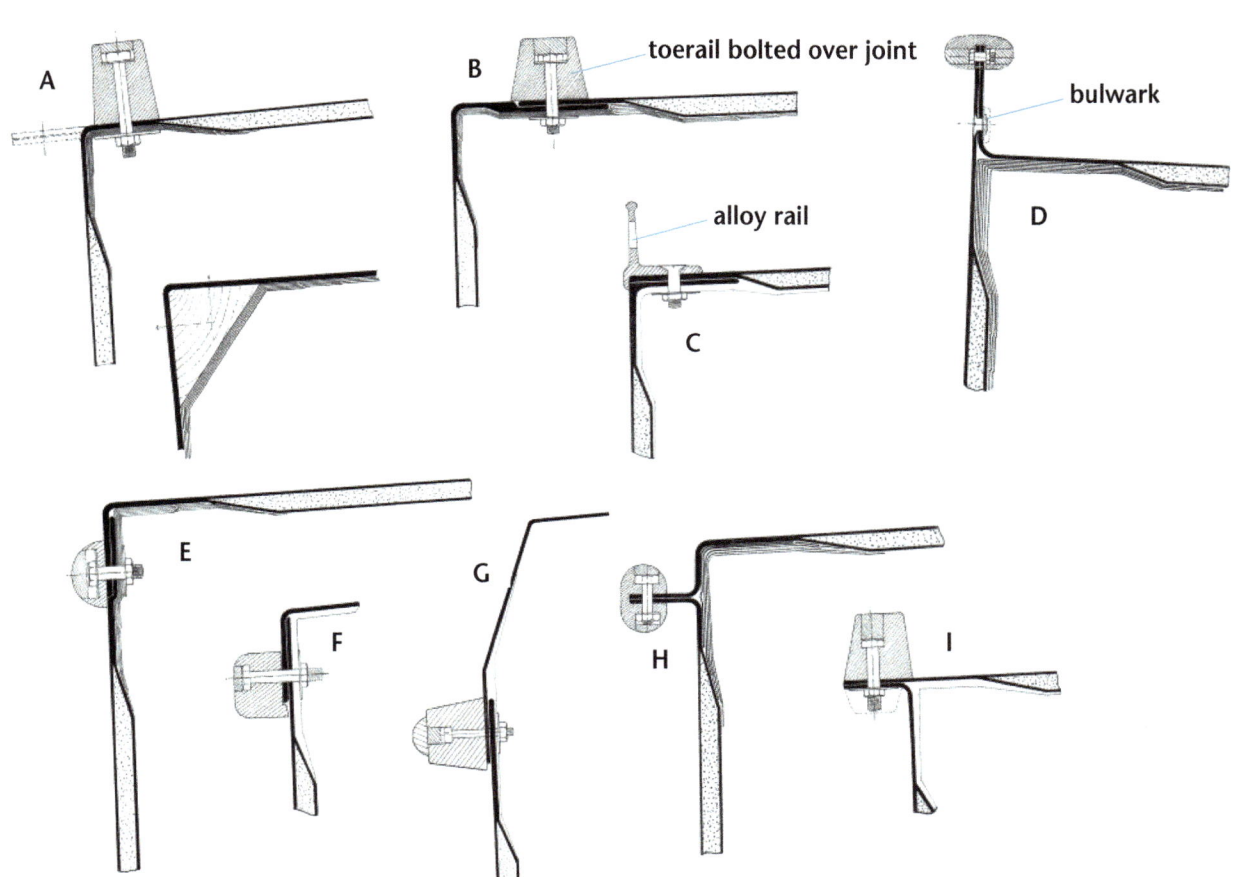

*Several hull-to-deck joints and how they are made. **A** shows a deck that is lowered onto an outward-turning hull flange. The deck is glassed to the flange on the inside, and the flange can then either be cut off (shown dashed) or capped by a rubrail. This method is not in common use today. **B** shows a much more common joint in which the deck is lowered onto an inward-turning hull flange and bolted down. To hide the joint, a toerail is often bolted over it. **C** shows a similar method, but with an alloy rail mounted over the joint. **D** shows a seam that turns upward to form a bulwark. If this joint is not properly made and scuppered, water may leak into the joint and down into the hull. **E**, **F**, and **G** show the most common hull-to-deck joint variation, in which the deck overlaps the top of the hull. **E** is a coffee-can joint, whereas **F** and **G** are shoe-box joints. In either type the hull and deck are bolted or screwed together horizontally, and often a rubrail is mounted on the outside of the joint. **H** and **I** show outward-turning flanges—a solid joint but one that sticks out from the side of the hull and is prone to damage from pilings and other boats.*

28 • HOW FIBERGLASS BOATS ARE BUILT

This deck was lowered onto an inward-turning flange and screwed into place. The toerail covers most of the joint, but a self-tapping screw is used at the stern quarter aft of the toerail termination.

will help to understand how hull-to-deck joints are made. While most builders use what is known as a coffee-can joint, there are others, and identifying them can be crucial in making the right decision on how to go about a repair.

This overview of fiberglass boatbuilding should provide the understanding you need to approach almost any fiberglass repair or restoration project. Bear in mind, however, that even a thorough knowledge of fiberglass boat construction can't prevent some changes to the interior layout of a newer fiberglass boat from being extremely difficult. This difficulty can't be helped—it's inherent to a method of construction incorporating hull pans, interior liners, and modular furniture installation. Changing an interior layout is a lot easier on an older boat with glassed-in bulkheads and stick-built furniture. And since that is precisely the sort of boat whose interior layout most likely needs updating, that's a good thing.

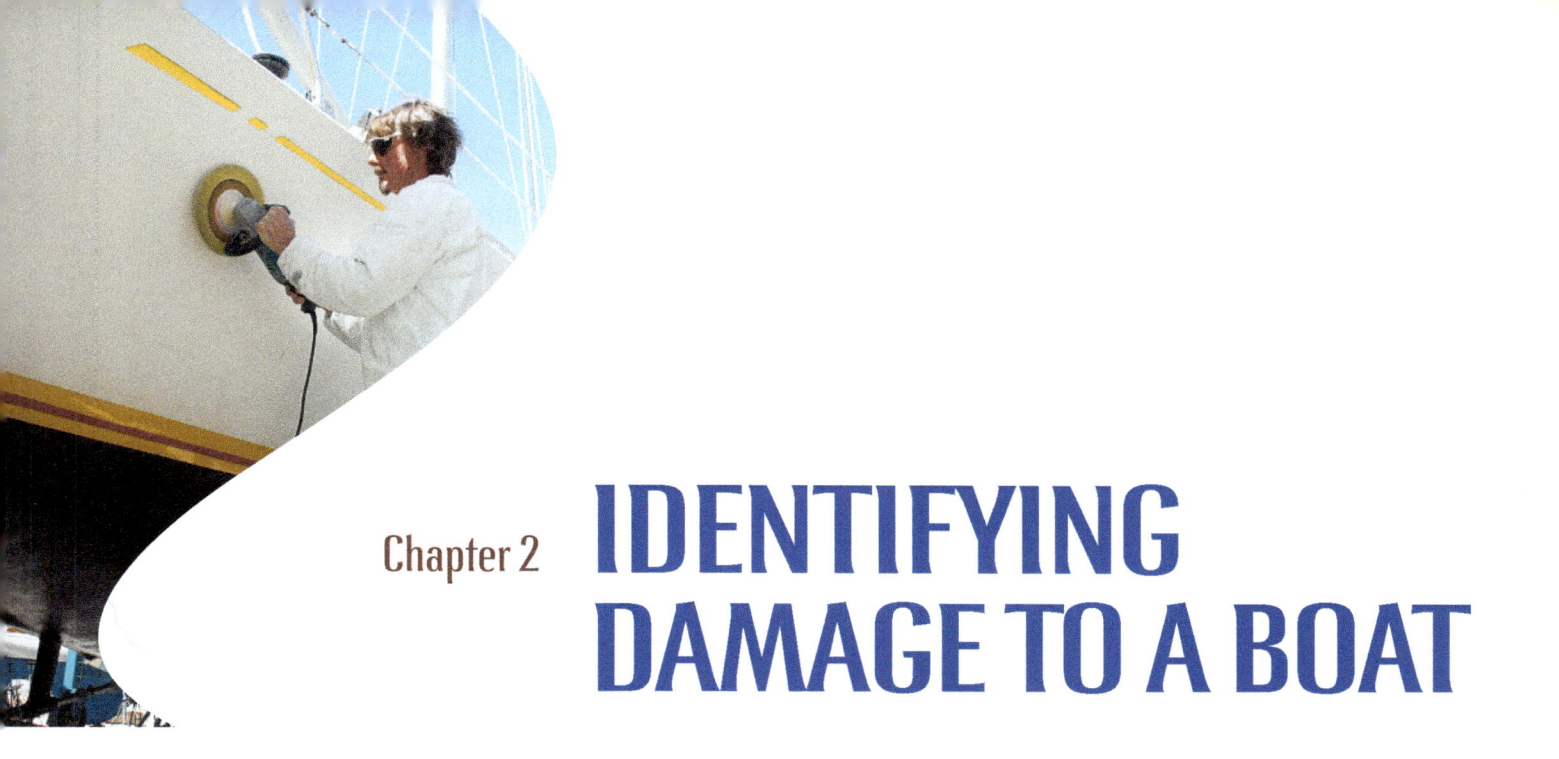

Chapter 2
IDENTIFYING DAMAGE TO A BOAT

Damage to a fiberglass boat is often obvious, but sometimes it can be hard to spot. Banging a boat's topsides against a piling or wall might produce no obvious gelcoat damage, yet inside the hull structural elements may have been broken, furniture may have shifted slightly, or a cabin sole board may now jam instead of lifting easily. Cabin or cabinet doors that jam could be a sign of trouble, especially if they didn't jam before.

Unless you are alert, saturation and delamination of a balsa deck core from moisture penetration through fastener holes or gelcoat cracks may be well advanced before it becomes apparent.

A grounding may produce only mild damage at the tip of a sailboat's fin keel, yet the force

These photos show core rot around an improperly installed impeller. Whoever installed the unit should have replaced the core around the perimeter of the hole with thickened epoxy (as described in Chapter 5 on page 94) so as to prevent moisture from reaching the core, but that did not happen. The problem was not discovered until the boat went on the rocks and suffered skin damage where the impeller was mounted. When the skin repairs were made, the rotten core was revealed by an area of darkened balsa. Additional core around this area was saturated but had not yet started to rot.

29

IDENTIFYING DAMAGE TO A BOAT

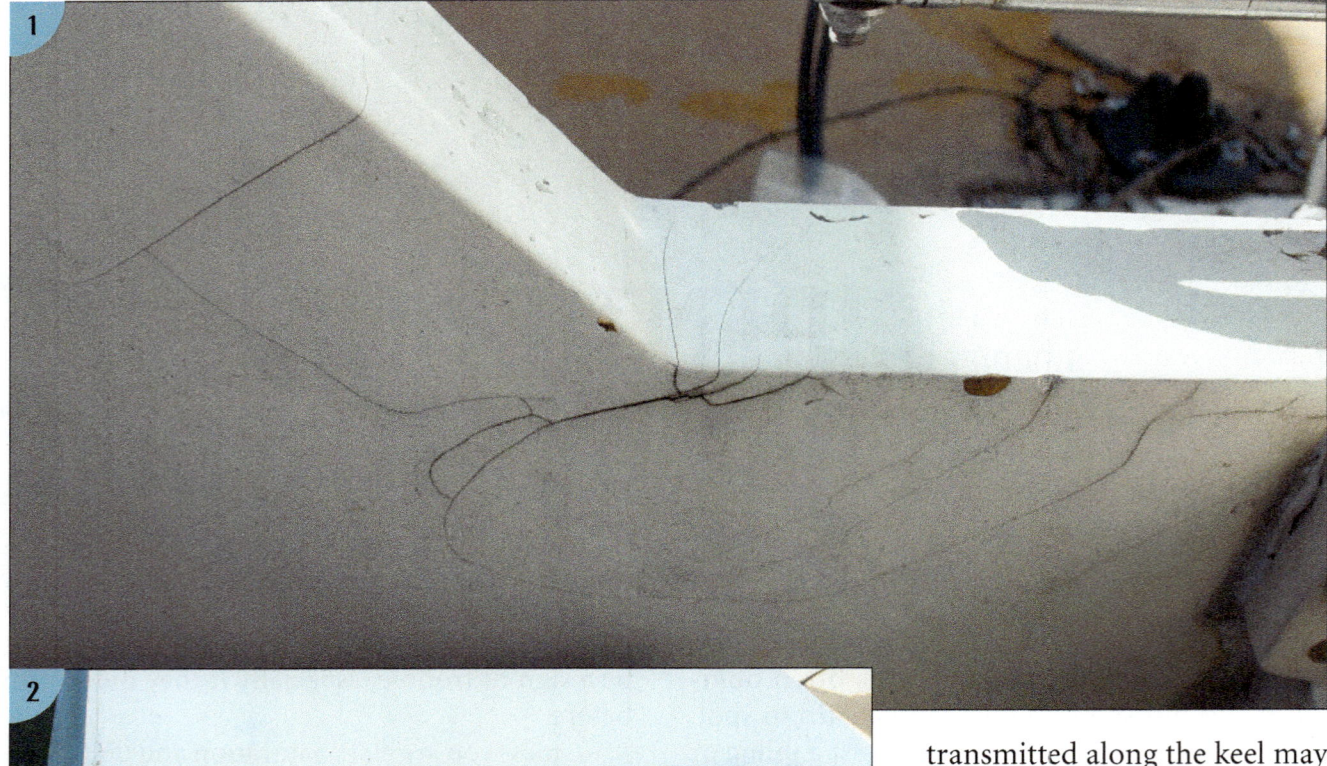

(1) Cracks around the transom cutout corners on an outboard-powered fiberglass boat are usually the first indication that water is getting into the plywood core. If the cracks are not repaired quickly, the entire core can get waterlogged and start to rot. (2) On the port side of the transom you can see damage in the corner (near where the rubrail lands) and screwheads breaking through the fiberglass skin. The most likely explanation for the screwheads is that an owner of the boat countersank the screws into the transom's plywood core in order to mount something inside the transom—perhaps something heavy, like a battery charger. This anonymous do-it-yourselfer then used either polyester or epoxy putty to fair the exterior holes flush with the surrounding gelcoat, and then perhaps painted the transom and called it good. But it wasn't good, as it turns out. Maybe the item that is fastened inside the hull has come loose or is bouncing around when the boat is under power, or maybe moisture has entered around the screwheads and rotted the plywood. Or maybe both things are happening, with each condition aggravating the other.

transmitted along the keel may have cracked the hull laminate at the forward or after end of the hull-to-keel joint. It might even have cracked an interior floor or stringer or a one-piece interior reinforcing grid (see Chapter 1). Just getting at interior structural damage might require the destructive removal of expensive joinery.

An awareness of how damage is caused and where it is likely to occur is an important prerequisite for making repairs to a fiberglass boat.

HULL DAMAGE

Some of the most common causes of hull damage are a lot less dramatic than collisions or groundings. Suppose, for example, that a large outboard engine mounted on a transom cutout has caused the corners of the cutout to crack. Those cracks might not look important, but most transoms of outboard-powered fiberglass boats rely on plywood cores for the strength and stiffness to withstand the engine's weight and thrust. The cracks might allow water to penetrate and eventually rot the plywood core, necessitating a major transom repair.

Rot in a transom's plywood core can occur for other reasons as well. On one powerboat that I restored, I discovered upon drilling into the transom that the entire core was completely rotten, and water literally poured out. The repair required removing and replacing the entire transom (see Project #4, Repairing a Rotten Transom, in Chapter 7). Most of this problem had been caused when the outboard was installed. The holes that were drilled through the transom for the installation were not properly sealed. Holes through any cored laminate—transom, deck, cabintop, or hull—should be drilled oversize, plugged with filled epoxy, and then redrilled to the fastener size, thus sealing the core edges around the hole perimeter from water ingress (see page 94 in Chapter 5 for this technique).

I thought I had finished restoring this 18-foot powerboat, but when I drilled bolt holes in the transom to mount an outboard engine, I found that the transom core was soaking wet. The entire transom had to be replaced. (See Project #4 in Chapter 7.)

Now consider hull damage resulting from impacts with docks, mooring buoys, floating debris, or other boats. Such impacts can create small cracks and marks that may look insignificant, but if these are shrugged off and neglected, bigger problems can result. Suppose your sailboat hits a semi-submerged log and receives a minor ding on the bow. Upon inspection, the damage does not seem like much, so you may be inclined to ignore it. But if the gelcoat has been broken, opening the laminate to water penetration, this will surely cause problems down the road. It may initiate delamination beneath the gelcoat, and in a cored hull it may lead to delamination of the vulnerable core-to-skin bond.

Impact damage to a powerboat is most often seen along the chines. Small chips, dings, and dents in this location are one clue to how old a boat is and how often or how hard it has been used. But impact damage can also occur to a boat's topsides when the boat bangs against a dock, a mooring buoy, or another vessel. This damage often shows up as a pattern of concentric circular cracks in the gelcoat, which, again, may lead to delamination or core damage.

Impact damage to unsupported fiberglass pan-

IDENTIFYING DAMAGE TO A BOAT

(1) *Damage to a bow is not always obvious. This ding, probably caused by hitting a floating object, is below the waterline and should be repaired before the boat goes back into the water. If left like this, with the gelcoat missing, water can penetrate into the underlying laminate and/or the core. Impact damage along the chines of a powerboat may not be structurally significant, but it can be unsightly and can affect the boat's value when sold. Severe impact damage needs immediate repair.*

(2) *Here we see chipping on the stem as well as the chine, possibly sustained in the same incident.*

els sometimes occurs in the absence of a collision or grounding. Consider, for example, a powerboat slamming into a head sea. If the topsides forward are fairly flat, and if a significant panel area forward is unreinforced by interior bulkheads and stringers, the topsides will flex (i.e., they will pant, or *oilcan*) each time the boat slams into a wave. Eventually this flexing will show up as a series of crescent-shaped gelcoat cracks, often near-vertical and near-parallel. Left unchecked, the cracks will penetrate the underlying laminate, and moisture penetration and more serious damage will follow. The proper fix is to add interior floors and/or longitudinals (using the techniques described in Project #2 in Chapter 7 for replacing rotten floors) and repair the gelcoat as described in Chapter 4. Any section of your boat's hull that you can flex with your shoulder when the boat is on jackstands is insufficiently reinforced on the interior.

Such damage may also occur on a chined powerboat's bottom—although this is less common—or in a sailboat's bow sections, although sailboats are less vulnerable due to their typically more convexly curved topsides and slower speeds. Some fiberglass boat repairers consider that this sort of damage is due to stress, not impacts, but the result is the same.

Crazing is a network of fine cracks in the gelcoat. Unlike stress or impact cracks, crazing has no focus or regular pattern. Rather, it looks like the irregular pattern of cracks you see in a surface of desiccated mud or in the shell of a hard-boiled egg that you have rapped with a spoon (see the photo on page 67). Gelcoat crazing is not uncommon on boats built decades ago with thick gelcoat. The solution involves grinding the surface, filling the cracks with epoxy, and painting the faired surface as described in Chapter 9.

Hulls can also sustain scrapes of various kinds from rubbing against objects, sometimes while being towed behind a car. For instance, a boat on a trailer can be scraped by overhanging branches or encounters with fences or walls. A hull can also be damaged as it bounces on the trailer supports, especially on bumpy roads. In some cases trailer damage can be extreme. I once saw a 40-foot yacht
(continued on page 35)

Hull Damage • 33

(3) Impact damage on the topside of a single-skin hull. Note the four separate star patterns suggesting four hard impacts, which may have occurred at different times. This damage needs to be fixed as soon as possible so that water cannot penetrate beneath the gelcoat, which can lead to delamination or blistering. If this were a cored hull, you would need to worry about saturation of the core or delamination of the core-to-skin bond.

(4) More impact damage, here on the bow of a boat that went onto the rocks. Much of this damage punched through the outer laminate and into the core.

(5) A close-up of the impact area. Notice how each impact has created its own crater in broken gelcoat and fiberglass. On this cored hull, the core in the damaged area may have to be replaced.

(6) When looking for impact damage to a boat, walk around the entire hull and look closely at all surfaces. Damage to this 56-foot yacht doesn't show up when you look squarely at the topsides. You have to view the topsides from an angle in order to discern the large area of impact damage, which a surveyor has enclosed with a chalk outline.

34 • IDENTIFYING DAMAGE TO A BOAT

(1) *This dinghy has been dragged repeatedly over a beach or other hard surface, wearing the skeg away. The core material in the skegs of many small boats is not glassed in place, so a breach in the exterior laminate may cause the boat to leak. Further, because the core material in the skeg is soft, it might even be pushed out of the hull altogether, resulting in a sinking.*

(2) *This photo shows impact damage to the chine. This is another small dinghy that has suffered from being dragged either on board or over a beach or dock. The chine is torn up and should be repaired, and the bottom is extensively scratched. The boat will need to be repaired using the techniques described in Chapter 4.*

Measuring Water Penetration

To check whether a laminate or core material has water in it, most surveyors use a moisture meter, which measures the electrical impedance between its terminals relative to a baseline reading taken on a dry part of the hull. An abnormally high moisture content puts a laminate at risk for blistering, core disintegration, or delamination. Thus, when wet spots are found, surveyors mark them for future repair.

Typically, a boat discovered to have a lot of moisture in it is put into a shed to dry over the winter, after which it is remeasured. If moisture is still present, the cutting starts. An infrared image (see the Infrared Surveys sidebar below) can often determine precisely how much of the boat needs to be cut away. The moisture meter shown in the accompanying photo can detect moisture up to 1 inch (25 mm) deep in the laminate. The scale shows whether the moisture level detected is within the normal range.

Moisture meters can be used with minimal training, but they are expensive. Try this test instead: On a warm, sunny day when your boat is on jackstands and its hull surface is bone dry, tape several squares of plastic freezer bags over several locations on the topsides and bottom. Seal each square with electrical tape around the entire perimeter. After 24 hours, see whether any moisture has condensed on the inside surfaces of the squares. If you see condensation in one or more places, consider hiring a surveyor to test your boat with a moisture meter.

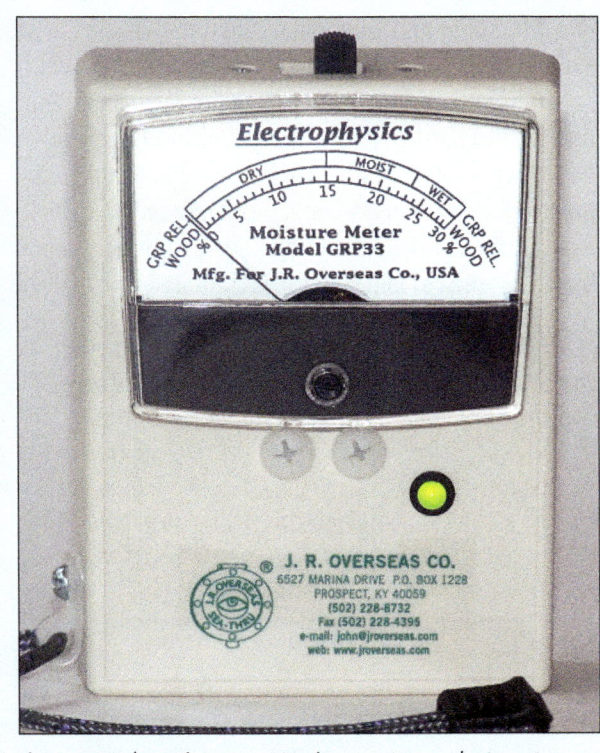

A surveyor's moisture meter is easy to use but costs several hundred dollars, so most boatowners do not purchase one of these instruments. (Courtesy Lee Ann Lyle, J.R. Overseas Company)

---

that had had its pulpits, mast winches, and a few other parts ripped out from being towed under a low bridge. Such severe damage from towing is rare, but lesser damage is not.

Delamination of a solid (i.e., uncored) fiberglass hull is rare, because the layers of a well-built laminate become chemically cross-linked while curing. But the bond between the core and the inner or outer fiberglass skin in a cored hull or deck is merely mechanical, not chemical, and that makes it vulnerable to delamination, which, if it occurs, will rob the hull or deck of much of its strength. Tap a cored hull every few inches with a plastic mallet or screwdriver handle. A sharp, ringing return suggests an absence of delamination, while a dull thud is reason to worry. Check the hull interior for explanations such as a bulkhead landing or gear stacked against the hull. If you find no other explanation, you may just have found delamination, and you may want to have a professional surveyor look at it. Delamination is not only hard to find but hard to repair—it is a job best left to professionals. When my son's Vanguard 15 sailboat was afflicted with an area of hull

(continued on page 38)

Infrared Surveys

Voids in a laminate or the failure of a secondary bond (including, notably, the bond between an inner or outer skin and a core) are virtually invisible to the naked eye and difficult to find without cutting into the areas being examined. A dull return when you tap with a mallet or screwdriver handle may cause you to suspect delamination, but further investigation without destructive cutting is difficult. The best approach is to check for the presence of water in the laminate using a moisture meter as described in the sidebar on page 35. An abnormally high moisture content suggests a saturated core that will need replacing, and the presence or absence of core-to-skin delamination becomes irrelevant. First make a test bore (using a hole saw and leaving the inner skin intact) to verify that the core is saturated. Then cut out the afflicted area of outer skin and core and rebuild the core and skin as outlined in the Repairs to a Cored Laminate section in Chapter 5.

But what if the moisture meter suggests a moisture content in the normal range? If you strongly suspect delamination, you can proceed with a test bore in order to confirm the diagnosis. If the test bore shows that the

(1) *Infrared testing can reveal problems that are not apparent to the naked eye. Here we see a deck as it appears from the exterior.* (2) *When the same deck is viewed using infrared technology, we can see that water has migrated into the core (the light yellow area at the top of the photo). Repairing this will involve removing the entire laminate over the water-laden core and replacing both the core and the deck.*

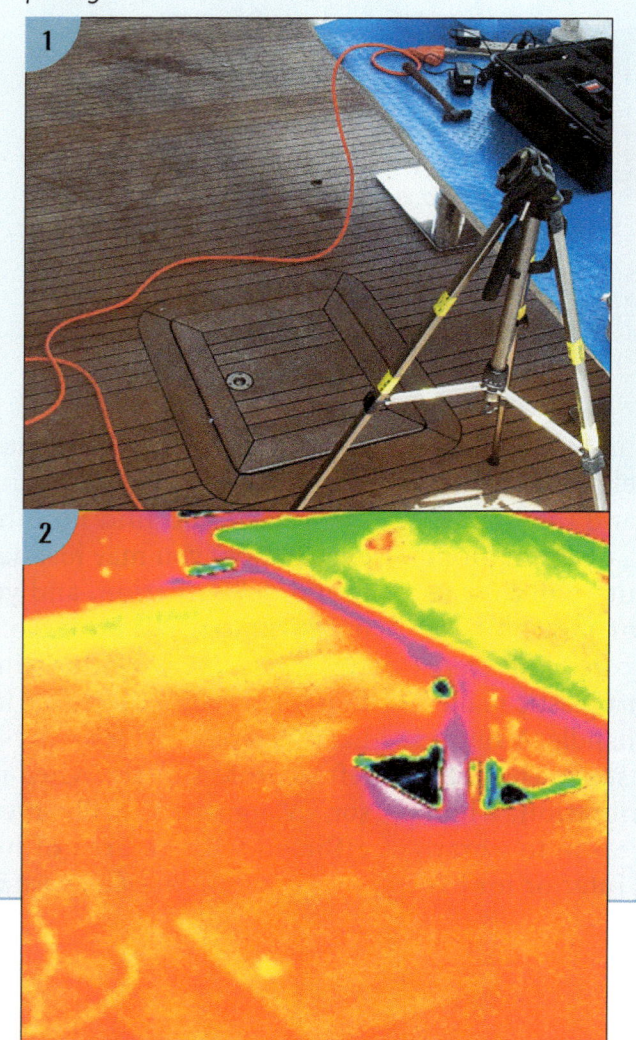

(1) *Hull delamination can be a problem on older boats. Without infrared testing, the only way to verify delamination and to pinpoint its exact extent is to cut into the hull, and even then it can be missed. Infrared imaging, in contrast, is completely nondestructive.* (2) *This hull appears to be in perfect shape, but the infrared photo shows otherwise. The light yellow patches are areas of either delamination or water penetration into the core. By drilling into one of these spots, a surveyor can ascertain the problem with minimal harm to the boat.*

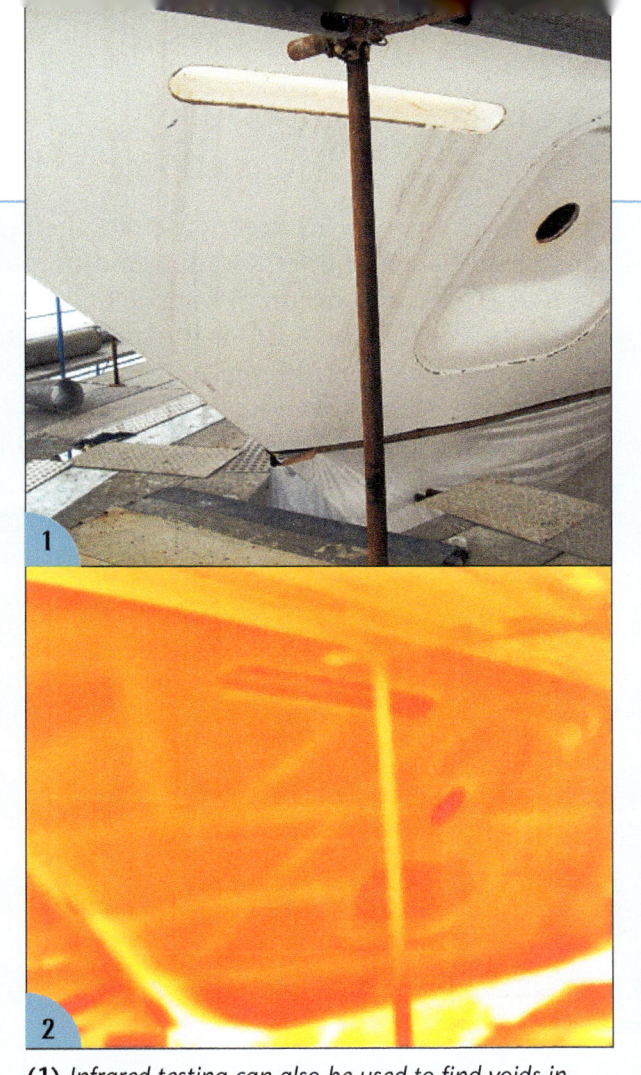

Hull Damage • 37

laminate is solid, simply fill the hole as described in the Repairs to a Single-Skin Laminate section Chapter 5.

One way to locate and investigate suspected defects without taking a boat apart is to have an infrared survey performed. An infrared image can "see" right through a fiberglass laminate and can tell you where voids, fractures, delaminations, wet spots, and other anomalies are located. The process relies on a temperature differential between the interior and exterior of the boat being surveyed. A differential as small as 10°F between the inside and outside of the hull can provide a reliable image of the laminate. Usually the surveyor concentrates on areas of the boat that are suspected to have problems. For example, a high reading on a moisture meter might indicate water penetration, or it might just be a false reading resulting from the builder having changed the resin or laminate slightly. An infrared image can provide a closer look at the laminate to resolve the question. Another benefit of infrared surveying is that it works with carbon fiber, whereas a moisture meter does not.

Infrared testing can also be used to verify that a boat is structurally sound and free of defects. For this reason, insurance companies often use it to establish the condition of a hull. They can find out with certainty if water has penetrated a boat's core or if an accident such as a grounding has caused structural damage to the hull. The findings are so reliable that they stand up as evidence in court.

(1) *Infrared testing can also be used to find voids in a laminate. Here a hull as seen with the naked eye.*
(2) *The same hull as viewed with an infrared camera. In this case there are no voids present, because no darker patches show up. Note how the hull framing can easily be seen through the laminate using infrared technology. (All infrared images courtesy Mark Ashton, Independent Marine Systems)*

(1) *This sectioned Volvo IPS system stern gland shows how it is laminated. The leftward-pointing knuckle is extremely hard to laminate properly, even for a skilled technician, because the fiberglass fabric tends to lift away from and bridge tight corners rather than conform to them.* **(2)** *A section through a foam-cored version of the same gland. Using shaped foam provides a more uniform laminate topology and reduces the possibility of voids in this critical part.*

38 • IDENTIFYING DAMAGE TO A BOAT

delamination, we had the repair done by a boatyard.

Damage from Going Aground

Going aground is a not-uncommon occurrence, especially in sailboats. The areas of potential damage from a grounding can often be deduced if you know the forces involved in the impact. As mentioned at the beginning of this chapter, forces transmitted through the keel may stress the hull laminate just above the keel's leading and/or trailing edge. This compression may move bulkheads or furniture inside the boat, or it may crack one or more interior floors or longitudinals. Just finding such damage can be difficult.

If a grounding is severe enough to crack fairing or filler from the keel, you should check the rest of the boat for damage. If you go from 7 or 8 knots to a dead stop, the top of the mast will

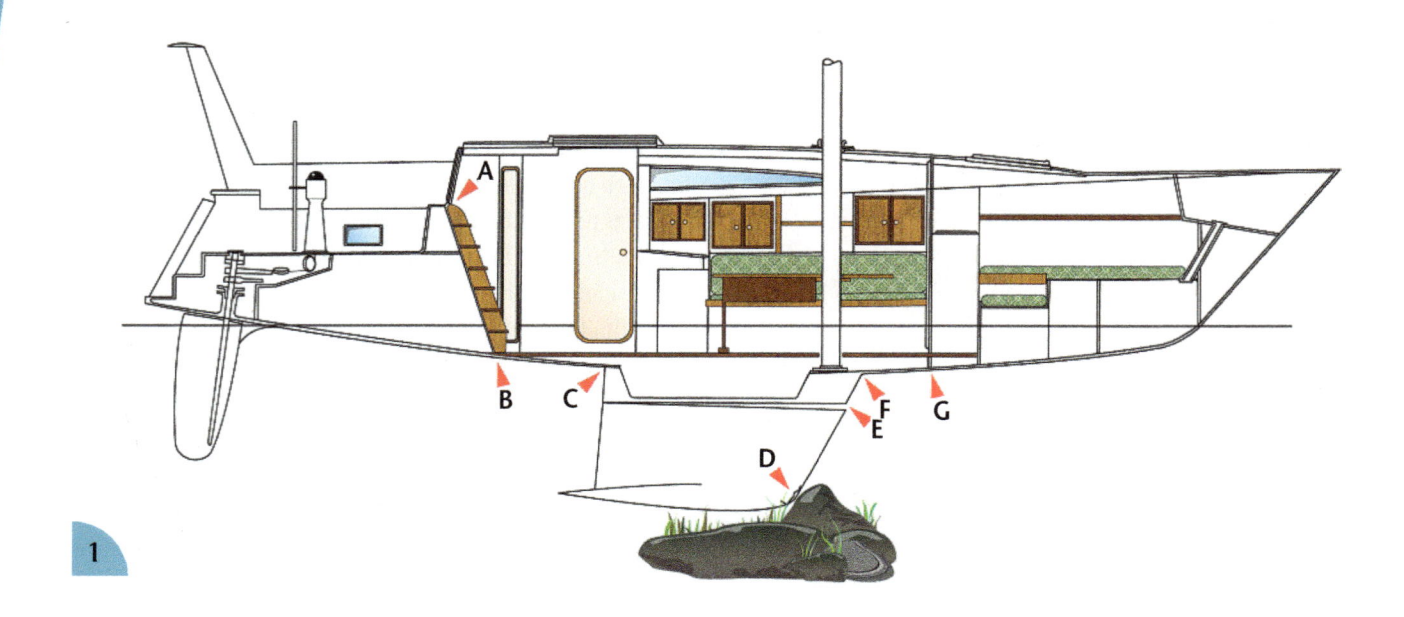

(1) The forces involved in a grounding or collision give clues about the kind of damage that may result. In this case it is not just the sailboat's keel **(D)** that is affected. The force of the impact transmitted through the keel may be enough to open the hull-to-keel joint **(E)** and/or fracture the hull laminate at the keel's leading **(F)** or trailing **(C)** edge. The boat's bulkheads **(G)** and its floors and longitudinals (or equivalent single-piece molded waffle reinforcing grid) should be checked, and so should its furniture (such as at **A** and **B**).
(2) The force of a grounding has opened a crack around the root of this keel. Before repairs can be made, the entire area will need to be ground back to ascertain the extent of the damage, and possible interior damage will also have to be checked. If the damage we can't see is serious enough, this boat could be declared a total constructive loss by its insurer—in which case some enterprising do-it-yourselfer might pick it up for a song and restore it to useful life.

Hull Damage • 39

(1, 2) Damage to the keel on this sailboat shows that it has gone aground heavily and spent some time on the rocks. Damage this extensive suggests that the entire interior needs to be checked carefully. (The repairs to this boat are discussed in Chapter 7.)

(3) The severe cracking between the hull sump and the keel on this sailboat suggests that it may have gone aground. The boat should be checked for interior damage.

(4) When a powerboat goes aground, the propeller or propellers may hit first, followed by the rudders. The propellers might break off, or the shaft might be bent upward. Either way, one or more prop blades might penetrate the hull. Or the shaft might be ripped out of the boat altogether, leaving a gaping hole where the shaft log was. If the bulkhead above the propeller shaft is forced upward, damage could occur at **A**, **B**, **C**, or **D**. If a shaft is ripped out, the engine may move aft as shown at **E**, and beds and engine mounts **(F)** may be damaged. You might also find that movement of the aft bulkhead has shifted other furniture inside the hull. In such cases a surveyor should be called in to ascertain the full extent of the damage before repairs are started.

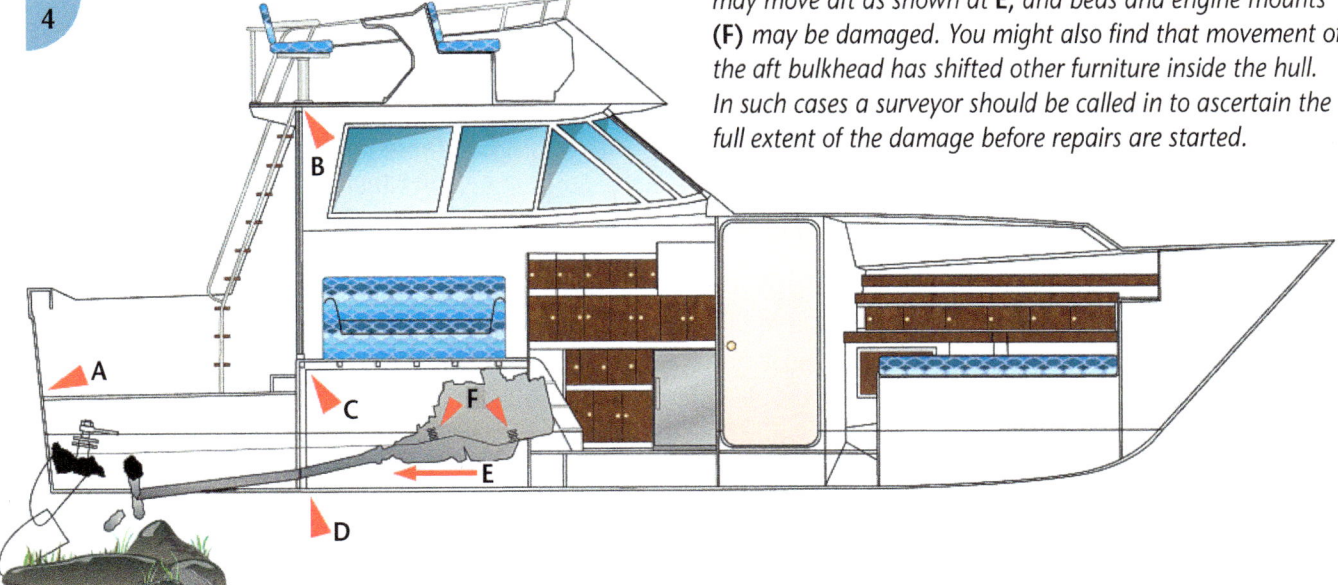

Hull Damage

whip forward and could strain the back of the mast step, so you'll want to look there for possible damage as well. You should also inspect the chainplates for signs of elongation and possible elongation of the chainplate holes in any supporting bulkhead. If the boat was built with a modular interior (as described in Chapter 1), an entire "block" of furniture may have shifted slightly. While this may not pose a structural problem, it can cause doors to jam and drawers to stick.

A powerboat hull may suffer grounding damage in areas other than those typically involved when a sailboat goes aground. For example, the propeller struts may be forced up into the hull, causing cracking of the hull skin. The engines may also move on their beds if the propellers were the first part of the boat to contact the sea bottom. All of this movement may cause furniture in other parts of the boat to move.

DECK DAMAGE

When assessing the condition of a fiberglass deck, look closely at its corners—that is, the corners of the cabin, cockpit, coamings, and chainplates. These are usually the first areas to show chipping or cracking. Because most decks are cored with

BLISTERS

Osmosis—commonly known as blistering—is caused by a chemical reaction between styrenes and other unreacted chemicals in polyester resins and the water in which boats float. When a fiberglass boat is built, both the gelcoat and the underlying laminate contain small pores (known as *voids*), microscopic cracks, dust particles, and other impurities. Molecules of water can slowly wick and permeate through the gelcoat via these tiny flaws, and can then react with uncured styrenes to form a mixture of glycol, hydrochloric acid, and acetic acids. These acids eat away at the cured resin, creating an osmotic pressure that draws still more water into the gelcoat. The eventual result, when the pressure of the liquid brew builds up far enough, is a gelcoat bubble with a diameter anywhere from a few millimeters to a few inches.

Most blisters originate within the gelcoat or on the interface between the gelcoat and the first underlying layer of mat. Such blisters are cosmetic issues, not structural, and repairing a few of them isn't a difficult undertaking. Wear goggles whenever you pop a blister, because the liquid is toxic and under pressure, and you don't want it squirting into your eyes. Scrape out the

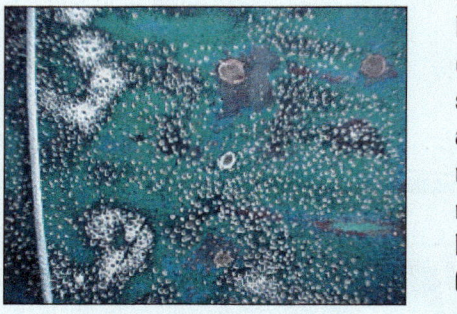

The sanded hull of this boat shows signs of osmosis.

blister with a knife, screwdriver, and scraper; wash and dry it; coat it with epoxy resin; fill it with thickened epoxy; and finish it with a barrier coat before reapplying bottom paint. Blister repair is discussed in more detail in Chapter 8.

A major outbreak of blisters is another matter. The only lasting fix may require peeling away the gelcoat and perhaps the first underlying layer of mat, a job that should be done professionally. A boatyard specializing in this work uses a mechanical gelcoat peeler to remove a predetermined thickness of the fiberglass. This device looks rather like a small 4- or 6-inch-wide (10 to 15 cm) planer on a flexible arm. It can be computer controlled to remove a precise amount of outer fiberglass skin. (On a cored hull, it might remove the entire outer skin down to the core material.) With the hull peeled, it is allowed to dry out. Quite often heaters are placed under the boat to facilitate the drying process. A moisture meter is used to determine exactly how much water remains in the hull. When it gets to less than 10%, the hull can be recoated. (See Chapter 8 for a more detailed discussion of osmosis.)

Deck Damage • 41

(1) *Stanchion bases are always a good place to look for potential damage to a deck. A person falling against a stanchion exerts a long lever arm on the deck, often causing cracks. The stanchions here have been bent inward, with resulting damage to the deck and the rail. Incidentally, this deck is fiberglass with a teak overlay. Usually a teak deck is screwed to the fiberglass subdeck, the screwheads being countersunk and bunged. Typically a builder beds the teak and the fasteners themselves in caulking so that moisture cannot get into the subdeck, but the fasteners nevertheless provide a possible route of moisture ingress. Even when this leads eventually to an interior leak, the leak may be some distance away from the actual problem. This can be one of the hardest moisture problems to find, and the search is best left to a professional surveyor who can trace it with a moisture meter or an infrared scan.*

(2) *This stanchion base shows signs of repair, which should lead a surveyor to check the area carefully for water migration into the core.*

foam or end-grain balsa, any water getting into the deck through these cracks can cause large areas to rot.

On outside corners of the deckhouse (and on hull corners—i.e., at the stem and transom), there may be voids between the gelcoat and the underlying laminate. These form when the hull or deck is molded, because fiberglass fabric tends to bridge corners in the mold rather than folding itself into them. Unsupported gelcoat tends to chip, and these breakouts, while merely cosmetic, must be puttied or they will admit moisture to the underlying laminate and cause more serious damage down the road.

On inside corners—for example, where cockpit sides meet the cockpit sole or where side decks

42 • IDENTIFYING DAMAGE TO A BOAT

meet the cabin trunk—the problem is not voids but stress. Repeated flexing of the deck can cause cracks to show up along the axis of a corner.

Another place to look for deck damage is around stanchion bases. If a crewmember falls against a stanchion, or if he uses it for support when boarding the boat from a dinghy, it can be bent outward; if he grabs the windward lifeline to try to keep his footing in a sudden heel, a stanchion can be bent inward. Either one is likely to open cracks in the gelcoat—often a series of cracks that radiate outward from the stanchion fasteners. If underlying deck core is crushed, the cracks will extend through the gelcoat and into the laminate. This is a great argument for replacing foam or balsa core with plywood core or solid fiberglass in the way of stanchion bases and other high-stress hardware, but builders don't always do this.

Damage to a deck. Note how these cracks radiate from the corner of a hatch. This suggests impact damage from a heavy object, perhaps while it was being dropped into the locker. There is another suggestion of impact damage in the lower left corner of this photo, and some of the cracks from the two damage centers are radiating toward each other. When a cored deck is involved, symptoms like this should cause you to question whether the cracks extend through the gelcoat and into the underlying laminate. If so, you need to ask if water has reached the core.

(1) *If you find cracks like these at the corner of a hatch or cockpit* **(2)**, *you might want to use a Dremel tool to cut a small V-groove into the crack to see how far the damage extends. (For more on Dremel tools, see Chapter 3.)*

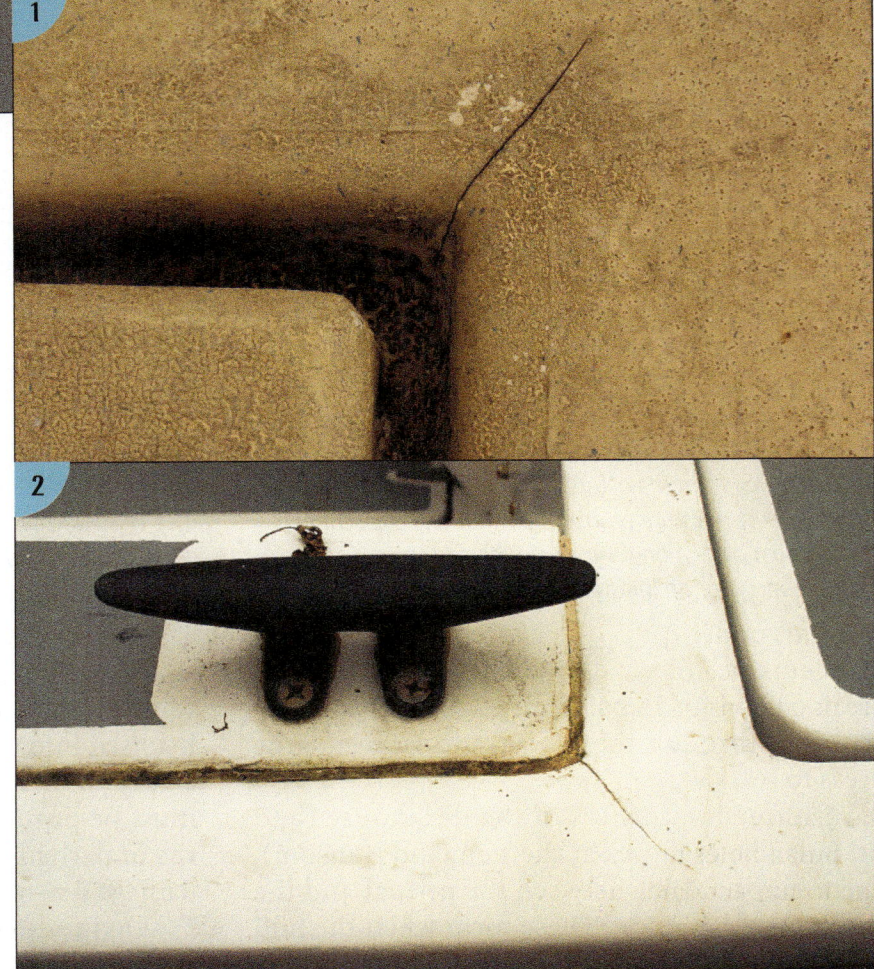

It's also a great argument for providing big backing blocks or plates under the deck for the stanchion bolts to pass through. Backing plates spread loads and provide a much more secure attachment, and any high-load deck hardware should have one. (See the drawing on page 96 showing backing plates.)

Deck damage may occur as well to the cockpit sole or to the area around a mast. These two areas are often damaged when crewmembers drop a winch handle or other heavy object. When inspecting a sailboat's cockpit sole for damage, you should also look around the steering pedestal base. If anyone has fallen or pulled against the pedestal or wheel, cracking may have occurred in this area. On a powerboat, cracks can arise on the corners of deck steps or where handrails are attached, as well as around the base of the windshield or the bases of any stanchions.

A noticeable swelling in a deck surface may indicate a delaminated skin-to-core bond, a waterlogged core, or both. This condition might also be accompanied by alligatoring (crazing) of the gelcoat, as mentioned above. Sound the deck surface with your plastic mallet or screwdriver handle, and treat dull returns with suspicion. A softness or squishing of the deck underfoot is a certain indication of core problems. Delamination and waterlogged cores must be dealt with as outlined in Chapter 5.

RUDDER DAMAGE

Rudders are perennial problem areas, and the problems can be wide ranging. The most obvious and extreme one is when the rudderstock lets go and the rudder drifts away from the hull. Other problems occur when tangs inside the rudder break, allowing the rudder blade to turn on the stock, or when part of the rudder blade snaps off because the stock has been cut too short inside the blade.

Small holes in the rudder laminate—whether due to impact damage or layup flaws—will allow water into the blade, making the rudder excessively heavy and perhaps eventually causing the

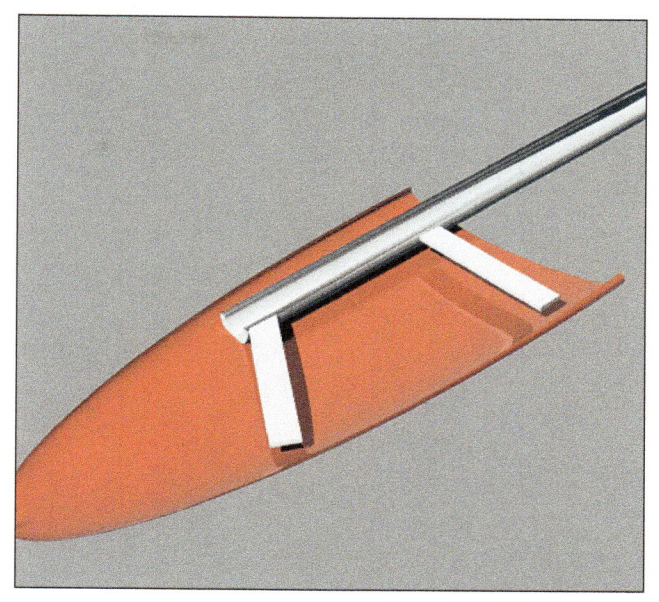

Common Practice: A production rudder typically consists of a fiberglass skin surrounding the rudderstock and flanges. The cavity is filled with closed-cell foam (not shown here). The stock is often untapered and therefore does not extend to the bottom of the blade, and this sometimes results in the blade breaking just below the end of the rudderstock. Flanges may be weakened when they are welded to the stock centerline, and they may subsequently break just aft of the weld. A better way to attach a flange, blade thickness permitting, is to bend it completely around the stock.

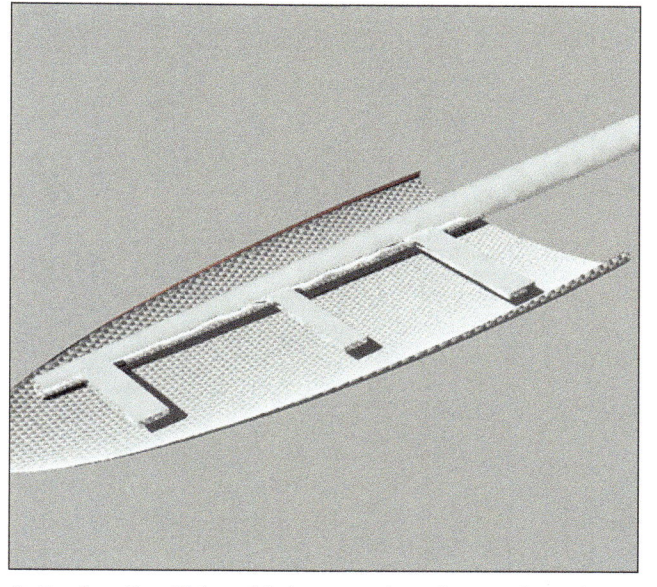

Better Practice: This rudder's tapered stock extends to the bottom of the blade, and the flanges are well spaced along the stock to ensure adequate blade support. Although it would be best to wrap the flanges around the stock, a lack of sufficient blade thickness often prevents this.

44 • IDENTIFYING DAMAGE TO A BOAT

(1) *Damage to rudders is fairly common. This rudder filled with water, which, as it drained, left a stain on the blade.*
(2) *Another rudder with a similar problem. Water draining from a gash has left a stain along the side of the blade. A waterlogged rudder must be cut open and dried out before repairs can be made. The fiberglass repair techniques covered in Chapter 5 apply to rudders as well as hulls and decks. See also the rudder fairing techniques described on page 115 in Chapter 6.*

core to disintegrate or the blade to delaminate. Most often a waterlogged rudder is discovered when the boat is hauled out for the season and the rudder continues to drip water from inside the core. The problem must be remedied before temperatures drop low enough for the water to freeze and expand. If this happens, ice can literally blow the rudder apart.

OTHER DAMAGE

Most furniture damage inside a boat is caused when people accidentally fall or when they drop or bang some heavy object. The resultant damage can range from dents and dings in woodwork to broken tables or bunks. Though joinery repairs are usually easy to make, they are not the province of this book.

A delaminated plywood bulkhead must be removed and replaced. Such damage can usually be prevented by pumping the bilges regularly.

ROT

It is easy to forget that a fiberglass boat is not immune to rot. A partial inventory of wooden parts includes balsa cores, plywood transom cores, plywood bulkheads (especially their bases, which can experience prolonged immersion if the bilges are not kept dry), cabin soles and their supports, and fiberglass-encased wooden floors, longitudinals, and engine beds.

Of the three prerequisites for rot—warmth, moisture, and air—moisture is the one you can most feasibly control. Keep your bilges dry, and keep moisture out of wooden core materials by following the precautions in Chapter 5 and elsewhere in this book. Replacing rotten wooden reinforcements is one of the projects discussed in Chapter 7 (see Project #2). Wood coated with epoxy resin is shielded from rot if the wood was dry and the humidity low when the epoxy was applied. (Moisture trapped under an epoxy coating can breed rot spores and cause rot.) Also remember that epoxy contains no UV filters, and if the wood will be exposed to sunlight you will need to varnish it with several layers of high-UV polyurethane varnish.

Damaged or rotting bulkheads are more serious problems, and repairing them requires a fair amount of work. The delaminated plywood bulkhead shown in the photo on page 44 is an extreme example of what can happen when joinery is immersed in standing water. Replacing this bulkhead will not be especially difficult, but the job could easily have been avoided just by pumping the bilges more often.

Most damage inside a hull, however, is caused by the forces unleashed by a grounding or collision. The damage may include broken reinforcing members, a cracked hull liner, or dislocated furniture modules as discussed earlier in the chapter.

Chapter 3
MATERIALS, TOOLS, AND BASIC TECHNIQUES

One of the many advantages of fiberglass as a boatbuilding material is that repairing it requires no great skill, although a good supply of patience often comes in handy. You need a small assortment of materials and tools—nothing esoteric or very expensive—and a basic understanding of their properties and how to handle them correctly. Those are the subjects of this chapter, as well as a few basic techniques and a few creative solutions that will serve you well through a wide range of repairs—the techniques and solutions illustrated in the chapters that follow.

MATERIALS

The basic materials of fiberglass repair are simply the fiberglass itself and the resin with which the fiberglass is coated. High-performance one-off boats are increasingly built with Kevlar, carbon fiber, or other high-tech reinforcements rather than fiberglass, but some 98% of boats in use today are built with ordinary fiberglass. The techniques for repairing Kevlar and carbon fiber laminates are pretty much the same as those outlined in this book.

Fiberglass fabric—whether roving, cloth, or chopped strand mat (CSM)—simply drapes like a bedsheet over any structure you lay it on. Only when you saturate the fabric with polyester or epoxy resin and allow the resin to harden does the fiberglass become frozen in the shape of the underlying structure. Thus, the fabric is of no use without the resin, but the reverse isn't always true. The resin alone has very little tensile strength, and structural repairs therefore require fiberglass reinforcement of some kind, but cosmetic repairs to gouges, cracks, chips, and dings can be done with putty (either polyester- or epoxy-based) or filled resin (again, either polyester or epoxy) alone. A repair to the topsides or deck of a boat will need to be matched to the surrounding finish—either with pigmented gelcoat or fairing putty that is then painted—and a deck repair may require the addition of a nonskid finish that matches the appearance of the surrounding nonskid. For more on finishing, see Chapter 9.

Fiberglass

As described in Chapter 1, fiberglass is made by extruding molten glass into very fine strands. For many production boatbuilding applications these strands are E glass, which has been in use since the late 1950s. The lighter, stronger, but much more expensive S glass favored by aircraft builders is not used on boats because of its expense (see sidebar page 12). A less expensive high-strength

S-2 glass has been developed for boatbuilding, but E glass is perfectly adequate for do-it-yourself repairs.

Once extruded, fiberglass strands may be chopped into short lengths and glued together to form CSM, as pictured on page 10. Or the strands may be made into yarns, and the yarns then woven into fiberglass cloth. Or a group of parallel strands may be bundled together to form rovings, which may then be woven into—you guessed it—woven roving.

Boatbuilders like woven roving because it is strong and because its coarse, thick weave builds up laminate thickness rapidly. But adjacent layers of woven roving do not form a good interlaminar bond, so they must be separated by intervening layers of mat, which

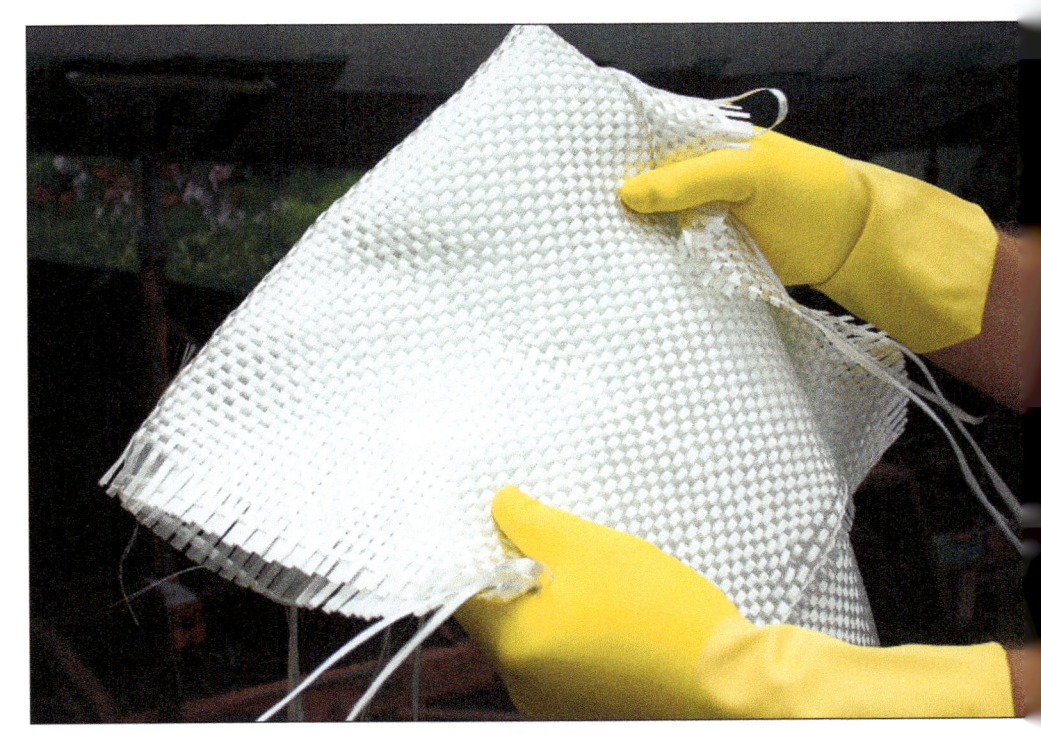

Gloves enable you to handle fiberglass (woven roving in this case) without getting shards in your fingers. These heavy-duty kitchen gloves can be worn even by those who are allergic to latex. Shears or scissors allow you to cut the material precisely; a face mask keeps fiberglass dust out of your nose and mouth; and safety glasses prevent airborne pieces of fiberglass from getting in your eyes.

provides superior interlaminar bonding. A laminate schedule in which layers of woven roving are separated and bonded by intervening layers of mat—with one or two layers of mat on the outside, under the gelcoat—is the basis of the majority of fiberglass boats we see on the water. For the convenience of boatbuilders, glass manufacturers offer a composite fabric sandwich that is woven roving on one side and CSM on the other, the two components being lightly glued together. The result, as pictured on page 11, is named after the weight of the material on each side, such as 1808 for 18-ounce woven roving combined with ⅞-ounce CSM (which weighs ⅞ ounce per square foot but 8 ounces per square yard).

In areas of high stress, however, the plain-vanilla schedule of mat and woven roving may not be the ideal solution. In a woven roving the warp and weft rovings are crimped at each crossing point, and when the laminate is loaded these crimps tend to straighten, rendering the laminate slightly elastic. For highly stressed areas of a boat, a nonwoven fabric may be the answer. To fill this need for boatbuilders, glass rovings are laid parallel on a flat surface and glued or cross-stitched together to form a unidirectional roving (see photo 2, page 11), which provides great strength along the axis of the rovings but not across them. To achieve great strength in two directions, a builder can adjust his laminate schedule to follow one layer of unidirectional roving with another turned 90 degrees, or he can use a biaxial roving, in which two unidirectional rovings have been sandwiched together, their roving axes at ±45 degrees to the length of the fabric (i.e., at right angles with one another). The result is pretty much the same.

When a third layer is added to the sandwich (with fibers at 0 and ±45 degrees to the length of the fabric), the result is a triaxial roving, and the addition of a fourth layer (with fibers at 0, 90, and ±45 degrees) forms a quadraxial roving. Builders orient the fibers in a laminate relative to the centerline of the boat. Generally speaking, fibers are run at 0, 30, 45, 60, or 90 degrees to the centerline.

You can use unidirectionals, biaxials, triaxials, or quadraxials for repairs, but most repairers use mat, woven roving, and/or cloth in order to hold down costs. Fiberglass cloth has a stronger strength-to-weight ratio than woven roving and yields a higher glass-to-resin ratio and a neater appearance in a layup. As mentioned in Chapter 1, a small inventory of 1½-ounce mat, 6-ounce cloth, and 18- or 24-ounce woven roving will suffice for the majority of fiberglass repairs.

If you plan to use epoxy resin for your repair, make sure your fiberglass fabric is suitable for epoxy. Not all are. Most of the cloth and mat products sold by marine retailers explicitly state that they can be used with epoxy as well as polyester resin.

Resin

The fundamental choice here is between polyester and epoxy resin. It's a fair bet that the builder of your boat used polyester, since the first use of epoxy in production boatbuilding wasn't until 2003, and it remains rare. The reason is simple: cost. Epoxy is stronger and forms better bonds in a laminate, but it costs about three times as much as polyester. Given the small amounts of resin needed for most repairs, however, you'll be less concerned with the cost differential than with the results. The biggest investment is your time, and you want a commensurate payoff in the finished job, so epoxy resin is often the best choice for repairs.

This is not true, however, of a repair you intend to finish off with gelcoat. Epoxy forms a strong secondary bond to underlying polyester, but the reverse is not true, and gelcoat is always polyester (or vinylester, which is a variety of polyester). So any repair that will be finished with gelcoat should be made with polyester resin. I also favor polyester resin for a large repair to a polyester-based hull or deck because I believe the properties of the repair will then be more compatible with the surrounding laminate. Cured epoxy is not just stronger but also less flexible than cured polyester, and a large repair of epoxy laminate in the middle of a polyester hull or deck could—it seems to me—create a "hard spot" (visible as a slight bump) that might induce stress cracks around its perimeter down the road.

Polyester Resin

The three basic types of polyester resin, in order from least to most expensive, are orthophthalic (ortho), isophthalic (iso), and vinylester. Early fiberglass boats were built with ortho resins, but when these were discovered to be susceptible to osmosis and blistering (as discussed in Chapter 8), most builders switched to iso or vinylester resins. Iso resins are more resistant to water penetration and also reduce osmotic blistering, while vinylesters appear to block osmosis altogether and provide superior tensile and compressive strength. Vinylesters are harder to use and more expensive, however, so their use in production boatbuilding has been confined mostly to gelcoat.

Polyester resins contain styrene in proportions up to 50%. The more styrene in a resin, the runnier it will be. Typically you purchase resin with the styrene premixed, and you add a catalyst just prior to use. Note that polyester resin eventually gels in the can, so try to buy fresh stock. Adding the catalyst initiates the polymerization of the resin. This curing, or hardening, process is an exothermic reaction—i.e., heat is given off—during which the mixture sets up into a solid lump, never again to be a liquid. This is why polyester is known as a thermosetting resin.

The catalyst, usually methyl ethyl ketone peroxide (MEKP), constitutes only a tiny proportion of the final resin volume; a little more hastens the cure, a little less retards it. MEKP is nasty stuff. It can cause blindness and certain cancers, so don't take chances with it. (And don't confuse it with methyl ethyl ketone, MEK, which is an industrial solvent often added to paints.) Once you have added MEKP to the resin and mixed it in well, you can add thickeners and/or pigments.

Another factor to take into account is whether your job calls for laminating resin or finishing resin. As its name implies, *laminating resin* is most often used for laminating layers of fiberglass. This resin is air-inhibited, meaning that it does not set up when exposed to air, but instead stays a little tacky to facilitate a strong, chemically cross-linked bond with the next layer of laminate. To make a laminating resin cure properly in air, you need to cover it with a plastic film (such as Saran wrap) or waxed paper, or coat it with polyvinyl alcohol (PVA), or add a little *tack-free additive* (TFA). TFA is a wax that floats to the surface of the wet resin and forms a waxy film beneath which the resin can cure normally. Rather than adding TFA or covering a fresh repair with Saran wrap, waxed paper, or PVA, you can simply purchase a *finishing resin*. If you plan on adding either another layer to your laminate or a structural part such as floors, however, laminating resin is the better choice; otherwise, you will need to remove the waxy film that a finishing resin forms by using a solvent or by grinding it away—or both. The resins available for purchase in most marine stores are finishing resins.

Polyester Putty and Gelcoat

Probably the easiest way to fix tiny scratches, gouges, or chips in a hull or deck gelcoat is with gelcoat putty, but you can only use it for small gelcoat repairs. Start with a neutral or white off-the-shelf gelcoat and mix pigment to match (as best you can) the color of the surrounding surface. The process is described in Chapter 4. Gelcoat putty is sold in both air-inhibited and non-air-inhibited formulations. For surface repairs you want the latter.

Unreinforced gelcoat may be too brittle to fill a deeper gouge, however. For that you can use a thickened polyester putty such as Bondo or a marine-specific equivalent, or you can thicken polyester resin to a putty-like consistency using many of the fillers described below for use with epoxy. Build your filler in thin layers and finish with regular gelcoat to bring the finished surface level with the surrounding area. I've seen it suggested that you can use glass snipped from cloth or rovings to thicken a resin, but don't do this. The ends stick out of the laminate and need to be ground back, and the resulting mess is almost impossible to get smooth.

Epoxy Resin

Epoxy is several times more expensive than polyester or vinylester resin, but I prefer it for many repairs because it smells less strongly of styrene and is easier to work with. It also makes a stronger repair with stronger interlaminar bonds.

Unlike the catalyst used with polyester resin, the hardener used with epoxy constitutes a significant proportion—10% to 50%—of the final mixed volume, and this proportion can't be adjusted to retard or hasten the curing. You might, however, be able to choose a fast or slow hardener. The resin will cook off quite quickly if you use a fast hardener, so mix only as much as you can use in 10 to 15 minutes.

While most manufacturers

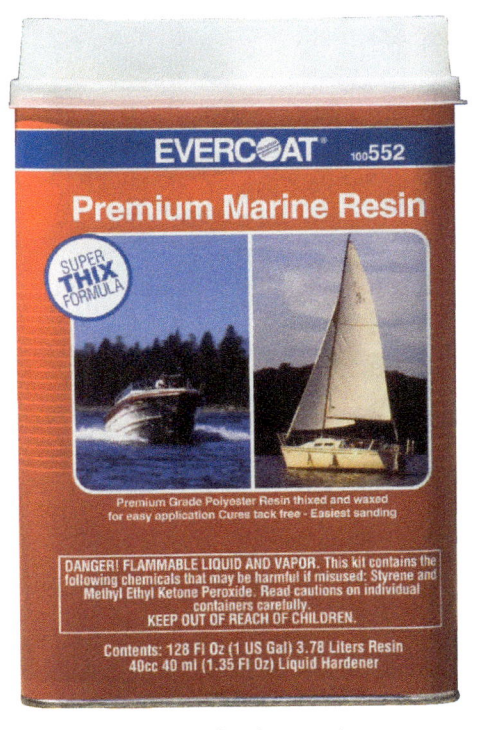

Evercoat polyester finishing resin.

tell you that epoxy will not set up in temperatures below 50°F, believe me it will. It can even set up in freezing conditions, although the process may have to be helped along by shining a heat lamp on the job. If you don't provide some form of heat, the epoxy may sag or remain sticky until it is heated enough to "kick" (start to harden). You must wear gloves and eye protection when working with epoxy; it is a potential allergen, and if you become sensitized to it you will not be able to use it. You'll also need respiratory protection if you're working in a poorly ventilated space. Proper precautions are outlined below. Note, too, that you can clean epoxy with household vinegar rather than using a solvent such as acetone.

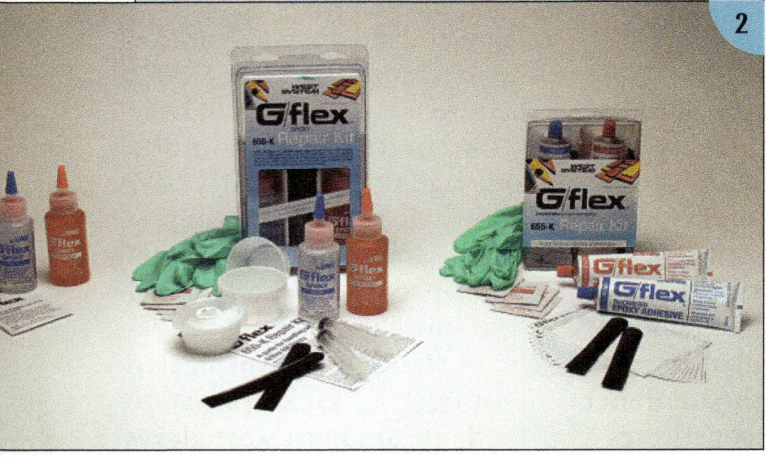

50 • MATERIALS, TOOLS, AND BASIC TECHNIQUES

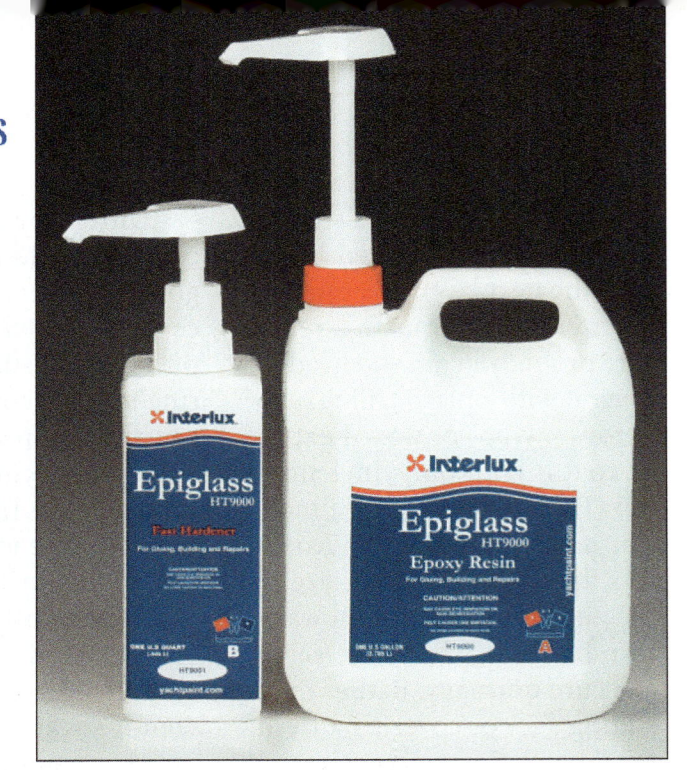

Epiglass epoxy resin and hardener from Interlux. It takes just a few drops of MEKP to cure a polyester resin, but epoxies are mixed in a 1:1, 2:1, 3:1, or 4:1 ratio of resin to hardener. (Courtesy Interlux)

(1) *WEST System epoxy resin, hardener, and metering pumps.* **(2)** *The company's G/flex epoxy remains flexible after curing. (Courtesy WEST System)*

The biggest problem with epoxy is that it has a tendency toward inflexibility and brittleness, which can cause a job literally to fall apart if the epoxy cracks. A new WEST System epoxy called G/flex is reputed to stay flexible indefinitely. I have used it and believe that it really does make epoxy an even more desirable material for fiberglass work, especially where a joint needs to stay flexible. It is mixed in a 1:1 ratio and is very thick, so it requires a lot of squeezing to get out of the tube. (Hint: Put the epoxy in a small plastic bag in case the tube breaks, and then gently stand on it until you have expelled the required amount. Keep the tubes in separate zippered plastic bags to ensure that they don't contaminate each other.)

As mentioned, gelcoat does not bond well to epoxy laminate, so you should use polyester resin for a repair you intend to finish with gelcoat.

Epoxy Putty and Glue

Epoxy is wonderfully versatile stuff. The unthickened resin is low in viscosity, and some epoxies—especially Epiglass—are less viscous than others. Use it for saturating the laminations of a fiberglass repair.

But to coat a core material or seal the exposed edges of a gouge, hole, or other damage that you are about to repair, you need to make the resin less runny, and you can do this by mixing in a little filler to thicken it slightly. You need to thicken the resin substantially to fill cracks, holes, and voids effectively; to fair a surface; or to glue hardware to a deck or bond two surfaces together.

Materials • 51

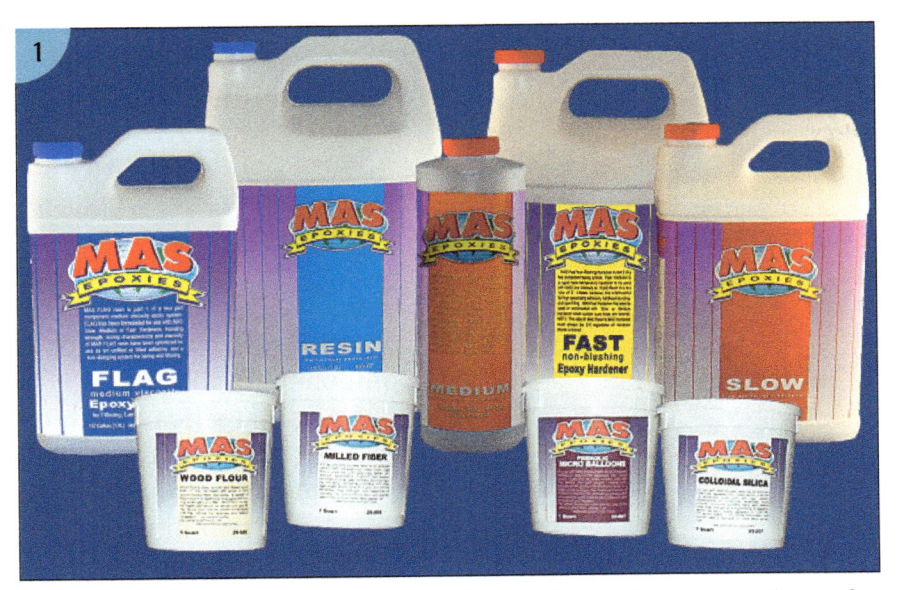

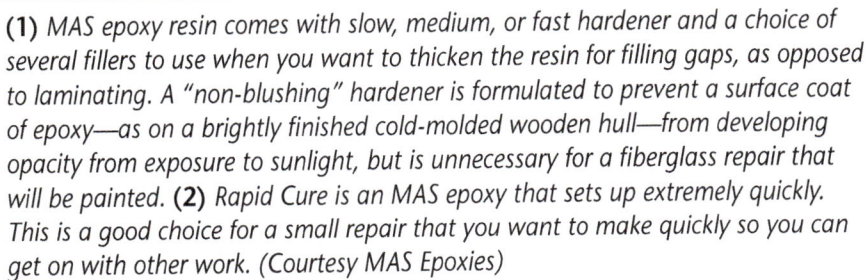

(1) *MAS epoxy resin comes with slow, medium, or fast hardener and a choice of several fillers to use when you want to thicken the resin for filling gaps, as opposed to laminating. A "non-blushing" hardener is formulated to prevent a surface coat of epoxy—as on a brightly finished cold-molded wooden hull—from developing opacity from exposure to sunlight, but is unnecessary for a fiberglass repair that will be painted.* **(2)** *Rapid Cure is an MAS epoxy that sets up extremely quickly. This is a good choice for a small repair that you want to make quickly so you can get on with other work. (Courtesy MAS Epoxies)*

Granted, you can purchase a prethickened epoxy putty such as Marine-Tex, but if you need epoxy for coating and laminating as well as for fairing, filling, and bonding, you can save money and get good results by making your own putty from the epoxy you have on hand and a variety of additives that are available for this purpose. According to the System Three epoxy manual, additives can be divided into four groups depending upon their function: thixotropic (i.e., thickening) agents, bulking agents, fillers, and pigments. The material you select depends upon the characteristics you want in the finished job. For example, if you want a nonsagging, void-filling epoxy putty, you can use colloidal silica, which is a thixotropic agent. Epoxy thickened with silica sets up very hard and requires a lot of sanding, however, so for surface fairing depressions and the like you might prefer to use microspheres instead, which yield a mixture that is easier to sand. Following are brief descriptions of the qualities obtained with various resin additives.

Note: The particles of all these fillers are very small. Wear a dust mask or respirator when using them.

Microballoons. Phenolic microballoons are a low-density filler material that gives a brown cast to the mixture. They are classified as a bulking agent, giving bulk but little strength to the mix. Typically, you can mix 15% to 20% by weight of mi-

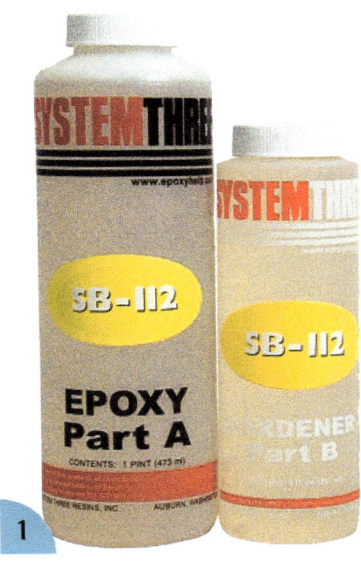

System Three epoxies **(1)**, *including a laminating resin* **(2)**. *(Courtesy System Three)*

MATERIALS, TOOLS, AND BASIC TECHNIQUES

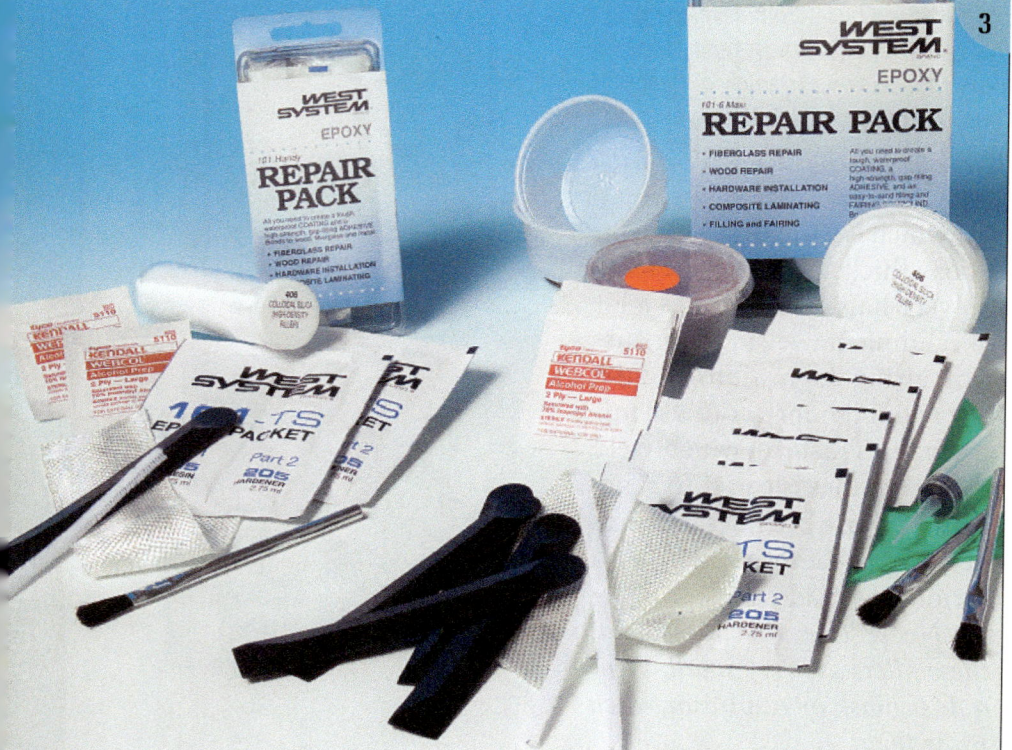

(1) WEST System products. Its 404 High-Density Filler is a thickening agent that creates a maximum-strength epoxy putty for hardware bonding, gap filling, or filleting. Its 406 Colloidal Silica can also be used in these applications. **(2)** WEST System's 501 White Pigment and 503 Gray Pigment. **(3)** The company also offers repair packs. The 101 Handy Repair Pack (left) includes enough resin, hardener, and high-density filler for one typical repair job. The 101-6 Maxi Repair Pack (right) includes both high-density and low-density fillers and will complete a half-dozen typical repairs. (Courtesy WEST System)

croballoons in an epoxy resin to create a fairing putty that will be easy to sand. When using a bulking agent to create a putty for filleting or for filling gaps, you should also add a thixotropic agent to help the resin retain its shape. A microballoon-silica mixture is often used as a filler compound for fillet joints.

Colloidal silica. Colloidal silica is a thixotropic agent that helps make an epoxy easy to spread and also prevents sags and drips while the mixture is drying. Often used in conjunction with other fillers, it gives the epoxy a slightly tan sheen. Manufacturers call it by various names, such as glue powder, Cab-o-Sil, or Aerosil. Colloidal silica makes a strong putty that resists abrasion well, which makes it hard to sand.

Microspheres or glass bubbles. Hollow glass microspheres, sometimes called glass bubbles, are a low-density bulking agent like microballoons. They are used to reduce the weight of resin, cut down on shrinkage, and make a surface that is easy to sand. Microspheres can be added to a resin mixture up to about 20% by weight and used to fill voids.

Microfibers. Microfibers are used to thicken an epoxy in order to obtain better adhesion when bonding wood or fiberglass. They can be made of milled or chopped fibers of glass or plastic. Microfibers are intended to increase the structural and gap-filling properties of the mixture as well as provide bulk. An epoxy mixture with microfibers retains much of its low viscosity but is thicker than the same epoxy with no additive. This quality enables the mixture to set up without bleeding out of the joint.

Pigments. The two most commonly used pigments for epoxy are white paste (titanium dioxide) and graphite (carbon) powder. Typically, white paste is added to a finish coat to make it easier to paint, while graphite may be added to a racing bottom to give self-lubricating properties to the hull. One drawback to graphite, however, is that it is conductive and can therefore set up a galvanic cell.

Other pigments come as a dry powder and are added to the epoxy after it has been mixed. When using colorants, add only a small amount at a time so that you can fine-tune the mixture to get exactly the color you want. Many manufacturers offer coloring agents that can be used with epoxy- or polyester-based resins and putties.

Mold Release Wax

After you lay fiberglass over or into a mold, wet it out with polyester or epoxy resin, and allow it to cure, there comes the moment of truth when you must remove the cured laminate from the mold. To ensure that the laminate doesn't bond to the mold, either cover the mold with plastic (such as a plastic sheet) or polish it with mold release wax. If you opt to cover the mold with a plastic sheet, you may find that the contact surface of the laminate comes away with creases or lines in it where the plastic was stretched. Extensive creasing is undesirable.

To make tooling that imparts no creases or marks to the laminated part, you need to coat the mold with mold release wax. This wax makes the surface of the mold slippery so that gelcoat or laminating resin will not stick to it. Since the wax coating is only a few microns thick, the laminate is a perfect replica of the mold. You can apply mold release wax with a cloth, polishing as you apply, or you can spray it on and polish it later.

TOOLS

You only need a few tools to work with fiberglass. Most are disposable, although a few can be used from job to job. Spatulas, mixing sticks, chip and foam brushes, cups and buckets to hold mixed resin, rubber gloves, a Tyvek suit (often called bunny suits or moon suits), and plastic sheeting can all be considered disposable, as you will use them only once or twice before throwing them away. Nondisposable tools include shears, rollers, resin pumps, resin measuring devices, heat lamps, and respirators.

Disposable Tools

If you're going to work with fiberglass and resins, you should have a supply of disposable gear on hand. You'll need wooden

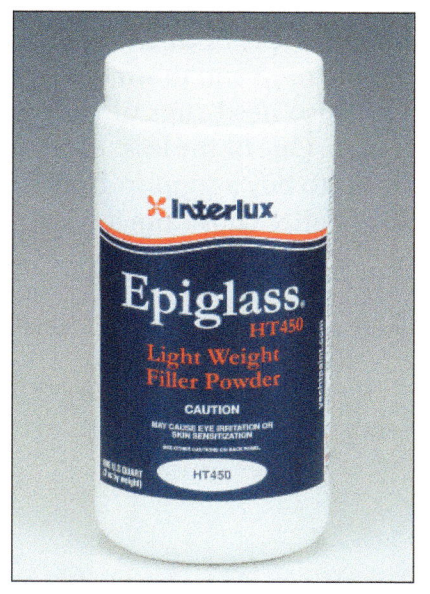

You can mix Interlux's Epiglass HT450 Light Weight Filler Powder with epoxy resin to create an easy-to-sand white fairing compound for filling gaps and bonding fillets. (Courtesy Interlux)

System Three's graphite powder creates a black coating for boat bottoms when mixed with epoxy resin. This is said to give a "faster bottom" to a high-performance boat, but note that graphite conducts electricity and can cause electrolysis when immersed in salt water.

System Three epoxy paste pigment.

MATERIALS, TOOLS, AND BASIC TECHNIQUES

mixing sticks both to stir hardener or catalyst into the resin and to stir thickening agents into it. You'll also need cups of various sizes to mix the resin in. One of the least expensive ways to obtain cups is to buy a supply of small and medium-size paper coffee cups from a convenience store. I also purchase inexpensive small paper buckets. These containers do the same job as the much more expensive ones sold by fiberglass suppliers.

You can use foam rollers for rolling resin onto fiberglass to wet it out. Be sure to buy rollers made for use with fiberglass resins, however. Conventional house painting rollers tend to fall apart when used to apply resins.

You can buy cheap foam and chip brushes and toss them out after using them. It is not worth the time and expense of using a solvent to clean them. There is no need to use a high-quality brush unless you are doing finish work, in which case you should buy one formulated for use with polyester or epoxy resin. I cut down chip brushes so that the bristles are about ½ inch long, which helps when you want to dab resin into cracks and crevices and into the weave of fiberglass roving or cloth.

To protect my hands when working with polyester or epoxy resins, I wear rubber gloves even for small jobs. For larger jobs, I also wear a Tyvek bunny suit to protect my clothes. Somehow or other the Tyvek always gets ripped, however, and resin finds its way in, so I also wear old clothes under the Tyvek.

Fiberglass strands can pierce your skin and respiratory membranes, so you should protect yourself when you work with fiberglass. Wear gloves and some form of eye protection. You should wear a dust mask when mixing thickeners into resin, because these contain microscopic particles that can get into your lungs.

(1) *Spreaders and wooden stirring sticks of various sizes are essential for mixing small quantities of resin. I bought the yellow spreaders shown here, but I made the off-white ones from a thin plastic counter mat. You can cut these thin spreaders to any shape and toss them out after using. Clean the spreaders by wiping them with acetone or some other solvent, but check the edge of a spreader after each use. If it becomes nicked, throw it out and use another.*

(2) *A pair of spreaders from System Three. Most resin manufacturers offer branded resin spreaders like these.*

Tools • 55

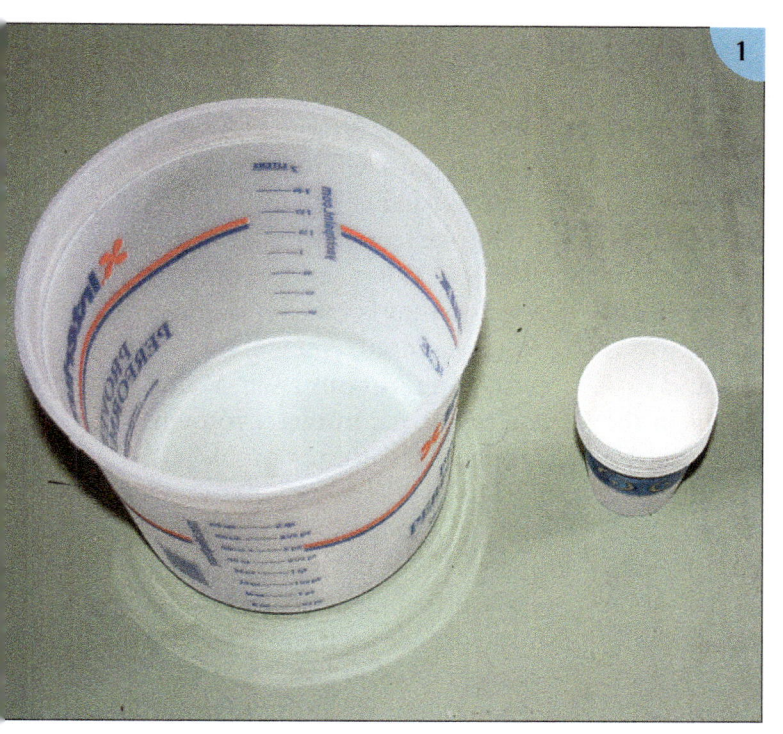

(1) Useful containers for fiberglass work range from small to large. The small paper cups shown here came from a local convenience store, where a hundred of them cost just a few dollars. The plastic bucket came from a paint manufacturer and is handy for mixing large quantities of resin.

(2) Calibrated resin cups like these from System Three make pouring the right amount of resin and hardener quite easy.

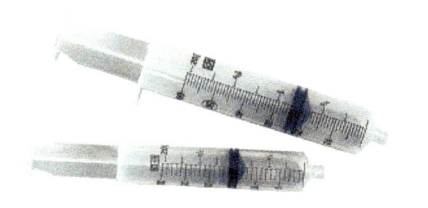

(3) A syringe is handy for squirting resin into an awkward corner or tight joint. WEST System and System Three, among others, offer syringes as small as 1 ounce and as large as a caulking tube. (Photos 2 and 3 courtesy System Three)

An assortment of brush sizes is handy. You can toss out the inexpensive chip brushes (left) and the foam brushes (right) after using them. Be careful when using chip brushes because they tend to shed hairs into the job. They are typically good for only one fairly quick application.

Styrene, phenols, and other chemicals are present in most resins, so you should use a respirator when mixing them (see below; a respirator is also preferable to a dust mask when you're grinding or sanding fiberglass). If you have any questions about the chemicals contained in a particular resin, ask for a copy of the manufacturer's material safety data sheet (MSDS). You can usually find it online at the manufacturer's website.

When doing fiberglass repair work, it is best to cover your work surface with a polyethylene sheet, even though it will tend to make the surface a little slippery underfoot (or under hand). This kind of sheeting can be obtained cheaply either as the special lightweight material sold by boatbuilding supply houses or as rolls of construction-grade polyethylene available at hardware stores. Plastic sheeting protects your workbench or your garage floor from spills, and when a job is done, you can quickly and easily wrap up all the debris in the sheet and dispose of it. Plastic sheeting is also useful when you need to set a lamination job down somewhere to cure. The sheet helps keep the resin from sticking to the underlying surface, and when the resin has cured, flexing the sheet usually dislodges any resin that needs to be thrown away.

A mold is another item that you can consider a disposable tool. When a fiberglass boat is built, as we saw in Chapter 1, a mold is used as the underlying structure to give the laminate its shape. When you are making a repair that is large enough to require a mold, you will have to make one of your own. When the repair is complete, you will probably discard the mold.

Nondisposable Tools

Nondisposable tools that come into contact with resin need to be cleaned after use. Most professionals use acetone, which dissolves the resin, for this job (vinegar can also be used). Again, wear gloves and try not to get acetone on your skin. (MAS Epoxies has developed an organic solvent called Bio-Solv that can be used in place of acetone and is said to be more user-friendly—see page 62.)

Scissors or Shears

You need to cut fiberglass cloth or roving into appropriately sized pieces for the repair. You can tear CSM with your hands, but this leaves a ragged edge and can put a lot of fiberglass dust in the air. It is easier and cleaner to cut CSM, like roving or cloth, with a sharp pair of scissors or shears.

Because these shears will get coated with resin if you use them while laminating, don't spend a fortune on them. An inexpensive pair of scissors works perfectly well for most weights of fiberglass fabric. If

Before starting any fiberglass work, don a pair of rubber gloves to protect your hands from the chemicals in the resin. Do not allow resin to contact your skin. You can become especially sensitized to epoxy resin, and once that happens you'll break out in a rash every time you come near it. These are latex gloves, but if you are sensitive to latex you can use nitrile gloves or buy a pair of heavy-duty kitchen gloves.

Tools • 57

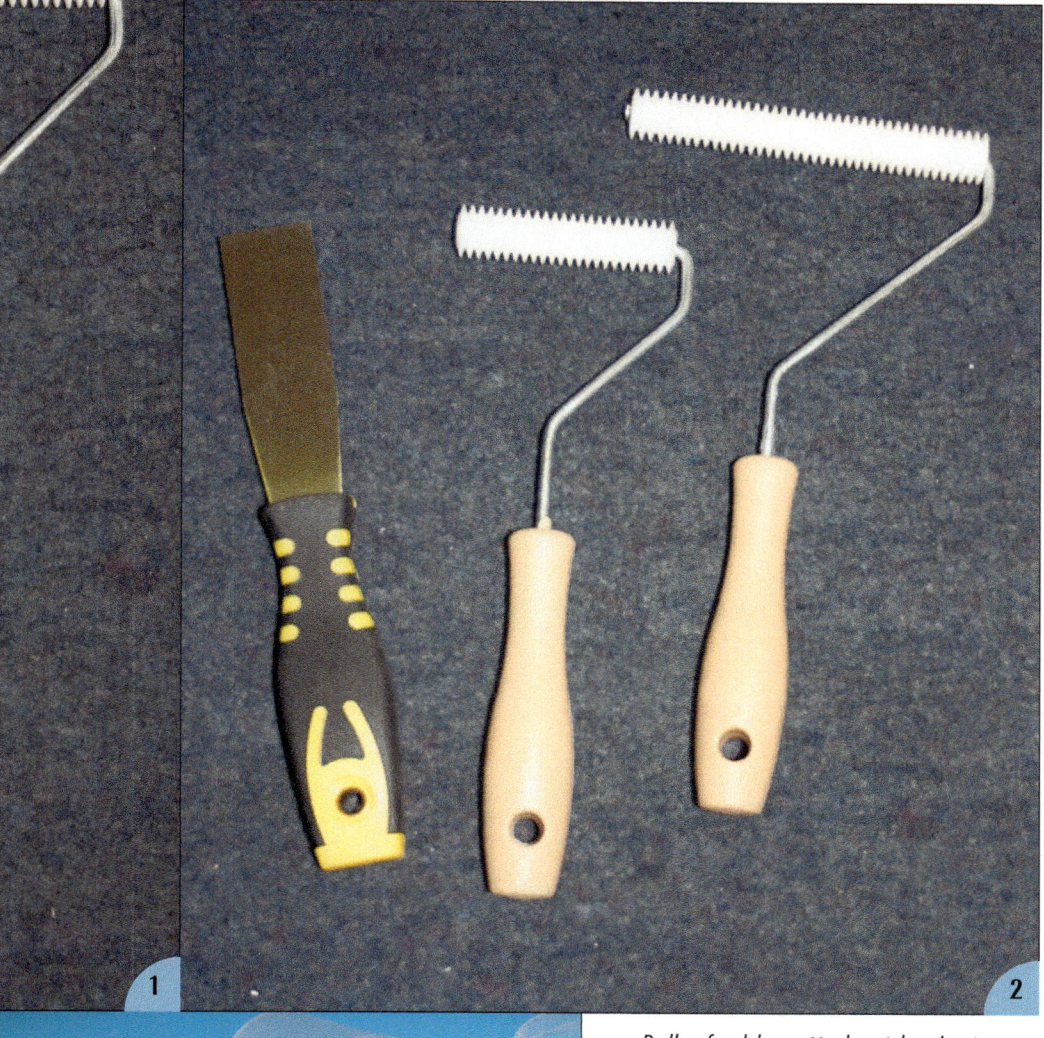

Roll a freshly wetted-out laminate with a plastic or metal roller to work all the bubbles out of the laminate. **(1)** A 5-inch (13 cm) roller. **(2)** A 5-inch and a 3-inch (75 mm) roller together with a spatula, which is handy for spreading thickened polyester or epoxy resin. When using a roller, work from the center toward the edges of the material to remove air bubbles while leaving the laminate undisturbed. **(3)** An assortment of foam rollers and a roller tray for applying resin to a job. Place the tray on a plastic garbage bag; when the job is finished simply dump the used rollers and other disposables on the tray and turn the garbage bag inside out to make cleanup easy and quick. (Photo 3 courtesy WEST System)

58 • MATERIALS, TOOLS, AND BASIC TECHNIQUES

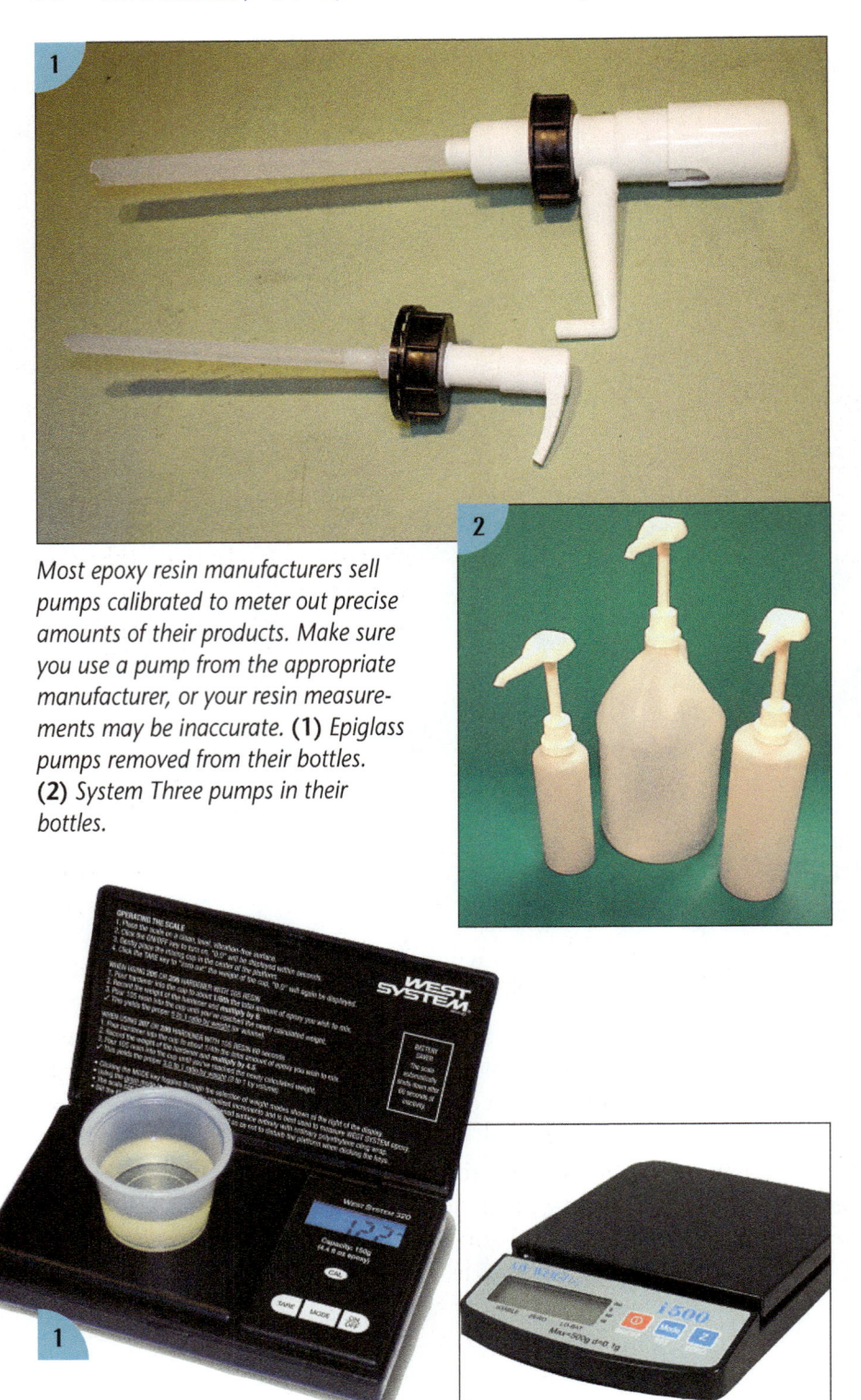

Most epoxy resin manufacturers sell pumps calibrated to meter out precise amounts of their products. Make sure you use a pump from the appropriate manufacturer, or your resin measurements may be inaccurate. (1) Epiglass pumps removed from their bottles. (2) System Three pumps in their bottles.

(1) The tiny WEST System resin measuring scale can be used to measure small amounts of resin. Simply set a cup on the scale, put the desired amount of resin in it, and add the required amount of hardener. Stir well, and your mixture is ready to use. (2) A scale from System Three for measuring small amounts of resin. (Photo 1 courtesy WEST System; Photo 2 courtesy System Three)

you are cutting carbon fiber or Kevlar, however, you will need a pair of heavy-duty shears.

Fiberglass Rollers
Fiberglass rollers made of metal or plastic are available from any fiberglass or resin supplier. These rollers are used to wet out the fiberglass and to eliminate air bubbles in the laminate.

Resin Pumps and Measuring Devices
Resin pumps dispense the exact amount of epoxy resin you need. Always be sure to buy the pump for the particular resin you are using. Virtually all the manufacturers have different formulations for their mixtures, so their pumps are not interchangeable. (When working with polyester resins, measure and mix the catalyst carefully. You can adjust the catalyst amount up or down for a faster or slower cure, but only within limits; sloppy measurements can result in a resin that cures halfway through a job or takes days to cure.)

Other resin measuring devices include balance scales and the WEST System scale for measuring small amounts of epoxy resin. To use one of these scales, put the desired amount of resin in a cup, weigh it, then calculate the proper weight of the finished mixture from the known ratio of resin to hardener. (For example, if the proper ratio of resin to hardener is 3:2 and you have 9 ounces of resin in the cup, you will need 15 ounces of mixed resin and hardener.) Add

You can clip a simple, inexpensive heat lamp on virtually anything and use it to keep the resin on a newly coated surface warm. This type of lamp is fine for small repair jobs, but for larger work you need to maintain a sufficient ambient temperature in the laminating room to ensure that the resin kicks properly. The recommended temperature range for proper curing of most resins is between 50°F and 80°F. The higher the temperature, the faster the resin mixture will kick. In general, a 50° increase in temperature cuts the cure time by about half, although you should not raise the cure temperature above 150°F without careful monitoring and vacuum bagging (see below) to get the best properties from the laminate.

Use an angle grinder to grind back pieces of fiberglass laminate when you need to make a scarf joint. You can get various grades of cutting disks; I prefer to use a 60- or 80-grit disk for fast cutting.

hardener until you achieve that weight. (Alternatively, it is more accurate to measure the resin and hardener separately and then mix them.)

It's a good idea to protect a scale from resin spills by placing it in a clear plastic zippered bag before use.

Heat Lamps

You can use a heat lamp to encourage resin curing in cool weather or help it kick faster in warmer weather. Some people prefer to use an infrared heat lamp, while others use a simple 100-watt incandescent lightbulb. There are also a few specially made heat lamps designed to kick a resin as quickly as possible to help prevent drips and runs.

Grinder or Angle Grinder

To cut back fiberglass (probably the most miserable job ever invented), you need an angle grinder and several different grades of grinding pads. When joining two pieces of fiberglass laminate, you must grind both sides of the joint to a taper, or *scarf*, to prevent a bump where the laminates meet. In general, the width of the ground scarf should be about nine to twelve times the thickness of the laminate.

Dremel Tool

A Dremel tool is a handy addition to your toolbox. It's like a handheld variable-speed drill but a lot more versatile. You can change the collets (the tiny collars that fit inside the chuck to hold the drill bit or other tool in place) and fit a wide variety of devices, from a tiny 3/8-inch-diameter (9 mm) drum sander to a 1/2-inch-diameter (12 mm) saw blade, a 3/4-inch (19 mm) cutting/grinding blade (wear a face mask when using the saw or grinder, as the blades can break apart), or a tiny, heart-shaped reaming bit that is ideal for opening a gelcoat crack into a V-shaped groove that you can fill with gelcoat putty. You can also get a buffing wheel of about 1-inch (25 mm) diameter, a tiny grinding wheel for putting an edge on a knife or other cutting tool, and brittle abrasive wheels for cutting small parts.

Some bits you can scavenge or get inexpen-

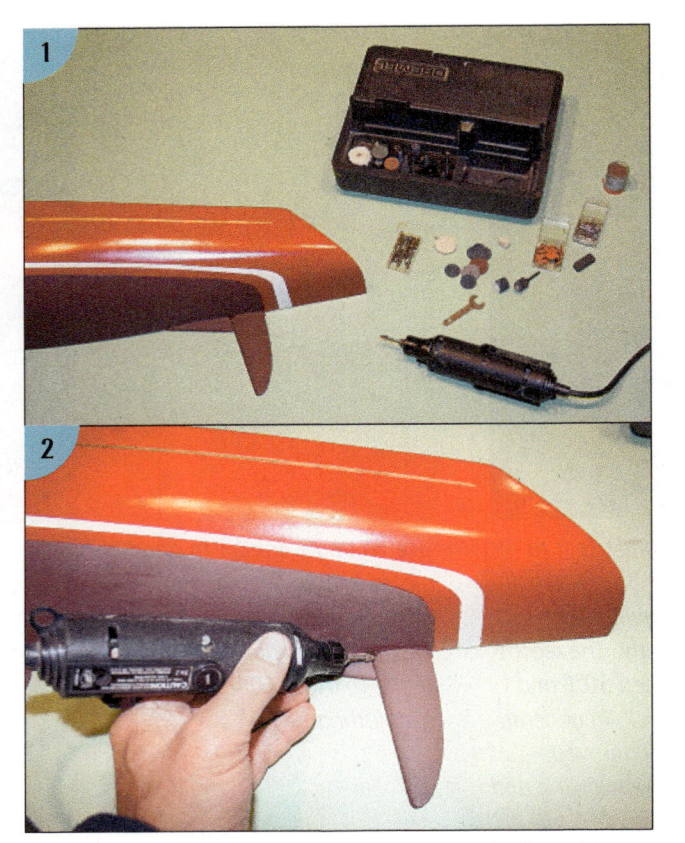

(1) *Using a Dremel tool (bottom right) on a half model. The tool's various bits and boxes of parts are also shown.* **(2)** *You can use the heart-shaped reaming bit to grind a sharp corner into a piece of wood or, as shown here, to remove the glue in a rudder-to-hull junction. You can also use it to open up a gelcoat crack for repair.*

sively. My dentist gave me a large selection of used drill bits and polishing wheels. The bits were no longer sharp enough for teeth but are ideal for carving wood, and I use the polishing wheels to polish small jobs for painting or finishing.

A complete Dremel tool and kit can cost less than $100. Since I bought my Dremel tool, new models, including an easier-to-use and easier-to-hold electric tool, have come on the market.

Respirators

Whenever you are using polyurethanes, epoxy primers, or other two-part paints; grinding or sanding fiberglass; or doing gelcoat work, you should use an organic vapor respirator. Good-quality respirators cost between $40 and $100, but they are worth every penny for the health and safety benefits they provide.

There are several styles of respirator suitable for fiberglass work. The most commonly used one is what 3M calls a disposable organic vapor respirator. It covers the operator's nose and mouth but does not provide eye and ear protection. A slightly better unit is the 3M professional respirator assembly with a 3M organic vapor cartridge.

If you want to upgrade even more, you can use the 6000 Series half-face respirator or the 6000 Series full-face respirator. As the names imply, the half-face does not provide eye protection, while the full-face protects the eyes as well as the nose and mouth. If you use the half-face respirator, you should use an eye shield with it to ensure that you don't get an eyeful of grit. I strongly recommend that anyone working with fiberglass should use a full-face respirator as a matter of course. If you combine that with a head sock that covers your hair, ears, and neck, a Tyvek suit, rubber gloves taped at the wrists, and a pair of boots, you should be fully protected from fiberglass dust and debris.

For spraying marine paints, the best respirator is a powered air purifying respirator (PAPR), which has a belt-mounted air purifier that blows fresh air into the face mask. For the best protection, you can use a PAPR with a high-efficiency cartridge. This style of respirator is expensive, however, and is most often used by professionals working in boatyards. For a person who is bearded or for some other reason cannot wear a face mask respirator, the 3M H-Series hood is an option that offers full head protection over a Tyvek suit.

Professional Tools That Are Nice to Have

If you want to do professional-level work, there are a few additional tools that you might want to acquire. For example, instead of using the rounded end of a spreader or spatula to make a nice smooth fillet or corner radius, professionals use a corner-radius tool, which looks like a miniature dumbbell with differently sized balls on either end. This allows them to select a ball of ideal radius for making a fillet or corner radius.

Another tool that is useful for repair work is a longboard, which professionals use to get a

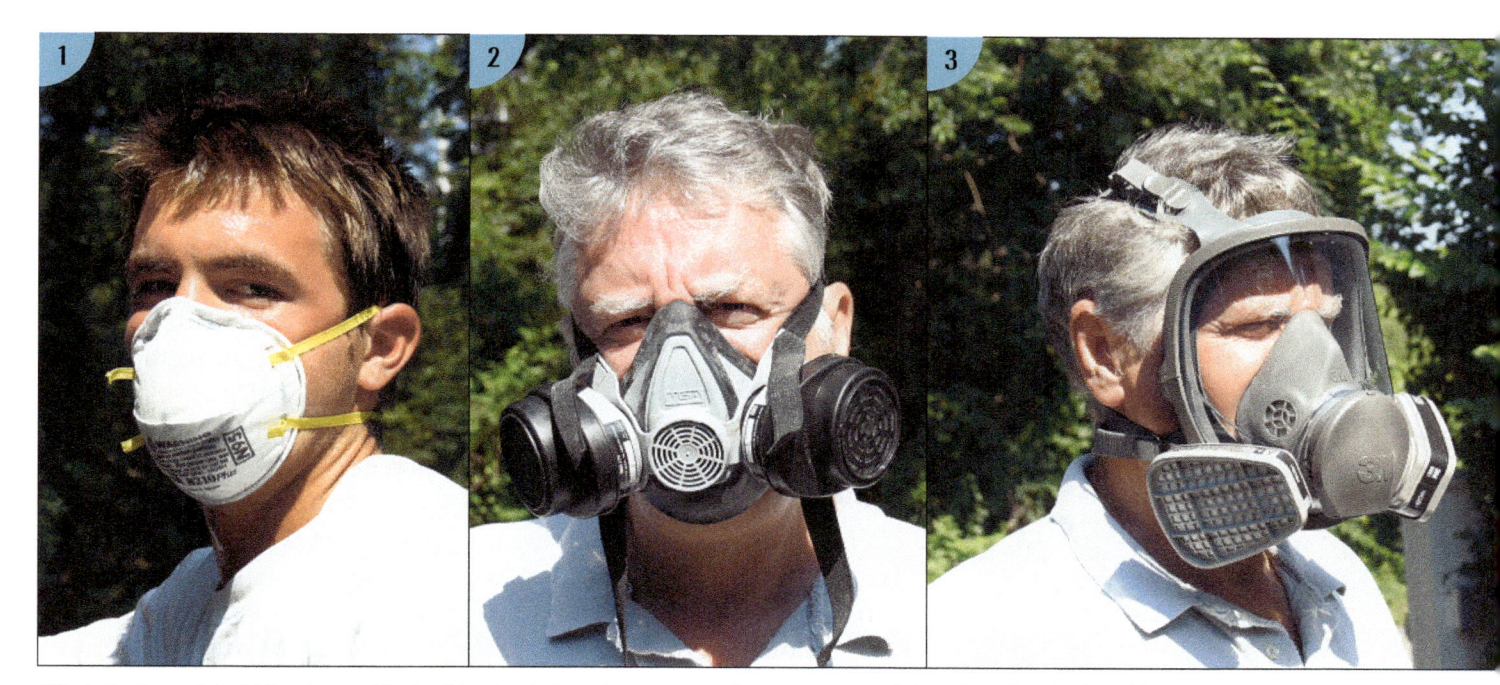

(1) *A dust mask held in place with double elastic bands provides better protection from sanding dust than a single-band mask, but a respirator is even better.* **(2)** *I'm wearing my half-face respirator here. This type of respirator is good for spray painting (when fitted with VOC control filters) and for dust protection (when fitted with dust filters) but does not protect your eyes from paint overspray.* **(3)** *Here I'm wearing a full-face respirator fitted with organic filters. A full-face respirator can protect your eyes as well as your respiratory system.*

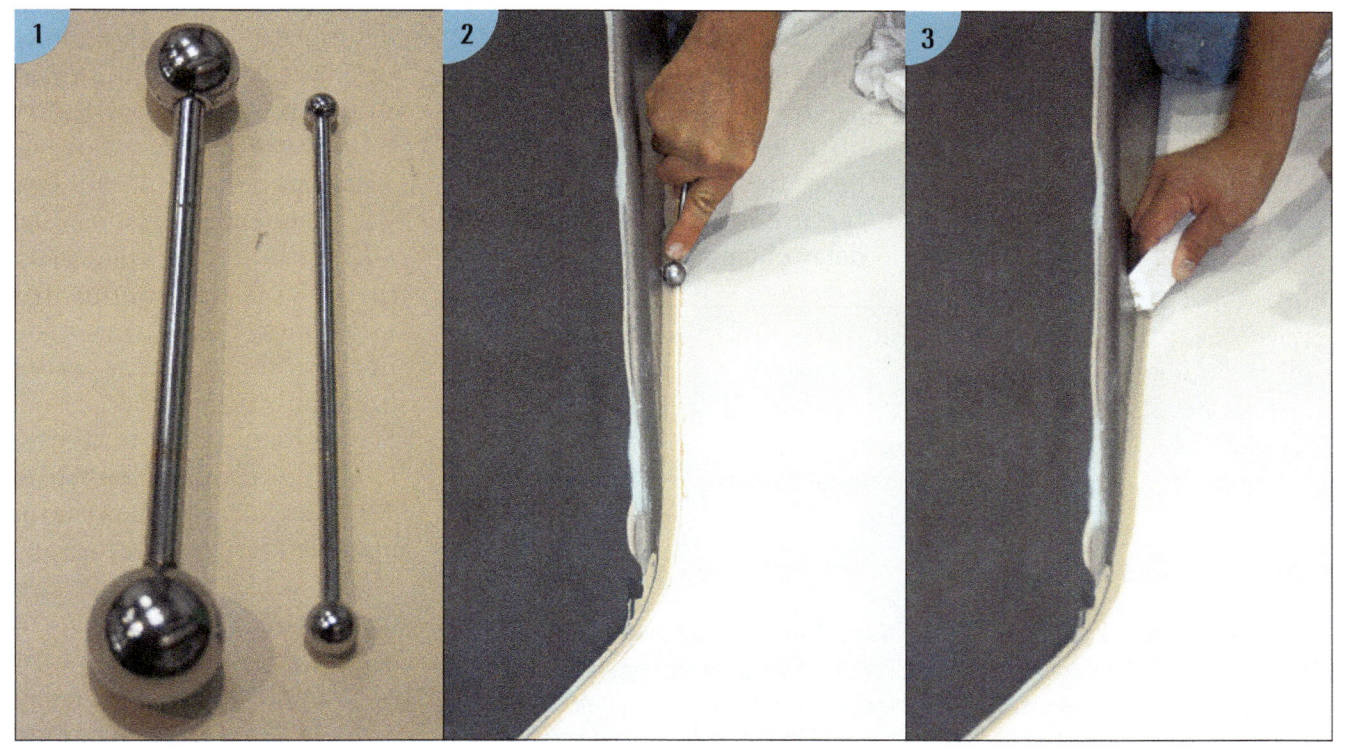

(1) *Two sizes of the corner-radius tool used by experts. A set of these tools costs roughly $50 to $100.* **(2)** *Using a corner-radius tool to impart a perfect radius to a fillet.* **(3)** *Here the operator slides a sharp edge along the corner fillet to remove any excess material.*

smooth, fair surface without bumps or hollows. Most boatbuilders keep a range of longboards on hand. Some are short—around 12 to 18 inches (30 cm to 46 cm) long—while others can be several feet long and require two or three people to operate. If you buy a longboard, make sure the correct grade of sandpaper is available for the board. Some boards can only use specific sizes of sandpaper that may not be available in all grades.

BASIC TECHNIQUES

Mixing Polyester Resin and Catalyst

When using polyester resin, mix only the quantity that you are likely to need immediately. First, pour the desired amount of resin into the pot, and then add the right amount of MEKP catalyst. Stir well from the bottom up so that the MEKP is thoroughly mixed in before you add any fillers or thickeners.

Most polyester resins need 1% to 2% of catalyst by volume. Relative to the hardener used with epoxy resin, this is both a much smaller and a more flexible proportion. You can use slightly less catalyst to delay curing in hot weather or slightly more to hasten curing in cool weather. Most resins in containers up to 1 gallon come with their own tube of catalyst. By making a pinhole in the spout, you can dole out a drop of resin at a time. About 400 drops constitutes 1 ounce, so you would need 8 drops to catalyze 1 ounce of resin at 2%.

Polyester resins contain styrene, otherwise known as vinyl benzene, which is a mild carcinogen. This is the chemical odor that is most obvious when you walk into a fiberglass assembly plant. You should avoid prolonged contact with the fumes. Polyester resin is also flammable, so you should not smoke when using it. In addition, you should take steps to avoid skin contact. Before you start to work, apply a barrier coat to your skin and wear rubber gloves. If you get MEKP on your skin, your skin will turn white. Remove it from your skin as soon as possible. Wash it off with plenty of soap and water rather than, as some builders do, rinsing it off with acetone. You can also use a new organic solvent from MAS Epoxies called Bio-Solv, which is reputed to be totally organic and can be used on skin without dire results. Follow any other steps that the manufacturer recommends.

If you feel the mixture getting warmer, it is starting to set up. The time that elapses from mixing until it sets up is known as the pot life. Polyester resins can create more heat than epoxies, so move a mixture that is getting warm outside the shop,

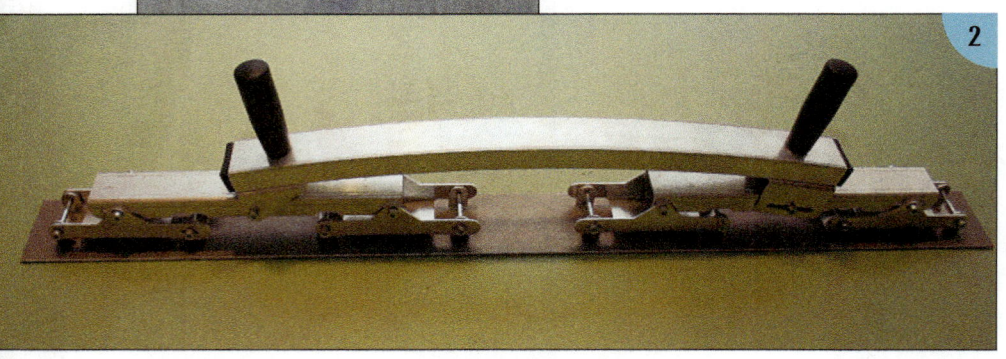

(1) A relatively short longboard that you can purchase from marine stores. The finest grade of sandpaper available for this board is 320-grit, which is about the coarsest grit you would want to use before a final coat of paint. If you'd rather use a finer grit, such as 400, you won't be able to use a longboard of this size. (2) A professional longboard with a flexible blade. This one comes from Flexicat Tools in the Czech Republic; their U.S. website is www.flexicat-usa.com.

place it on a nonflammable surface, and let it kick off. It may smoke; do not inhale the fumes. Do not put it in the trash until it is cold. A number of boat shops have burned down because hot resin was thrown into the trash, where it ignited other flammables.

Mixing Epoxy Resin

Before mixing epoxy, read the instructions carefully to get the proportions right. Each manufacturer formulates its own mixing ratios. Epiglass resin uses a 4:1 ratio, most WEST System epoxies use a 3:1 ratio, MAS epoxy is mixed in a 2:1 ratio, and WEST System's G/flex epoxy needs a 1:1 ratio. Getting your proportions just right will be a lot easier if you use the manufacturer's pumps. Check the pumps carefully if they have not been used for a while, however. Sometimes a pump opening gets clogged over time, causing you to dispense less than you want.

The next step, before starting to mix, is to don rubber gloves so that you will not get epoxy on your skin. Again, epoxy is an allergen, and people can become highly sensitized to it over time. Eventually they may break out in a rash every time they use it, and there are stories of boatbuilders who have been forced to stop working with epoxy altogether. If you plan on adding a thickening compound, wear a dust mask so that you don't inhale the thickener.

When you're reading the manufacturer's MSDS and/or instructions, check the pot life of the prod-

Bio-Solv, new to the market, is advertised as a much safer alternative to acetone. (Courtesy MAS Epoxies)

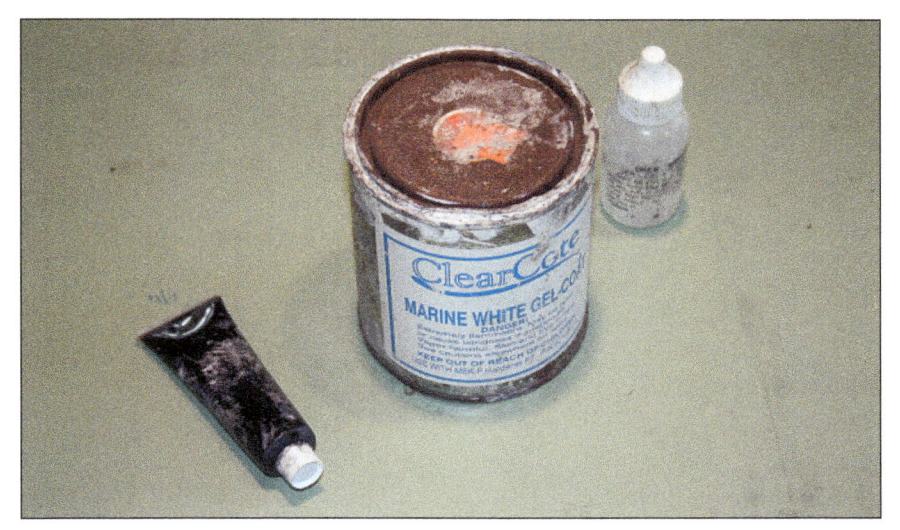

You can purchase small cans of resin (in this case, gelcoat resin) suitable for most small repair jobs at your local chandlery or marine products distributor. Be sure to measure out the resin carefully in order to get a good, strong bond. The bottle to the right rear of this photo contains MEKP, while the tube in the lower left contains a black coloring agent. It only took one or two drips of the black pigment to turn white gelcoat from this can the right shade of gray to repair the 420 shown in Chapter 4.

uct. Some epoxies harden very quickly. For example, MAS epoxy with fast hardener can kick off within 7 minutes. This means that you must have everything ready to work on before you mix the batch.

MATERIALS, TOOLS, AND BASIC TECHNIQUES

To mix epoxy, squirt or pour the desired amount of epoxy into a paper or epoxy-resistant cup and then add the hardener. Stir the mixture well. Make sure you dig into the corners while stirring, and that the mixture acquires a uniformly silky-smooth consistency. You should spend at least 2 to 3 minutes stirring the epoxy and hardener mixture. As soon as it is mixed thoroughly, you can use it. If you plan on using a thickener, you should thoroughly stir the epoxy and hardener mixture first and then add the thickener. Once it is prepared, you should use the thickened epoxy as quickly as possible.

If your epoxy kicks off in the cup (you'll feel the cup getting warmer and warmer), take the cup outside and set it on concrete or some other fireproof surface. As with polyester resin that is kicking, *do not* throw uncured epoxy into the trash. It generates a lot of heat as it kicks off (I have seen it literally smoking), and it can set the trash on fire.

Thickening Polyester or Epoxy Resins

There are a few more tips for adding a thickener besides just making sure that the resin and the hardener (or catalyst) are mixed together thoroughly first. Before opening the thickener container, you should put on a dust mask. Thickeners are fine powders of colloidal silica, microballoons, glue powder, or even plain sawdust, and they can easily become airborne and get into your lungs. Once the container is open, measure out the thickener carefully and pour it into the already well-stirred resin mixture. Stir in the thickener gently. If you stir it too vigorously, you'll spill it. Make sure the entire mixture is well wetted before applying it to the job.

Wetting Out and Rolling a Fiberglass Fabric

To learn how to roll fiberglass properly, place a pane of glass flat on your workbench. Polish it with mold release wax, then dry-fit a square of CSM to it. Cover the layer of mat with a similarly sized square of cloth, then wet out the two pieces of fiberglass with whatever resin you are using. Use your chip or foam brush to apply the resin until the fabric is saturated. It will be uniformly transparent when saturated; areas of white strands indicate resin starvation, so work more resin into those areas. An excess of resin is less than ideal, but resin-starved areas are worse, so be judiciously generous in your resin application.

When the laminate is thoroughly wetted out, roll it with a metal fiberglass roller, working from the center outward. After two or three strokes, lift the pane of glass and inspect it from the underside. You should see very few bubbles. If bubbles are present, roll the patch again, then lift the glass and inspect it a second time. You should see fewer bubbles. If you continue to roll the fiberglass, you are apt to increase the number of bubbles as the thickening resin starts to make the fiberglass lift off the glass sheet. When this

(1) *Epoxy should be mixed carefully. Be sure to measure out the correct proportions of epoxy and hardener for the particular epoxy you are using. Stir the mixture well for at least 2 to 3 minutes, making sure that you scoop the epoxy out of the corners of the pot.* **(2)** *Then, and only then, add your filler powder and stir it in.*

happens, you've gone too far. You want the minimum number of bubbles.

When working on an actual job (not just a pane of glass for practice), you should wet the surface with a foam roller dipped in polyester resin mixture, just as you would paint a wall with house paint. Then press the fiberglass reinforcement fabric onto the wet resin and roll it over with a foam roller dipped in resin. After the fiberglass has been fully wetted out (again, you can judge this by the transparency of the strands), roll it carefully with a metal fiberglass roller to eliminate voids.

You will probably not be able to get rid of voids and bubbles entirely just by rolling the laminate, however. To reduce bubbles to an absolute minimum, some do-it-yourselfers like to vacuum bag their work.

After coating the repair surface with well-mixed resin, lay your fiberglass in the wet resin. Add a little more resin on top of the fiberglass and roll it out to ensure that the entire surface is wet. Work from the center toward the edges to eliminate air bubbles. (Courtesy System Three)

Vacuum Bagging

As you become more experienced working with fiberglass and resin, you may decide that you want to get a better (i.e., lower) resin-to-reinforcement ratio. The resin-to-reinforcement ratio in a hand-laid fiberglass laminate is typically about 70:30. This is adequate but not ideal. A builder (or a repairer) can make a stronger, lighter laminate by adding more fiberglass relative to resin.

Professionals can get a 65:35 ratio in a traditional layup, but reducing that ratio further while at the same time ensuring that the fiberglass reinforcement is fully saturated with resin is difficult without special techniques. To achieve this, many builders and some repairers use *vacuum bagging*. With this technique the laminate is laid up as normal, but when the layup is complete the entire job is covered with a sacrificial covering, often Peel Ply (see page 17), which allows resin to seep through it. Then a bleeder cloth or other membrane that allows air and resin to flow through it is placed on top of the Peel Ply. That is followed by an airtight plastic membrane with a specially plugged hole to which a vacuum is applied; the vacuum sucks out air and pulls some of the resin from the resin-rich laminate through the Peel Ply and into the absorbent layer.

Amateur builders and repairers will find that the vacuum created by an air compressor or even a vacuum cleaner is adequate for this job, but don't use either one unless you don't mind getting resin accidentally sucked into the appliance. A professional will probably have access to a vacuum pump to draw the air out of the layup.

When the Peel Ply and absorbent material are removed at the end of the vacuum-bagging process, resin comes with

66 • MATERIALS, TOOLS, AND BASIC TECHNIQUES

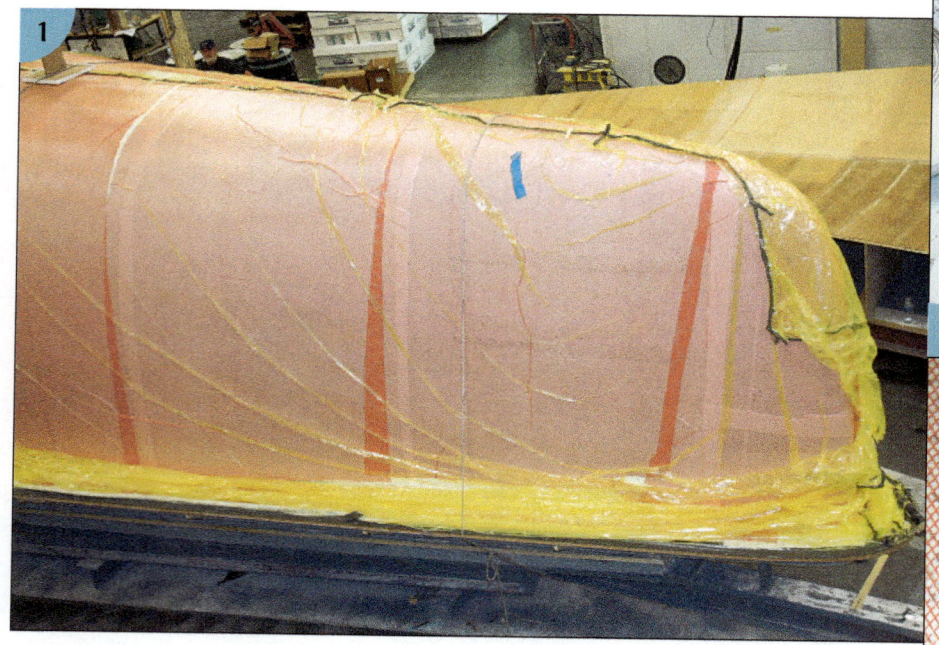

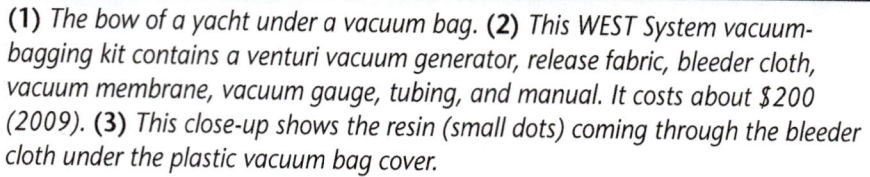

(1) The bow of a yacht under a vacuum bag. (2) This WEST System vacuum-bagging kit contains a venturi vacuum generator, release fabric, bleeder cloth, vacuum membrane, vacuum gauge, tubing, and manual. It costs about $200 (2009). (3) This close-up shows the resin (small dots) coming through the bleeder cloth under the plastic vacuum bag cover.

it, and the laminate has fewer voids. Whereas a typical hand-laid laminate contains about 15% to 20% voids, a vacuum-bagged laminate might have only 1% to 2% voids. Meanwhile, the resin-to-reinforcement ratio can be reduced to 40:60—i.e., more glass than resin—anything less than which may yield a "dry" laminate without enough resin to hold it together. The Do-it-Yourself Vacuum Bagging sidebar on page 138 describes how to use a vacuum bag in greater detail.

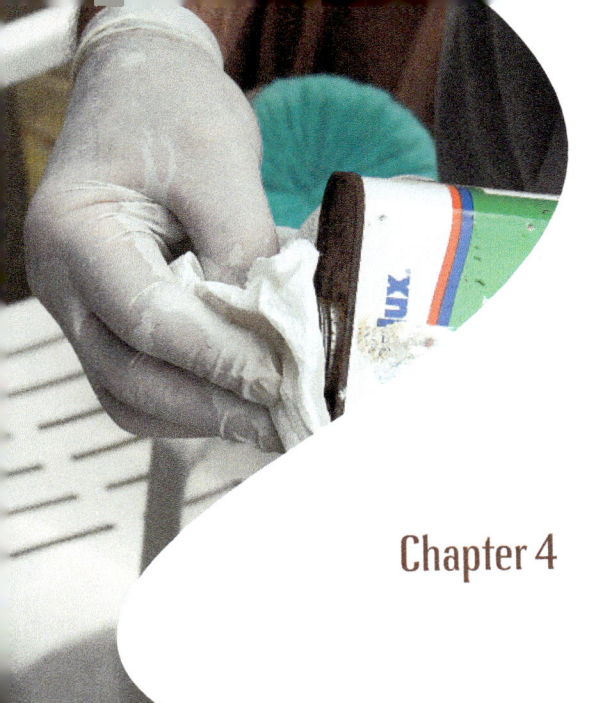

Chapter 4
GELCOAT RESTORATION AND COSMETIC REPAIRS

As we saw in Chapter 1, the gelcoat is the outer layer of pigmented polyester resin that protects an underlying fiberglass laminate from abrasion and wear. When a fiberglass hull or deck is formed in a female mold, the gelcoat is applied first, sprayed to a uniform thickness against the mirror-smooth polished interior surface of the mold. The gelcoat thickness is 10 to 20 mils (a mil is a thousandth of an inch), making it an order of magnitude thicker than a coat of paint. Unlike a coat of paint, it is also chemically cross-linked (not just mechanically adhered) to the fiberglass laminate that follows it into the mold. When a hull or deck is removed from its mold, its gelcoat should be not only beautiful but highly durable.

But gelcoat is not immune to deterioration. Over the years its surface may oxidize, becoming porous and therefore dull with a powdery, chalky appearance. The thickness and uniformly dispersed pigment of the gelcoat prove advantageous at this point, because the oxidized gelcoat can be removed with rubbing compound and a polisher to reveal the like-new gelcoat beneath it—shiny, brightly pigmented, and with minimum porosity. Less commonly, depending on how it was made and

(1) *This crazed gelcoat is too far gone to be resuscitated. It will have to be sanded off, and the topsides will have to be filled and painted or re-gelcoated to make them shiny again. Had the owner acted sooner, he could have addressed the problem by dewaxing the topsides, sanding the crazed gelcoat thoroughly, priming with a high-build epoxy primer, filling gouges and other flaws with epoxy putty, applying a second coat of high-build epoxy primer, and then applying a polyurethane topcoat. (See Chapter 9 for more on finishing.) It would still have been a lot of work, but at least he wouldn't have had to sand off the crazed gelcoat entirely.*

GELCOAT RESTORATION AND COSMETIC REPAIRS

(2) This oxidized gelcoat could have been restored with aggressive compounding, but the hull had sustained other damage and the owner decided to paint the boat. (This is the hull of the J/24 owned by my son; other repairs to this boat are described in Chapters 5 and 7.)

(3) This gelcoat looks as if it hasn't been polished or waxed in years. If the owner continues to neglect it, it could end up looking like the gelcoat in the preceding photos. Restoring it will require aggressive compounding with an abrasive rubbing compound (see the buffing compound sidebar on page 72), followed by waxing and polishing.

applied, gelcoat may harden and yellow slightly with age. If applied *too* thickly it may crack and craze, making repairs to it extremely difficult.

In general, hard gelcoats are formulated for enhanced resistance to fading and discoloration from ultraviolet light but are more prone to cracking as the hull flexes in a seaway. Soft gelcoats are more resistant to cracking but more likely to chalk and fade. On the underwater portion of a hull, many builders (since the early 1990s) use a vinylester gelcoat that is much less permeable to water migration into the hull laminate and therefore helps prevent osmotic blistering. Some builders apply an epoxy barrier coat over the gelcoat for the same reason.

GELCOAT RESTORATION

We'll focus here on topsides gelcoat, but the procedures for deck, cabin, and flybridge gelcoat are the same, with one big exception: You do not want to apply wax to nonskid deck surfaces, because doing so would defeat the purpose of the nonskid.

There are four steps in the process of restoring a moderately tired topsides gelcoat to tip-top shape: (1) cleaning the topsides; (2) getting out heavy stains such as rust stains or black streaks around the exhaust; (3) removing any oxidation and buffing the surface; and (4) doing a final waxing and polishing. Many manufacturers offer one-step products that clean, remove oxidation, and apply a layer of wax in a single application. Such products are tempting because they save time and effort, but I don't think they do as good a job as the more laborious multistep approach unless the gelcoat is only slightly dirty and oxidized to begin with. In all other cases, the boat never seems quite

Gelcoat is about 10 to 20 mils thick, or the thickness of five to ten sheets of copy paper. It is designed to provide a shiny, attractive outer layer that protects the boat's surface from UV and other forms of degradation. This hull has black gelcoat, which tends to heat up in sunlight and eventually show print-through of the woven fiberglass laminate beneath it. White gelcoats do not heat up so much and are less likely to show print-through.

as clean or the final finish quite as glossy.

If your gelcoat is *really* tired, there remains another possible solution short of painting the topsides: You can apply a clear, paint-like polymer finish such as Poli Glow, NewGlass2, or Vertglas to bring back the gloss. We'll return to these products below. Once you have the gelcoat gleaming again, you should take steps to keep it that way with ongoing maintenance.

Cleaning the Hull

The first step is to give the entire hull a general cleaning with fresh water, a good sponge, and a good boat soap to remove water-soluble dirt and debris. There are lots of boat soaps available. Star brite (www.starbrite.com) makes Boat Wash and Sea Safe Boat Wash, Super Spray Boat Cleaner, Instant Hull Cleaner, and Super Green Cleaner, among other products. 3M (www.3M.com) makes Marine Boat Soap, and Sudbury makes Boat Zoap Plus (www.sudburyboatcare.com). CRC Industries (www.crcindustries.com) makes the highly concentrated MaryKate Super Suds, and marine retail chain stores offer their own brands. Some people simply use dishwashing soap, but you have to rinse it off thoroughly before it dries or it will leave alkaline streaks. For this reason you should use a pH-neutral soap, and for the sake of environmental friendliness you should select one that is also biodegradable and phosphate-free. The ideal soap is nonstreaking, leaves no waxy deposits, and gets the topsides squeaky clean. After you have finished cleaning the hull, wipe it down with a soft cloth and let it dry.

I've tried most of the boat soaps, and they all do a pretty good job. You'd be hard pressed to tell the differences among them unless you were to make product comparisons while cleaning different sections of the same boat on the same day. I've noticed a tendency for some petroleum-based cleaners to leave a slight yellowish tint over time. Experiment to discover your own preferences.

Removing Stains

With the surface dirt removed, we come to the hard part of cleaning a hull. Getting out stubborn stains is a real problem, and few cleaners do a perfect job. If you want an excellent gelcoat restoration, however, you'll need to get out the stains before you wax the topsides.

I've tested a number of stain removers. Most are acid based (oxalic acid) and remove 75% to 80% of a stain. Few will remove a stain completely in the first pass unless the stain is mild. Deeply ingrained stains are hard to get out entirely even with several applications.

Davis (www.davisnet.com) makes a fiberglass stain remover called FSR (Fiberglass Stain Remover), a mild oxalic acid gel that is excellent for removing the yellow staining that inevitably appears on a white hull after a season in less than pristine water. Simply apply a small amount, and the yellow wipes off with no rubbing whatever. For a variety of other stains, I have tried Inter-

70 • GELCOAT RESTORATION AND COSMETIC REPAIRS

The Interlux line of boat-care products. (Courtesy Interlux)

GreenClean Boat Soap from Trac Ecological Marine Products. (Courtesy Trac Ecological)

CRC Industries' MaryKate On & Off Hull & Bottom Cleaner contains hydrochloric, phosphoric, and oxalic acids for stain removal. Wear rubber gloves and eye protection when you work with an acid-based stain remover. (Courtesy CRC Industries)

lux's (www.yachtpaint.com) Heavy Duty Stain Remover followed by its Light Duty Rubbing Compound and find that that they do a good job. If that fails, CRC Industries makes the MaryKate On & Off Hull & Bottom Cleaner that incorporates hydrochloric, phosphoric, and oxalic acids. This is a potent cleaner, however, and should be used with caution.

Jan Mundy, former editor of *DIY Boat Owner* magazine, reports that "Interlux Stain Remover does an amazing job on just about everything: algae, grease, blackened inspection ports, and well-cured seagull poop. Apply it with a chip brush, let it sit for 5 to 10 minutes, agitate the area with a soft bristle brush, and hose off. Any parts you missed will be clearly visible. This cleaner," Mundy adds, "contains a mild oxalic acid solution that doesn't harm surfaces and is not so toxic that you need to wear a moon suit and work upwind of it."

When you're trying to remove tough stains, it is important to let the product sit on the affected area for the recommended "cure" time before you rub the surface with a non-scratching brush or pad. Also take note that when using strong acids or solvents, you should be sure to wear gloves, protective clothing, and eye protection—or better still, a face mask and respirator. You definitely do not want to get an acid-based cleaner in your face and eyes or breathe the fumes. The last step after using most boat-cleaning products is to rinse the surface well with plenty of fresh water.

Even the most diligent efforts with a stain remover may fail to remove extremely tough stains completely. Those caused by rust are particularly stubborn. Even when you use a specially formulated rust remover, a shadow of the stain may remain. In such cases, you may have to follow the stain remover with a rubbing compound. 3M makes several professional-series rubbing compounds and pastes that are designed to remove heavy stains. Be forewarned, however, that rubbing compounds, also called buffing compounds, contain microparticles of silica that abrade the gelcoat to remove marks. These compounds range from white (least aggressive; finest silica particles) through intermediate shades of tan to dark brown (most aggressive; coarsest silica particles), as described in the sidebar on buffing compounds on page 72. You should choose the least abrasive compound that will do the job, and you must be careful not to rub too heavily or you will go through the gelcoat.

If even an aggressive rubbing compound fails to remove a stain, you may need to give the area a good wet sanding with 360- or 400-grit wet-or-dry sandpaper. This is likely to cause other problems, however. It will leave scratches that you will then have to buff out with a serious rubbing compound, and by the time you've done all that you may well have worn away the gelcoat, exposing patches of underlying laminate. See the Repairing Abraded Gelcoat section later in this chapter, and don't get this aggressive if you can help it.

Removing Oxidation

As mentioned, oxidation is dulling, chalking, and increased porosity of the topside gelcoat caused by exposure to ultraviolet light, weather, and salt water. If your hull lacks its former luster when dry, wipe the gelcoat with a slightly moist sponge. If the sponge comes away with a chalky smear on it (white if the gelcoat is white), the hull is oxidized. If there is no chalky residue on the sponge and the hull becomes shiny and bright when wet, the gelcoat is not oxidized, just faded. In that case, a good waxing and polishing may be all it needs.

Many boats, however, will be found to have oxidation. A buffing compound such as Shurhold's (www.shurhold.com) Yacht Brite Buff Magic will remove mild oxidation. You can apply and buff a compound like this by hand, but most professional boat detailers use an electric buffer revolving at about 2,000 rpm to 2,500 rpm. Apply the compound sparingly and work in a circular motion over a small area before moving on to the next area, which should slightly overlap the one before.

Products for removing mild oxidation also come in liquid form, such as Interlux's Light Duty Rubbing Compound. For very lightly oxidized gelcoats, some people prefer a one-step product such as those from Seapower Products (www.seapower.com) and 3M that clean and wax at the same time. These are essentially hybrid products—waxes that contain some rubbing compound. At the mild end, these cleaners and waxes are more wax than compound. At the aggressive end, so-called restorer waxes are more compound than wax. By using a hybrid product you can avoid a follow-up waxing, but if you're attacking stains as well as oxidation, you risk covering a stain with a layer of wax and making it harder to remove.

Shurhold says Buff Magic removes rust, stains, and oxidation. The compound is meant for light oxidation, and its abrasive particles are finer than those in a more aggressive rubbing compound. The best compound to use is the least aggressive one that will do the job. Shurhold claims that its abrasive particles wear finer with continued buffing, thus providing a prewax polish while removing oxidation. (Courtesy Shurhold Industries)

Again, as a general rule, you want to use the mildest, least aggressive rubbing compound that will do the job. Eventually, as the years go by, you may rub right through the gelcoat, but you'd like that time to be later—maybe even after you sell the boat—not sooner.

To restore a heavily oxidized gelcoat, however, you will generally need a heavy-duty rubbing compound. Examples include Evercoat's Heavy-Duty Fiberglass Rubbing Compound and Star brite's Liquid Rubbing Compound for Heavy Oxidation. Many other manufacturers make compounds formulated to remove heavy oxidation, among them Meguiar's (http://marinerv.meguiars.com) Oxidation Remover, Vertglas (www.vertglas.

com) Oxidation Remover, and 3M Super Duty Rubbing Compound. Do not buff a hull with Soft Scrub or other household products. The grains of silica and kaolin clay in boat-buffing compounds are much smaller than those in products made for the home. Consequently, household products will leave a dull finish rather than buffing to a shine as boat-rubbing compounds do.

Again, although you can apply and buff a rubbing compound by hand, an electric buffer with a 10-inch (25 cm) buffing pad will make the work go faster, especially if you have a large area to do. Look for a machine with variable speeds and a dual buffing-polishing action. Such tools range between $75 and $300. Be sure to use a specially made buffing pad as well, which typically has a 1-inch (25 mm) wool pile. A new pad works best. I prefer the 3M pad with the Hookit SBS system because it stops rotating if it gets stuck instead of continuing to rotate and eventually burning out. (The Hookit system is rather like having a Velcro backing on the pad rather than a mechanical means of fastening it.) After using a pad, wash it out carefully and store it in a zippered plastic bag to keep it free of contaminants. Before using the pad again, "refluff" it using a spur or a comb made especially for this purpose.

Prewax Finishes

Before waxing your boat—especially if you've had to do some aggressive compounding to remove oxidation—you might want to apply an intermediate polish. These finishes usually come from the car industry and are aimed at removing swirl marks, filling scratches, and giving a highly polished sheen to a surface. For example, after compounding and before waxing, you can use Finesse It II Glaze, a car-polishing product from 3M, to impart a brilliant shine to your hull. Glaze removes swirl marks and levels the gelcoat to give a deep, even shine. Glaze does not contain any UV blocker, so you will

A NOTE ON BUFFING COMPOUNDS

Buffing compounds are pigmented roughly according to grit level, with white being the least aggressive and brown being the most aggressive. Remember that it is the grit in the compound that actually does the work.

The medium in which these microparticles are suspended liquefies when pressure is applied, in order to lubricate the buffing pad. Try out the compound you have purchased on a small area where the results will not be seen—like under the transom. Only if you are satisfied with the outcome should you proceed to other parts of the boat. When working with an electric buffer, be sure to keep the pad moving for best results. If you continue to work in one spot for several minutes, you can generate a lot of heat, which is not desirable. If you are generating a lot of heat even while keeping the pad moving, either back off on the pressure or use a little more compound.

Bruce Johnson of the Jamestown Boat Yard using an electric buffer to cover a large area quickly. Johnson buffs one small area at a time before moving on to another. Working in this fashion, you can buff an entire boat in a few hours. Tyvek suits make sense for messy jobs.

Electric polishing and buffing machines and pads. The machine at right is an inexpensive (under $50) dedicated polishing machine from Rockford. The polisher shown at bottom is a battery-powered low-speed unit by Ryobi (about $40 to $75). The variable-speed Makita buffer/polisher (about $150 to $200) used by most professional boatyards is shown at top. At the left are various Hookit buffing pads from 3M. These pads stick to the buffer pad by means of a Velcro-style backing.

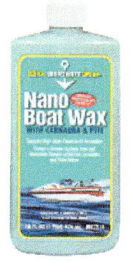

Like Eagle One's NanoWax, CRC Industries' MaryKate Nano Boat Wax contains a UV blocker and is meant as a finish wax. Both products contain carnauba, the traditional basis of a marine wax, and both manufacturers claim that their products fill and eliminate tiny scratches and swirl marks to achieve a highly polished finish. (Courtesy CRC Industries)

have to wax the gelcoat within a week or two.

Another product used to remove swirl marks (also coming from the car industry) is NanoWax, from Eagle One (www.eagleone.com), a spray-on carnauba wax product that is designed to conceal any marks and scratches left by compounding and to achieve a high-gloss shine. It takes its name from the nano-sized particles it contains, which are reputed to penetrate deeply into the surface being polished. It does contain a UV blocker to prevent fading from sunlight, and need not be followed with a finish wax. MaryKate Nano Boat Wax is a similar product.

Another alternative is Interlux's Teflon Wax Sealer, a product that can be used with or without a follow-up wax. It protects against UV, seals any micropores or cracks in the gelcoat, and provides a shiny, low-friction surface. It is easily applied with a cloth and requires only light buffing.

Final Waxing

Once you have removed all the oxidation from a fiberglass hull, the finish step is to apply and polish a coat of wax. Waxing a hull protects it against UV degradation, helps cut down on oxidation, and also aids in keeping the hull clean by sealing gelcoat pores.

Long gone are the days when boat waxes were simply wax. Most "waxes" today do contain some traditional carnauba wax, but they also include a blend of polymers and glossifiers. A quick check of labels on some of the waxes in a local marine store showed that they contain petroleum distillates, naphtha, and hydrocarbons as well as carnauba wax. Manufacturers recommend that you wear a respirator when using these waxes to protect your lungs from the distillates—although I have yet to see anybody in my local boatyard actually follow this precaution.

Once applied, lightly polish a boat wax with a pad designed for the purpose. You can also buy a polishing machine (similar to the buffing machine mentioned above) for about $75. These machines run at lower speeds (700 rpm to 2,000 rpm) than a buffer and should be used only for waxing. A variable-speed buffer-polisher like the Makita pictured above will polish as well as buff.

Interlux Premium Marine Wax—representative of the many marine waxes available—can be followed with Interlux UV Protectant & Wax Sealer to make the glossy wax finish last longer. Interlux now offers both these products with a Teflon additive, which, the company claims, provides a harder, more dirt-repellent, durable finish. (Courtesy Interlux)

Wax needs heat in order to bond to the gelcoat. In general, you'll need a minimum of about 50°F over several weeks for a good bond to form. In hot weather, the wax may dry before it has a chance to bond fully to the gelcoat, so you might have to wait for cooler weather, avoid working in direct sunlight, or work fast!

One trick to consider when you finish boating for the season is to clean your boat's hull and then wax and polish it. An autumn waxing will keep the topsides clean and protected through the winter, making the spring cleaning and waxing easier or perhaps even unnecessary. Do not, however, leave a late-season application of wax unpolished over the winter. I've heard it suggested that this provides even greater protection to the gelcoat—the idea being that winter temperatures are too low for the wax to bond to the gelcoat to occur, so that in the spring you can wash off the wax with water or buff it to bring up the shine. All it takes is one warm day to bond the wax, however, and then you will have great difficulty polishing it. This happened in my local boatyard, and the bonded but unpolished wax had to be painstakingly removed.

Polymer Coatings

In most cases, a rubbing compound (as mild as possible) followed by waxing (possibly with an intermediate polish if the oxidation was severe) should bring the shine back to a boat's topsides. But if you're still not satisfied, you may wish to apply a polymer coating that reacts with the surface of the gelcoat to give it a good shine. This approach can be tried before you resort to your last and much more expensive option of painting the topsides as described in Chapter 9. As mentioned earlier, Poli Glow (www.poliglow-int.com), New-Glass2 (www.newglass2.com), Star brite Glass Cote, and Vertglas are among the leading polymer coatings. I applied two coats of Vertglas to one boat, and when I was done it looked great, but I had to recoat it with the polymer two seasons later to maintain the shine. Further, if you later want to paint the topsides, you will probably have to sand off the polymer coating so as to apply the paint to the original gelcoat.

Maintaining the Finish

To maintain the finish of your gelcoat, rinse it with fresh water after each time you use your boat. Some people add a little water-soluble wax to the rinse water to help maintain the UV protection throughout the season. Make sure that when you are alongside the dock, your fenders are clean and do not have grit or contaminants on them. If you keep felt or terry-cloth jackets on your fenders, they too should be clean and free of grit.

GELCOAT REPAIRS

Repairing Abraded Gelcoat

As mentioned earlier, a boatbuilder typically sprays gelcoat into the female hull mold before starting the hull laminate. The ideal thickness of this sprayed-on gelcoat is 10 to 20 mils, which may

Gelcoat Repairs • 75

This hull topside has been badly abraded by a fender, and the area will need to be cleaned, wiped with solvent, and sprayed, brushed, or rolled with gelcoat pigmented to match the surrounding gelcoat. An exact color match will be difficult or impossible to obtain. The owner may opt instead to paint the entire topsides (or maybe just one side of it), as covered in Chapter 9, in which case the abrasion could be repaired with epoxy fairing putty rather than gelcoat.

not sound like much but is many times thicker than a coat of paint. (Although some builders use heavier gelcoats, these can shrink and crack in a manner reminiscent of desiccated mud.) It is easy to abrade through the gelcoat if you get a little overly enthusiastic with a gritty rubbing compound. On the other hand, when stains are deeply embedded in the gelcoat, rubbing hard to remove them is often a necessity. You may even have to grind into the gelcoat to get out a very stubborn stain.

If you grind through your boat's gelcoat, the best thing to do is to mask off the entire area around the repair and respray it with new gelcoat. You may have to thin the gelcoat in order to force it through the spray head of a Preval-type sprayer (which you can find in most marine stores) or a small gun set at light to medium air pressure. Spray the gelcoat with long, parallel, overlapping strokes to cover the surface, then immediately apply a second coat on a diagonal to the first, then apply a third on still a third orientation. Each coat should add about 5 mils of thickness, so add a fourth if you wish to build up a 20-mil thickness. You can also apply new gelcoat with a brush or foam roller—possibly with some thickening agent to prevent sagging, or in several layers of very thin gelcoat, or both. Experiment on a pane of glass before you tackle the hull, and be prepared to do a bit more sanding prior to buffing the surface to a high polish.

The biggest problem with applying fresh gelcoat is the difficulty of getting a good color match, especially if the old gelcoat has faded. Even "white" gelcoat comes in many shades, and you will have to be careful to make as close a match as possible. Mix the right pigments in the right proportions into white gelcoat to match the surrounding surface. You can get a colorizing gelcoat pack from your local marine store. Do not add catalyst (MEKP) to the gelcoat until you're happy with the color. The last thing you want is for the gelcoat to kick before you've gotten the color right. When you're happy with the color, catalyze a small subsample to see what happens to the color when it kicks. Most gelcoat colors change slightly as the gelcoat sets; dark colors, especially, will usually become lighter when cured.

Repairing Dings and Scrapes

Dings and scrapes can be inflicted in a boat's topsides while docking or when a tender pulls alongside. If the scrape is cosmetic—i.e., if it is shallow and does not go completely through the gelcoat—it can be fixed at your leisure. Deeper dents and scrapes made by harder knocks may penetrate the gelcoat, however, requiring more immediate attention to prevent water from wicking into the underlying laminate. A color change will usually appear when gelcoat has been penetrated. Your topsides may be white, while the underlying laminate may be blue or green, which will show up even in a small scratch if you look carefully at it.

A gelcoat repair kit. At bottom center is a can of white gelcoat paste, and to its right is a tube of coloring compound. The remaining items (proceeding counterclockwise) are a can of thinner/solvent for wiping down the surface to be repaired, a cup or container for mixing the gelcoat with pigment, and a small container of MEKP catalyst. As a general rule, you need one or two drops of catalyst per ounce of gelcoat, but follow the manufacturer's instructions and err toward the low end of the recommended amount for a longer working time. You want at least 30 minutes before the paste starts to harden, but more is better and 2 hours is probably ideal. The catalyst must be mixed in thoroughly (for at least 2 to 3 minutes) to avoid pockets of undercured repair. Wear rubber gloves for this job.

Unless prevented by furniture or a hull liner, check the inside of the hull, too, to be sure the laminate isn't cracked or otherwise damaged.

Years ago, when my sons were sailing Optimist dinghies, I routinely repaired cosmetic scrapes on the hull bottoms caused by well-meaning regatta volunteers helping pull the boats on dollies up the concrete boat ramp. The dollies were designed for children, and the adult volunteers carried the dolly handles far too high, which caused the hindquarters of the boats to bump along the concrete. I always repaired the damage using Clear Cote (see photo page 63) two-part gelcoat, which comes in a can with a small tube of MEKP catalyst. The job was relatively easy because the scratches and scrapes were small and never penetrated deeply into the fiberglass. I lightly sanded the damaged area, wiped it with acetone or DuPont's (www2.dupont.com) Prep-Sol (now I use Bio-Solv, which was introduced in Chapter 3), mixed the gelcoat resin and catalyst, and applied it with a plastic spatula. After it hardened, we wet-sanded the hull bottoms with emery paper, working from 220- to 400-grit. (These dinghies were dry-sailed and thus didn't have bottom paint.)

Deeper scrapes are somewhat more onerous to repair. Gouges that extend into the underlying laminate cannot be repaired with gelcoat putty alone—you need a thickened polyester or epoxy putty to get more structural strength.

I remember, for example, the dings one of my boats received in its cradle beside the driveway when a heating oil delivery truck backed into it. These dings penetrated through the gelcoat and into the underlying laminate, so I first pried around the edges of the damage to see if more laminate had been loosened by the impact than was immediately apparent, and to check for any signs of delamination or radiating damage. Finding no structural damage, I removed the loose laminate and gelcoat from the periphery of each ding, then ground tapered scarfs into the edges so that the repairs could be faired in.

Since this boat of my own design had been laminated with S glass and epoxy resin, I decided to use Awlfair—a trowelable epoxy fairing compound developed by the makers of Awlgrip (www.awlgrip.com) polyurethane paint—for the repairs. Awlfair is a professional fairing compound and is not readily available to do-it-yourselfers, but you can get a perfectly acceptable substitute by making up a batch of epoxy thickened with microballoons (see Chapter 3). Had the boat been laminated with polyester resin (as most are), I could have repaired the dings with either thickened polyester or epoxy putty, but my preference in these circumstances is epoxy because it's easier to mix, stronger, forms a stronger secondary bond with the underlying laminate, and doesn't give off the strong styrene odor of polyester resin. If you intend to surface the repair with gelcoat (which does not bond well to epoxy), then you should use polyester putty, but if you intend to sand and paint the repair, the better choice in my view is epoxy.

I first wiped the area of the repair with a solvent, then coated it with unthickened epoxy for a good bond. (You can thicken this base coat slightly if

Repairing dings and scratches in gelcoat. **(1)** I lightly sanded this small ding in the transom of this dinghy before wiping it down with a solvent. **(2, 3)** I prefer a slow-drying solvent to keep the sanding residues in suspension long enough to be wiped off. Some people use acetone for this, but acetone dries extremely quickly and can leave residues on the surface. Bio-Solv is a good, recently developed alternative. **(4)** I filled the damage with a gelcoat paste. Don't try to fill the crater completely in a single pass. Instead, apply a layer of gelcoat and let it harden for 24 hours or so, then sand the area to improve the mechanical bond of the next layer. Wipe with solvent, and note how well the pigment of your repair matches the color of the surrounding gelcoat. Adjust the pigment accordingly as you mix your final batch of gelcoat paste, then apply this coat to fill the remaining dimples. **(5)** Allow the repair to set up for another 24 hours, as I did, before sanding to a smooth, fair finish. The tinted repair shown here does not quite match the color of the surrounding gelcoat—it's a hard thing to get perfect.

Gelcoat Repairs

necessary to keep it on the repair surface.) Then I prepared the epoxy fairing compound and applied it in layers using a flat trowel. I made each layer about ⅛ inch (3 mm) thick, let it harden, and then sanded it before applying the next layer. I have found both then and since that if I apply a heavier layer—say ¼ inch (6 mm) thick—the resin sags and makes the cleanup harder. If each layer is reasonably thin, it will cure throughout, but if you add more layers before the ones beneath are properly cured, you may delay the curing of the bottom layers and get enough heat buildup to distort the job.

I kept adding layers of epoxy until the repair was flush with the surrounding surface, then I wet-sanded the repair using finer and finer paper until it was smooth enough for painting. I applied Interlux's two-part Epoxy Primekote undercoat, followed by Interlux's two-part polyurethane Perfection paint to match the hull color.

When there is structural damage to the underlying laminate, even more work is required. You will need to grind away the edges of the dent or gash to remove loose material, to ensure that you've removed all delaminated fiberglass from the perimeter of the damaged area, and to ensure that the repair can be easily feathered in. A slope of 9:1 to 12:1 from the deepest penetration of the damage to its perimeter is considered desirable; if the gash is ⅜ inch (9 mm) deep, you should grind a scarf about 4 inches (10 cm) wide to each side of it. Then, if needed, you should apply a fiberglass patch as described in Chapter 5. When the patch has set up, apply thin layers of epoxy resin and microballoons (as described above) until the damaged area has been built up flush with the surrounding surface. After that, it is simply a matter of sanding and painting as described above and in Chapter 9.

If a crack in a laminate is deep but neither wide nor long, you can widen it for repair—and at the same time remove loose laminate—with a V-shaped bit on a Dremel. Lacking a Dremel, you might be able to accomplish the same thing with an old church key–style can opener. Once you open the crack enough to inspect its depth, you'll know whether a thickened polyester or epoxy resin will suffice for the repair. If the crack is deep enough, you may want to lay a thin strip of fiberglass roving in the V-slot. (Peel it from a woven roving or use unidirectional tows.) Wet out the fiberglass and build up the repair until it is level with the surrounding laminate, then apply gelcoat or paint the job.

Repairing Crazed Gelcoat

On some early fiberglass boats you may encounter crazed gelcoat—that is, gelcoat that has hardened and become covered with a random network of small cracks. These cracks are not only unsightly, they can allow moisture into the underlying laminate. This is especially problematic for a cored hull or deck, where moisture can easily disrupt the core-skin bond, but even a single-skin hull can suffer blistering or internal delamination from invading moisture.

To repair crazing, first sand the crazed area with 100-grit sandpaper, then wipe down the surface with a solvent such as Interlux's 2333N Reducing Solvent or DuPont's Prep-Sol. Do not use acetone for this, as it is fast-drying and may not keep wax and grease in suspension long enough for you to wipe them off. Repair any dents, gouges, or other flaws with a thickened epoxy putty as described above, sand again (this time progressing to 150- to 220-grit) to ensure a smooth hull, and wipe down with solvent again. Follow this by undercoating with a primer. If you are using a two-part topcoat (such as Interlux's Perfection), you will want to use a two-part primer (such as Interlux's Epoxy Primekote). If you are going to paint with a one-part topcoat, however, a one-part primer is appropriate. For best compatibility, you should use a primer and topcoat from the same manufacturer. Sand the primer coat with 220- to 320-grit if you think you will need two layers of topcoat, and/or 320- and then 400-grit prior to the final topcoat. You can either roll and tip the topcoat or have a professional spray it for you. Hull finishing is described in detail in Chapter 9.

A severe case of crazing—such as that pictured in the first photo of this chapter—may require you to grind away the crazed gelcoat al-

Gelcoat Repairs

together, in which case you will need to replace it either with new gelcoat (vinylester as opposed to polyester for underwater portions of the hull) or with an epoxy fairing compound such as Awlfair, which can be troweled on much like spackling compound in a home. Awlfair is a professional product, however, and you may have to resort to mixing thickener into an epoxy or polyester resin. Boatyard workers use battens and specialized techniques to fair a hull, but you can achieve good results on your own by fairing a section at a time and building up the fairing in layers no more than 1/8 inch (3 mm) thick. After the last layer of fairing compound has set, the hull should be long-boarded to ensure that it is fair and smooth.

Repairing Centerboards, Rudders, and Keels

The centerboard and rudder of a small sailboat are easily damaged. These parts have fine edges, and the trailing edges in particular are often banged on things when the blades are removed from the boat or from a transport vehicle. Dings in the body of a blade can be repaired as described above, but repairing a dinged edge is more difficult.

The trailing edge of a foil is usually sharp (within the tolerances specified by a one-design class or manufacturer rules), but a razor-sharp trailing-edge repair is easily damaged again, so I prefer to incorporate a slight bluntness in a

Shaping the trailing edge of a centerboard or rudder. (1) I ground the thick trailing edge of the rudder thinner to meet one-design class requirements, and faired nicks and dings in its trailing edge with thickened epoxy putty. I then sanded it with 100-grit paper, coated it with an Interprotect epoxy barrier coat, sanded it with 220-grit, painted it with high-build epoxy primer, sanded that with 400-grit, and finally painted it with a bottom paint formulated for racing. (2) A close-up view shows some of the dings that have been repaired with epoxy and now need fairing, as well as the small flat on the trailing edge. (3) This shows the well-rounded leading edge of the rudder before the final fairing. After coating the rudder with bottom paint I sanded with 400-grit wet-or-dry sandpaper in order to obtain a racing finish.

80 • GELCOAT RESTORATION AND COSMETIC REPAIRS

The trailing edge of this keel terminates in a ⅛- to 3/16-inch (3 to 4 mm) flat, which towing tank testing has shown will actually cause less resistance than a razor-sharp edge. A perfectly sharp trailing edge is extremely hard to achieve in any event, and is also prone to chip or break.

trailing-edge repair. An edge thickness of about 1/16 inch (2 mm) for a dinghy and about ¼ inch (6 mm) for a larger sailboat does not appear to affect performance, and in fact may actually help it by creating a vacuum behind the foil. Water drawn into this void stays attached to the blade longer, which may enhance the lift obtained from the rudder, centerboard, or keel.

Properly fairing the leading edge of a foil is also important. The leading edge needs a parabolic cross section to the extent permitted by the class rules. A parabolic leading edge encourages water flow to stay attached to the blade, which again gives it more lift.

Years ago I repaired an assortment of Optimist centerboard and rudder blades that had sustained chips and gouges in their leading and trailing edges. I repaired the deep gouges and missing chunks with Interlux's Epiglass epoxy resin thickened with microballoons. I made the mixture about the consistency of putty and carefully tapered the repairs to conform to the edges of the blades. I then allowed the epoxy to cure overnight under a heat lamp so it would be ready for sanding the next morning. I finished the repair as described in the photo caption on page 79.

Repairing Nonskid Gelcoat

Gelcoat in general is slippery, so deck surfaces require some form of nonskid in or on the gelcoat to provide positive traction underfoot. When you repair or replace a nonskid deck surface, there are several ways to renew the nonskid. You can apply a paint with nonskid compound; you can apply strips of nonskid tape; you can make a permanent nonskid surface with gelcoat and a coarse-nap foam roller; or you can adhere a nonskid mat.

Painting on Nonskid

Many paint manufacturers make nonskid paint. Interlux offers Interdeck, and both Interlux and Pettit (www.pettitpaint.com) sell a nonskid compound that can be added to any of their regular deck paints. Using pigments, you can match the color of the nonskid areas to the rest of your deck. If you do not want to buy a proprietary nonskid compound, you can sprinkle finely crushed walnut shells over wet, freshly applied paint and then repaint the surface, although I am told that this creates a slightly muddy color. If you sprinkle your freshly painted deck with sand and then paint over it, the result will be a terrific nonskid surface that also, unfortunately, acts like sandpaper on your clothes and skin.

To apply a nonskid paint, mask off the area to be painted, wipe it down with a solvent, and roll on the paint with a coarse-nap roller. Don't paint over the surface with a brush or you'll knock some of the particles off and reduce the nonskid quality. See Chapter 9 for more details.

One advantage of a nonskid paint is that it makes the surface of a later repair relatively easy to blend in. It is harder to match a nonskid deck pattern when you make a repair.

Nonskid Tape

Several manufacturers make strips of nonskid tape, but most

Gelcoat Repairs • 81

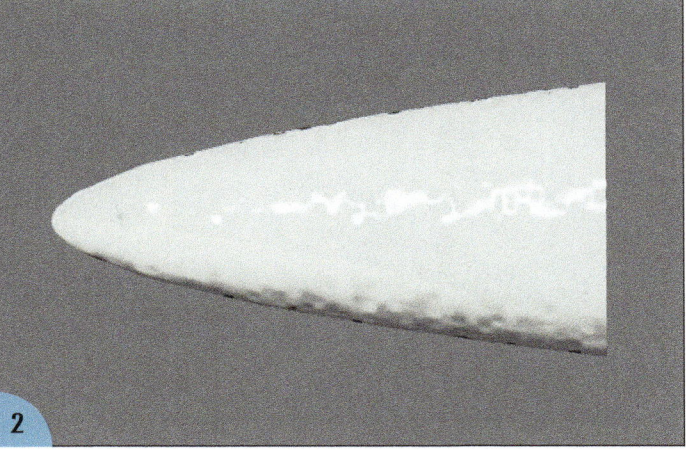

(1) *The leading edge of a rudder, keel, or centerboard should be shaped to a parabolic section* **(2)**. *Water impinges on the foil at the boat's leeway angle (generally 2 to 5 degrees from the foil's fore-and-aft centerline), and this flow needs to remain attached to the foil's windward surface in order to create the lift that enables the boat to sail to windward. A sharp leading edge does not allow this.*

(1) *Another example of a minor repair. This boat was backed into by a truck while it sat in the yard. The hull had been faired using a white filler, some of which was knocked off when the truck hit the boat. The repair was to fill the damaged area with a fairing putty made of Epiglass thickened with filler powder. This was smeared over the job, sanded back, undercoated, and then topcoated to match the existing color.* **(2)** *The finished job after it had been repaired and the hull repainted. You can hardly tell that it has been damaged.*

GELCOAT RESTORATION AND COSMETIC REPAIRS

Nonskid tape can be used in many places to help prevent slips and falls. (1) On the foredeck of a launch it provides more secure footing for a crewmember tending lines. (2) On a foredeck hatch it transforms a slick surface to a "sticky" one.

boatowners use the 3M brand. It comes in green or black and can easily be cut to the desired length. Round off the corners to help prevent them from lifting, then simply wipe the surface where the tape will be applied with solvent, peel off the tape backing, and stick the nonskid in place. I find that it is easier to position the nonskid properly if you first "dry-fit" it (i.e., place it in position with the backing still in place) and trace the outline with a grease pencil. Then peel off the backing, align the tape with the pencil marks, and smooth it into place. You do not want to have to remove and re-lay the tape, because it will not stick as well the second time.

The many places where the use of a nonskid tape makes sense include Plexiglas hatch covers, around the base of a mast where you might work in wet weather, and on the treads of companionway or flybridge stairs. Any walking surface that might get wet and slippery is a good candidate for strips of nonskid tape.

Applying Nonskid Gelcoat

Just as you would when applying nonskid paint, you must mask off (using painter's masking tape) the perimeter of the area you want to cover. Sanding may not be necessary—the worn nonskid should already have a fair amount of tooth—but you should clean the area well and wipe it with solvent. Mix the catalyst into the gelcoat and then add a nonskid compound to it. Or you can omit the compound and just thicken the gelcoat—say with microfibers—and apply it with a foam roller to impart good roughness to the surface. (Try this on a test surface before turning your attention to the deck.) The bumps will slowly degrade if the gelcoat takes a while to kick, so in cool weather you should be a bit more generous with catalyst and put a heat lamp on the job to kick the gelcoat quickly. When the gelcoat is semi-cured, remove the masking tape carefully. Do not walk on the surface for at least 24 hours or until it is completely hard.

Applying a Nonskid Flex-Mold Pattern

None of the previous approaches to renewing nonskid will match an existing molded-in nonskid pattern. There are ways to do that, however, including Flex-Mold, a relatively new product developed by Gibco and marketed in the United States by MAS Epoxies. The idea is that you apply premixed gelcoat to the deck and then press a section of Flex-Mold mat into the resin as it is hardening. The mat is coated with mold release wax, so you can peel it off easily once the gelcoat has kicked, leaving a nonskid pattern imprinted in the gelcoat.

I tested the product on a project boat that needed its nonskid renewed. First, I made a rubbing of the boat's existing nonskid so that the supplier could match its texture and pattern. To do this, I simply taped a sheet of blank white paper over the existing nonskid and rubbed it with charcoal (you can also use a soft lead pencil). I scanned the rubbing to create a digital file that I e-mailed to MAS Epoxies. A few days later a rubberized Flex-Mold mat sample measuring about 2 inches by 3 inches (50 mm by 75 mm) arrived at the shop.

The nonskid gelcoat on this engine box was applied with a foam roller over the existing gelcoat. Often the gelcoat is pigmented to make it stand out from the white gelcoat around its perimeter.

I tested this sample on two or three small, discrete areas of the deck from which hardware had been removed, and which therefore now needed nonskid. Choosing one such area, I spread a small amount of gelcoat and pressed the Flex-Mold sample into the wet resin with a weight on it. Once the gelcoat had set up sufficiently, I peeled off the mat. The resulting diamond-shaped nonskid perfectly replicated the existing nonskid surface.

Having thus ensured that the pattern matched, I masked off a larger area of the deck on which the existing nonskid was badly worn, and I ordered a larger mat with which to renew the nonskid. I roughly sanded the area with 100-grit paper on a random orbit sander—a fairly simple job, since most of the area was degraded anyway. Where the sander damaged the masking tape, I laid down new tape. Then I wiped the area with a solvent to remove any grease or other impurities and rolled on a thin layer of white polyester gelcoat. I then pressed the Flex-Mold mat into the wet gelcoat and left it there until the gelcoat kicked.

Once the gelcoat had cured, I painted the area with Interlux's Interdeck to make it completely nonskid and to match the other parts of the deck. You do not need to paint with Interdeck, but in this case the remainder of the deck had been painted, and I wanted a color match.

The big advantage of this system is that you can get a Flex-Mold mat that exactly matches what your original deck looked like and try it

84 • GELCOAT RESTORATION AND COSMETIC REPAIRS

out. If it doesn't work, simply sand it off and do it again. There are literally hundreds of patterns of nonskid; MAS Epoxies, working with the Gibco Flex-Mold Company, has many of them available as of this writing. You can find out more at www.masepoxies.com.

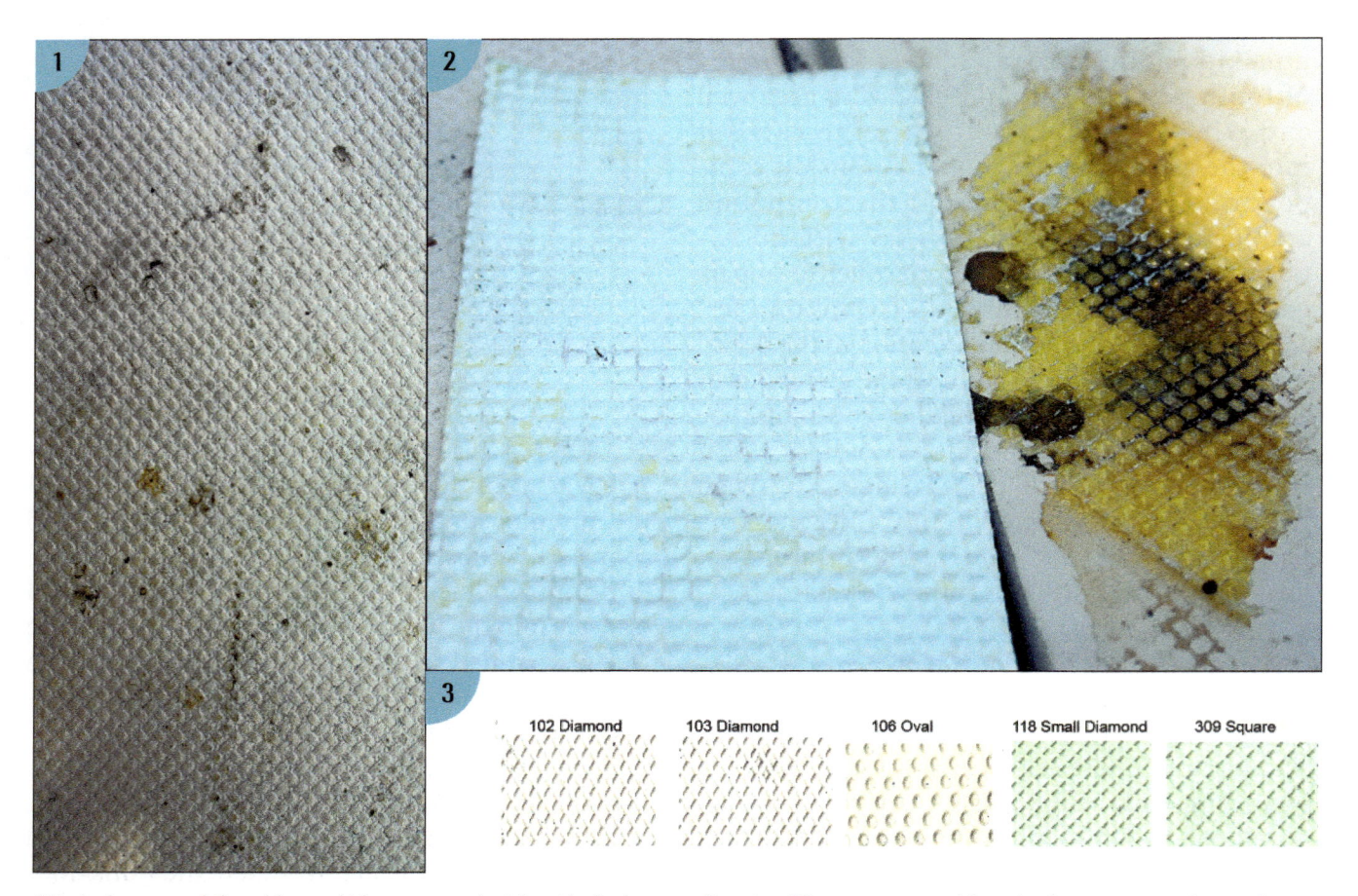

(1) *A close-up of the old nonskid on my project boat's deck. You can see how the gelcoat has oxidized and worn.* **(2)** *A test sample of Flex-Mold is at left, and the nonskid pattern made from it is at right.* **(3)** *Flex-Mold samples from MAS Epoxies. There are several hundred patterns to choose from, so you will need to make a rubbing of your deck, then contact MAS Epoxies to find one that matches.*

Chapter 5
MINOR STRUCTURAL REPAIRS

The projects in this chapter range from filling a hole in a hull or deck to joining a bulkhead to a hull and making a *splash*, or mold, for a boat part that needs to be replaced. Most of the work is straightforward and will give you the skills needed to tackle a more difficult project like those discussed in Chapter 7.

The good news hidden in the previous paragraph is that repairing a hole in the hull of a fiberglass boat—even a good-sized hole right through a laminate—is a fairly simple job. Ease of repair is just one more advantage of fiberglass construction.

Always wear proper protective gear when working with fiberglass, resins, and solvents—even for small jobs. After the resin has set up, you should continue to protect yourself from the fiberglass "needles" that can pierce your skin in the most unlikely and uncomfortable places. Be forewarned that grinding fiberglass is one of the more unpleasant jobs anyone can do.

BEFORE YOU START ANY REPAIR WORK

Before you begin any job, gather all the tools you'll require (there aren't many; see the Tools section in Chapter 3) and form a clear idea of the work that must done, as well as what the finished job should look like. Take steps to protect the parts of your boat that are not going to be touched. For example, if you are going to work on the inside of a hull, remove or cover cushions and furniture to protect them from fiberglass dust. Such measures require little time or money and pay off in less cleanup and aggravation.

A cheap polyethylene sheet keeps fiberglass dust from invading areas where it isn't wanted. This simple step ensures that those who use the boat after the repairs are made will not get fiberglass dust in their food or on their pillows. The polyethylene covering is simply taped in place while the work proceeds, then thrown away when the job is done.

A polyethylene sheet will also protect cushions and furniture from resin drips, although it can make a cabin sole slippery underfoot. And when you work on a boat exterior in a shed or garage, paper or polyethylene on the floor will catch drips of resin and small scraps of fiberglass that might otherwise accumulate and make the floor uneven.

When working on fiberglass, you should understand what type of laminate you are dealing with and how it was laid up. A hand-laid laminate generally contains more resin than one that was vacuum bagged. Boatbuilders commonly begin the laminate with a layer (or sometimes two lay-

86 • MINOR STRUCTURAL REPAIRS

(1, 2, 3) *The fiberglass on this boat will be ground back, which will spread fiberglass dust everywhere. To avoid removing all the interior fittings and cushions and having to painstakingly clean the boat after the repair work is done, the workers have taped polyethylene sheeting over all areas not involved in the repair.*

ers) of chopped strand mat (CSM) immediately under the gelcoat to help prevent print-through from the woven roving that follows. CSM sprayed with a chopper gun may be thicker than if it was hand laid or vacuum bagged. You might also try to find out what type and weight of fiberglass reinforcement was used in the original laminate, and match this if you can. Four layers of 6-ounce cloth comprise an insufficient repair for a hole through four layers of 24-ounce woven roving. You will have to use a lot more layers of the lighter cloth to prevent the possibility of structural failure down the road.

Perhaps the easiest way to ascertain the original laminate schedule is to call the builder (if still in business) and ask. You'll be surprised how much builders will tell you. If that fails, contact the designer to find out what was specified. If you can't locate the builder or designer, just aim to replicate the original laminate thickness using an acceptable schedule of mat, roving, cloth, or hybrid fabrics as discussed in the Fiberglass section in Chapter 3. Older boats, especially, were overbuilt to begin with, and if you match the original laminate thickness, chances are your repair will have strength to spare.

In addition, you will need to determine whether the laminate is single-skin or cored (see pages 9 and 16 in Chapter 1, including the cross section of a cored laminate pictured on page 19). The former is most often found below a hull's waterline, although on many boats (especially those built prior to 1980) it may extend through the topsides as well. When a laminate is cored, 40% of the total skin thickness is typically in the outer skin, and 60% is in the inner skin. The most common use of a cored laminate is for decks, where great rigidity is required. By separating the deck's inner and outer skins, a core creates a beam-like structure that eliminates flexing (also known as *trampolining* or *oilcanning*) without greatly increasing the weight of the deck. This chapter looks first at repairs to single-skin laminates and then discusses repairs to cored ones.

Your choice of repair techniques will depend on whether you can get access to the back of the damaged area. When you do not have access (as might happen if a hole breaches a buoyancy tank, for example), your job is more difficult. We'll cover repairs with and without access to the back.

REPAIRS TO A SINGLE-SKIN LAMINATE

Patching Screw Holes

Patching a hole in a single-skin laminate is relatively simple if the hole is small (such as that left by a screw or bolt) and you have access to the back. All you need to do is tape over the back of the hole and fill it with a thickened resin mixture. I prefer epoxy to polyester for this kind of repair because it is easier to thicken and sets up fairly quickly. By using fast-acting hardener when you fill small holes, you can get the repair to set within a few minutes. If you have a lot of holes to fill, however, mix only a small amount of epoxy at a time, or it will kick before you are halfway through your project. Despite using thickener and fast-acting hardener, the initial repair is likely to leave a surface dimple when it hardens (due to shrinkage and absorption around the hole edges), in which case you will have to apply a second, surfacing coat to make the repair flush. Finish the repair with color-matched paint. I like to use an epoxy primer and polyurethane topcoat as described below and in Chapter 9, but a visit to a marine store or catalog will show you other good options as well.

Patching Larger Holes with Access to the Back

Patching a larger hole is more time-consuming than filling screw holes, but the job is not difficult if you have access to the back of the hole as well as the front. We'll assume the worst-case scenario here—a hole that has penetrated or seriously compromised the entire laminate thickness. If only the outer layers of the laminate are damaged, the repair job will be easier because your backing is already in place.

You can repair a hole all the way through the laminate from either side or from both sides, depending on circumstances. I prefer to laminate the repair inside as well as outside the boat whenever possible—as illustrated in Project #5 in Chapter 7—especially when the inside surface will be visible to the boat's occupants.

Either way, the first step is to mark the perimeter of the damaged area. Tap with a plastic mallet or screwdriver handle to ascertain where the dull report of delaminated fiberglass is replaced by the sharp knock of uncompromised laminate, and use a permanent marker or grease pencil to outline the damaged area. This is the line you will cut or grind to.

Before cutting or grinding, however, check inside the hull to make sure no bulkhead, bunk framing, or other interior structure will be affected. If you find an interfering member, you will have to either cut it from the repair or make your repair from the outside.

If the area you need to remove is large, you can cut it out with a saw. A circular saw works well on a flat surface such as a transom. A Sawzall reciprocating saw is often the best choice for an irregularly shaped repair on a curved surface. If the repair area is relatively small, however—say under 1 or 2 square feet—you shouldn't need a saw and can instead grind back the damage with an angle grinder to leave the edges of the work tapered for the new fiberglass.

Grinding is a miserable job, but it is slightly less miserable when you use an angle grinder as discussed on page 59. It is critical to grind away a wide enough tapered shelf around the hole to ensure good adhesion for the repair. One rule of thumb is to grind the scarf, or shallow slope, at least 3 inches (75 mm) wide. A better guideline, however, is to make the scarf width around the hole nine to twelve or fourteen times the thickness of the fiberglass laminate. In the case of a ½-inch-thick (12 mm) laminate, this might mean a scarf about 6 inches (15 cm) wide all the way around the hole. If you're laminating the repair

88 • MINOR STRUCTURAL REPAIRS

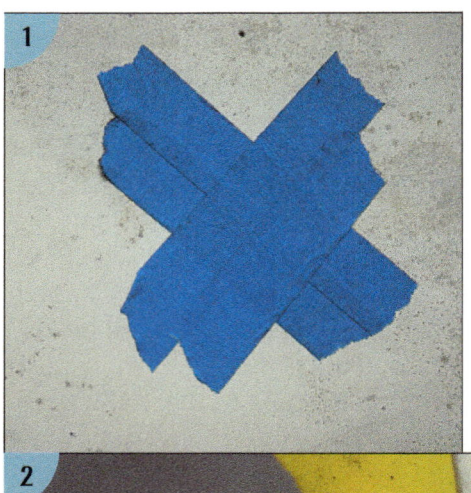

Fixing a screw hole with access to the back. **(1)** Cover the back of the hole with masking tape so the resin won't leak through. **(2)** Use a spatula or scraper edge to push thickened resin into the hole. (I have used ordinary resin to make it visible in this photo, but normally I'd use a white thickened gelcoat resin so the hole is coated with gelcoat.) **(3)** If your spatula or straightedge is too large to cover the hole easily, use a thin mixing stick or cut a spatula down to a narrow strip. **(4)** If the screw hole is deep—as it might be with a cored hull—fill a syringe with thickened resin and inject the resin into the hole to get a fully filled screw hole. **(5)** Scrape the spatula across the area to ensure that the resin in the hole is flush with the surface. Making it smooth while the resin is wet is easy—it is a lot harder to sand off the resin after it has set up, plus at that time you run the risk of sanding away some of the gelcoat.

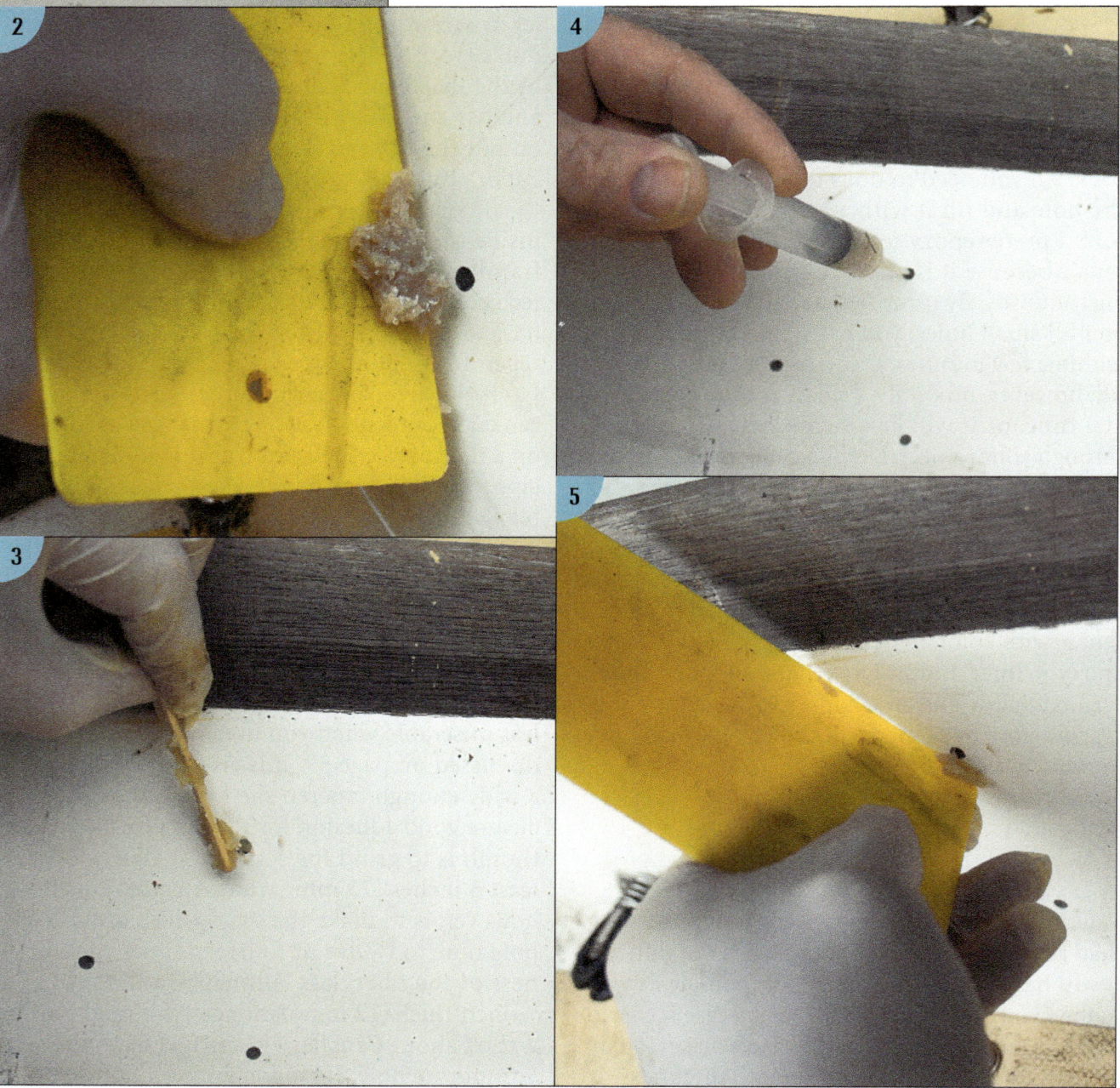

from the inside as well as the outside (my preference), you'll want to make scarfs both inside and outside. Orient the grinder so that it throws dust away, not toward your face. If the grinder spins clockwise, for example, use the top (12 o'clock) portion of the disk on the work.

Next you'll need backing on the inside or outside of the hole to laminate your repair against. If the hole is small (a ½-inch-diameter/12 mm hole left by a removed through-hull, for example), you may be able to back it adequately with painter's masking tape, just as described above for filling fastener holes. If the hole is larger, however, you'll need a stiffer backing to ensure a strong surface to roll your laminate on. In this case you can use narrow strips of thin plywood (¹⁄₁₆ to ³⁄₁₆ inch/ 2 to 4 mm thick) to make a temporary backing for the hole. If the hole is in the hull, I prefer to start the repair from the interior, so I tape a piece of plastic sheeting over the damaged area on the hull exterior, then screw the plywood strips over the sheeting with machine or sheetrock screws. (For patching these screw holes later, see above.) Alternatively, a thin sheet of Formica or Plexiglas several inches larger than the hole might provide a sufficiently stiff backing when taped to the hull with duct tape. It will depend on the hull curvature in the area of the repair. Don't be afraid to experiment.

If the hull curvature is pronounced in two directions, make the plywood strips narrower and extend them far enough beyond the hole perimeter that they approximately conform to the hull shape. If the hole is wide, use thicker plywood to provide adequate backing support. In extreme cases (a big hole in an area of the hull with pronounced compound curvature), you can take a mold off an adjacent hull section or the matching section on a sister ship, as described in the Replacing Missing Parts section later in this chapter (see page 102).

It might seem counterintuitive to laminate against an exterior backing when you are later going to add more layers on the outside. After all, won't these initial layers applied from the inside conform to the hull's exterior surface, leaving no room for the layers you plan to apply on the outside? This is true in theory, but in practice the backing creates a flat spot that you will have to build up to the surrounding surface with outside layers, and it all works out.

With the prep work done, you can start laminating the repair. If you know the original laminate schedule, it is helpful to replicate this in the repair. If you do not know the original schedule, you will have to improvise. Most single-skin hulls are laid up using alternating layers of CSM and woven rovings, but what fabric weight should you use for the job? Few of us keep ten or twelve different weights of fiberglass materials on our workshop shelves, so you'll have to either order by the job or choose from the one or two standard weights and formats you happen to have on hand. Some ¾-ounce or 1½-ounce mat, some 18-ounce woven roving, and some 6- to 12-ounce cloth should cover all needs. (Remember that mat is sold by the square foot, and roving and cloth by the square yard, so 1½-ounce mat is slightly heavier than 12-ounce cloth.) Another option is 1708 or 1808 knitted fiberglass, which is made from 17-ounce (or 18-ounce) biaxial roving (two plies of rovings, each ply oriented at 45 degrees to the fabric's long axis and at 90 degrees to its mate) stitched to a layer of ¾-ounce mat. In what follows we'll assume that you're making the repair from mat and either roving or cloth.

Cut a piece of mat large enough to cover the hole with 1 to 2 inches (25 to 50 mm) of overlap onto the interior scarf all the way around. You can lay the patch against the backing to dry-fit it. Make another patch of mat, one of cloth, and several additional patches alternating between mat and cloth to build up the new laminate, then put them aside. Each patch should overlap the one beneath it by at least ½ inch (12 mm) all the way around.

Now it's time to mix as much polyester or epoxy resin as you think you can apply before it kicks off. I have said elsewhere that I prefer to use epoxy for many repairs, but I make an exception when patching a large hole in a boat built with polyester resin. Epoxy is stronger, less elastic, and (except for some specific brand names, such as WEST System's G/flex epoxy) slightly more brittle than polyester. When my son and I repaired his J/24 (see Chapter 7), for example, we worried that an epoxy-based patch in the middle of its polyester-based hull would create a hard spot that might stress the hull when it worked in a seaway, so we used polyester instead. However, epoxy will work as well.

Mix your resin in a large, shallow dish. If you use a deep cup, the resin will kick before you are done. With a fast hardener, the pot life of some epoxy resins is only about 7 to 10 minutes. If you have a big job and do not want your epoxy to kick early, use a medium or slow hardener, but remember that on a vertical surface an epoxy resin with slow hardener or a polyester resin with light catalyst tends to sag.

When the resin is ready, paint (using a cut-down chip paintbrush) or roll a layer of resin over the backing and the ground-back edges of the hole. Then lay the first patch into the wet resin. Wet the patch using your cut-down brush and roll it flat to remove any air bubbles. When rolling, make sure that you use a roller made for use with resins, and work from the center toward the edges.

Build up your laminate, wetting out each layer of mat and cloth, and when two or three layers are in place, let them harden. Then add two or three more, and proceed in this fashion until you've built up the interior surface flush with the surrounding surface. Now you can remove the exterior backing.

You will now find out if the exterior surface of your repair is smooth and fair. More often than not it will show bumps, creases, or bulges where the backing failed to lie fair or the laminating resin bled under the backing. The resin may also have seeped up onto the outside scarf in places. These high spots will need to be ground down before you laminate the exterior layers.

Then lay up two or three layers on the outside, each one

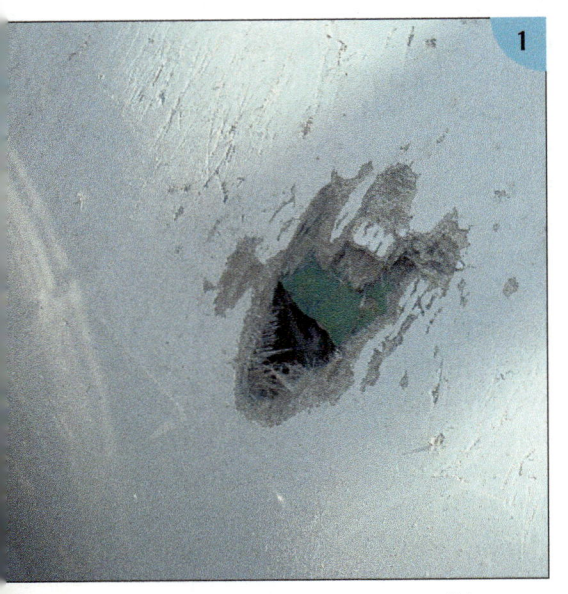

(1) *Major damage on a small boat. This dinghy pounded on the rocks for several hours. You can see how a rock punched through the hull and left the gelcoat severely scratched.* **(2)** *The damaged area has been cleaned and ground back. A thin piece of plastic-covered plywood has been wrapped around the outside of the hull, and a layer of fiberglass applied from the inside. Note the irregular outline of the hole. Grind only until you reach undamaged laminate. There is no need to grind or cut a smooth perimeter.*

overlapping the one beneath, just as on the inside. Let these harden, then add more layers until you've finished the repair laminate flush with the surrounding surface. Try to keep the new layers as even as possible with the ground-back edges of the hole, or you will have to do a lot more grinding later. And don't wet out too many layers at once or the laminate might generate too much heat and distort while curing.

If space is tight and it is not possible to do a lot of rolling on the fiberglass, you might want to use the following technique, known as a wet layup: Wearing rubber gloves, dip the precut fiberglass patch into the resin, then lay it on a plastic-covered table and use a squeegee to remove most of the wet resin. (Drain this resin back into your dish.) Finally, lay the patch into the hole, either pressing or rolling it into place. This is a messier method than laying dry cloth and then wetting it out, but it's easier when space is tight.

Remember that you won't be able to work with the area for at least 24 hours—longer if the ambient temperature is cooler. If the ambient temperature is below 55°F, either heat the area or postpone the job until the temperature is warmer. If you try to work in cool temperatures, the resin will usually run down the side of the job before it has time to set up, and you will get a mess.

When the repair is hard, grind or sand back the exterior surface so that it is slightly below the level of the hull surface. Use a flexible batten to make sure you have a slight depression. Next, trowel a fairing compound of thickened epoxy resin (with the consistency of peanut butter) over the hole to get the surface as smooth as possible. Use your long batten to make sure this surface coat is as fair as possible to the surrounding hull, then let it cure. (See the photo sequence for Project #5 in Chapter 7.)

Sand the faired area with wet-or-dry paper, progressing through finer grits up to 220, and mask it off, then apply an epoxy primer either by spraying it or by rolling it on and tipping with a brush. I usually use Interlux's Epoxy Primekote, but you can use any primer that is compatible with the final paint layer.

When the epoxy primer has dried, apply a second coat of primer if necessary (sanding with 220- to 320-grit between coats), then apply the first coat of the two-part polyurethane topcoat. After that has dried, sand back the surface with 320- to 400-grit wet-or-dry. Pay particular attention to the edges where you masked off the paint job. You'll need to sand away any ridges.

Now comes the final topcoat. I prefer to spray the entire side of the hull to be sure that the paint color matches. Often even the same hue of paint from the same manufacturer will have a slightly different cast from one can to the next. To prepare the side for spraying, mask off the remainder of the hull using masking tape and paper. Wrap in plastic anything that might get overspray on it. You'll be surprised how far overspray can travel, so when in doubt, cover up the area. Proceed with spraying only when everything is protected.

If you cannot spray the job, I suggest using Interlux's Perfection, a two-part polyurethane that has been developed for brushing. You should still carefully mask off surfaces that are not to be painted. Then apply the Perfection with a roller and use a dry brush to "tip" the paint and get it smooth. When finishing the last stroke, put your brush on the masking tape at the top of the paint job and gently pull it to the masking tape at the bottom of the job. Now remove the brush. This way you won't leave a brush mark in the topside paint. Finally, let the paint set, and the job is done. Painting is covered in greater detail in Chapter 9.

Patching Holes without Access to the Back

If you can't get access to the back of a hole—for example, if access to the inside of the hull is prevented by a hull liner or a tank—your task becomes more difficult but by no means impossible. To accomplish it, you must insert the backing material through the hole from the outside. As before, your first step is to cut or grind the damaged area back to undamaged

92 • MINOR STRUCTURAL REPAIRS

Repairs to a Single-Skin Laminate

(1) *This hole opened into a watertight compartment, which gave no access to the back of the hole to make a repair. I ground back the edges and then inserted a thin slat of wood with a dab of thickened epoxy on each end into the hole. To clamp wood in place while the epoxy set, I screwed a second piece of plastic-covered wood to it with a sheetrock screw. (I placed the second piece against the outside of the hull, with the edges of the hole forming the "filling" of the resulting sandwich.) When the epoxy on the backing piece had set up, I removed the exterior wood and sheetrock screw, leaving the backing piece in place. I then laminated fiberglass with epoxy resin over the hole, covering the area that had been ground back.*

(2) *Here I have faired the laminate smooth but have not yet sanded it. It also still needs to be painted to match the rest of the boat. I painted the finished hull with Interlux's Perfection as described in Chapter 9. If the boat had been repaired using polyester, I could have finished it by spraying with gelcoat, but that can add a lot of extra weight. A paint layer weighs less.*

laminate, then grind the edges of the hole into a shallow slope of sufficient scarf width—except that in this instance the scarf will be solely on the hull's exterior. Then you need to make a backing piece that is flexible and bendy enough to pass through the hole but large and stiff enough to span the hole from the inside and make a sufficient backing. I like to use a section of light but strong Formica plastic laminate (or equivalent). Cut a large enough piece to overlap the hole by 1 inch (25 mm) or so all the way around, and screw a couple of sheet-metal screws partway through the piece in the middle so that you can easily reach the screws when the piece is in position. Bend the piece as necessary to get it through the hole, then "butter" its perimeter with thickened epoxy. Gripping the screwheads, pull the piece against the inside of the hole—or rig a twine or wire bridle to the screwheads and tie that off under tension to hold the piece against the hull until the epoxy kicks. When the epoxy hardens, remove the screws and proceed with the repair.

If you can't get a single large backing piece through the hole, you can cut it into two or more pieces that will abut each other on the inside of the hole. If you can gain access to the back of the hole (for example, there might be an access hole some distance away), cover your sheets with polyethylene to prevent the fiberglass from sticking to them. Screw through the outside laminate into the backing strips to hold them in place. If you cannot get access to the back, use the lightest, thinnest pieces of material you can use because they will stay in the boat. Instead of screwing through the outer laminate into the backing pieces, simply put a dab of epoxy on the end of each piece and glue it into place.

Now you can build your repair laminate as described above. The finished repair will have one or more thin pieces of Formica-type laminate fastened to the back of it, but only you will know that.

REPAIRS TO A CORED LAMINATE

Most repairs to a cored laminate require removing and replacing the core material. This procedure involves careful grinding and filling to ensure that the finished job fairs perfectly with the surrounding area of the deck or hull. Removing core material may be easy it if has rotted . . . or very difficult if the original builder achieved a good bond between core and skin. The only way to find out is by tackling the job.

The outer and inner skins of a cored hull or deck are often laminated from a basic polyester resin and fiberglass reinforcement—the tried-and-true, decades-old combination. The fiberglass reinforcement may consist of individual layers of CSM and woven cloth or roving (usually the latter in original construction), or it may be a material that combines CSM and roving, such as a 1708, 1808, or 2408 biaxial as described earlier in the chapter. Alternatively, on high-tech yachts, the laminate sandwiching the core may be graphite (carbon fiber), Kevlar, or high-strength S glass. (Note that drilling through carbon fiber or Kevlar is so difficult that I advise you not to try it without approval from the designer or builder.)

The core material used for a composite also varies. It may be end-grain balsa (which can rot if water penetrates into the core through fastener holes or cracks) or a closed-cell foam such as Divinycell or Corecell. Foam cores do not rot, but they can be crushed, or the core-to-skin bond can delaminate. On high-tech boats the core may be Hexcel or another aramid honeycomb. To save weight and expense, high-strength core materials are sometimes incorporated with slightly smaller safety factors than those observed for more conventional materials, so again you should consult with the yacht's designer or builder before drilling into one.

Filling a Hole in a Cored Hull or Deck

Holes in cored hulls or decks are a slightly different kettle of fish from single-skin holes in that you need to replace the missing or damaged core in addition to doing the glass work. Let's assume for the moment that the hole penetrates the entire sandwich, including the inner skin. There are several ways to repair this, but what works best for me is to find a piece of foam or balsa core material that is larger than the hole. I then mark the diameter of the hole on the foam or balsa and cut it to size. I like to cut it just slightly larger than the hole in order to ensure that it provides a good press-fit. I then coat its edges with thickened epoxy, fit it into position, and then laminate the inner and outer skins over the core, so that no backing is needed.

Let's look at the repair in a bit more detail, using as an example the hole left by a removed through-hull. You first need to ascertain that the exposed core edges in the hole are intact, free of rot, and well bonded to the skins. Tap and probe to test this, and ream out disintegrated core until you get back to solid core. Seal the exposed core edges with unthickened or only slightly thickened epoxy; then, if necessary, build the core back to the hole perimeter with thickened epoxy.

Working both inside and outside the hole, grind scarfs 2 to 3 inches (50 to 75 mm) wide into the inner and outer skins around the hole's perimeter. Next coat the edges of the core material replacement with thickened resin and push-fit the piece into the hole, leaving it while the resin hardens. If the fit is snug, the core will not move when you lay fiberglass over it.

When you are ready to begin the fiberglass work, start by prewetting a piece of CSM that overlaps the hole by about ½ inch (12 mm) all

94 • MINOR STRUCTURAL REPAIRS

Repairs to a Cored Laminate

Repairing a cored laminate. **(1)** A depthsounder was removed from the bottom of a hull, leaving a 2-inch-diameter (50 mm) hole. The first step on the exterior side of the repair is to grind a scarf into the outer skin around the hole to make sure there is enough meat to make the repair. With the fiberglass ground back, make up a small piece of foam or balsa core the same thickness as the core material and cut it for a snug fit in the hole. **(2)** Press this plug into the hole after coating its edges with thickened epoxy. **(3, 4)** Then glass over the repair on the outside, sand it back fair with the surrounding hull bottom, and undercoat it with an epoxy primer such as Interlux's Epoxy Primekote. You can then fair this with 320-grit sandpaper and coat the entire boat bottom with bottom paint. Repair the inner skin in the same way except that fairing and finishing isn't necessary.

the way around. Lay it in place and cover it with a piece of cloth or woven roving that overlaps the CSM by ½ inch all the way around. Keep applying alternating layers of mat and cloth or roving, each one slightly larger than the one beneath, until you have built up the repair to just below the level of the surrounding skin. Then fair the repair as described above.

If there is a small area of damage to the outer skin and core but the inner skin is still intact, your job is simpler. Use a core bit or hole saw to cut out the damaged skin and core to the depth of the inside laminate. You want to leave clean, undamaged core around the hole, and the inner skin will have only a small hole from the hole saw's pilot bit. As before, grind a scarf into the outer skin and fill the hole with a matching core. Glass it over and fair the repair as above.

Installing a Fitting on a Cored Deck

Let's say that you have standing water on your deck and want to install a drain, which entails making a hole through the deck's core. This fix can lead to major problems if you are not sure what you are doing. In particular, you can significantly damage the core if you do not seal the area around the drain properly.

A standing rule should be that whenever you drill *any* hole in a cored deck—whether for a drain, a hardware fastener, a solar panel cable, a handrail fastener, or anything else—you should first drill an oversized hole, then seal the exposed core edges with epoxy or polyester resin thickened only to the extent necessary to keep it in place while it cures, and finally fill the hole with thickened epoxy or polyester resin.

Only then should you drill a hole of the correct size through the resin plug, leaving a seal of resin around the hole to ensure that the core stays watertight. To drill and seal a hole for a scupper drain or other large-diameter installation, use the following procedure.

1. First, check behind the area where you are going to drill to make sure that you are not drilling into wires or furniture. Drilling into the stereo system or high-voltage wires could make your hair stand on end!
2. Once you are sure you can successfully drill the spot, drill an oversized hole through the core, but leave the inner skin in place.
3. If you have penetrated the inner skin, either by design or by accident, place a sheet of polyethylene plastic (in a pinch, a plastic

Holes in a cored deck. **(1)** *If you are going to drill a hole through a cored deck, you should be sure that the exposed core edges are sealed. Otherwise, water may penetrate the core and cause rot or core-to-skin delamination.* **(2)** *First, drill a hole that is larger than you actually need, leaving the inner skin intact if possible. If any part of your hole has penetrated the inner skin, back it with a block of wood that is covered with polyethylene sheeting to prevent the resin from sticking to the wood. Then seal the exposed core edges with epoxy thickened enough to keep it in place while curing.* **(3)** *Fill the hole with thickened epoxy, but do not fill the entire hole in one shot. The heat created by the resin setting up might cause a fire. Instead fill about ¼ inch (6 mm) at a time and let the resin harden before adding more.* **(4)** *When the resin is level with the top laminate, drill the correctly sized hole through the resin plug, making sure that you have at least ⅛ inch (3 mm) of resin all around the hole. Now you can install your fitting knowing that moisture cannot get into the core material and that the epoxy plug will act as a compression column to prevent loaded hardware from crushing the core.*

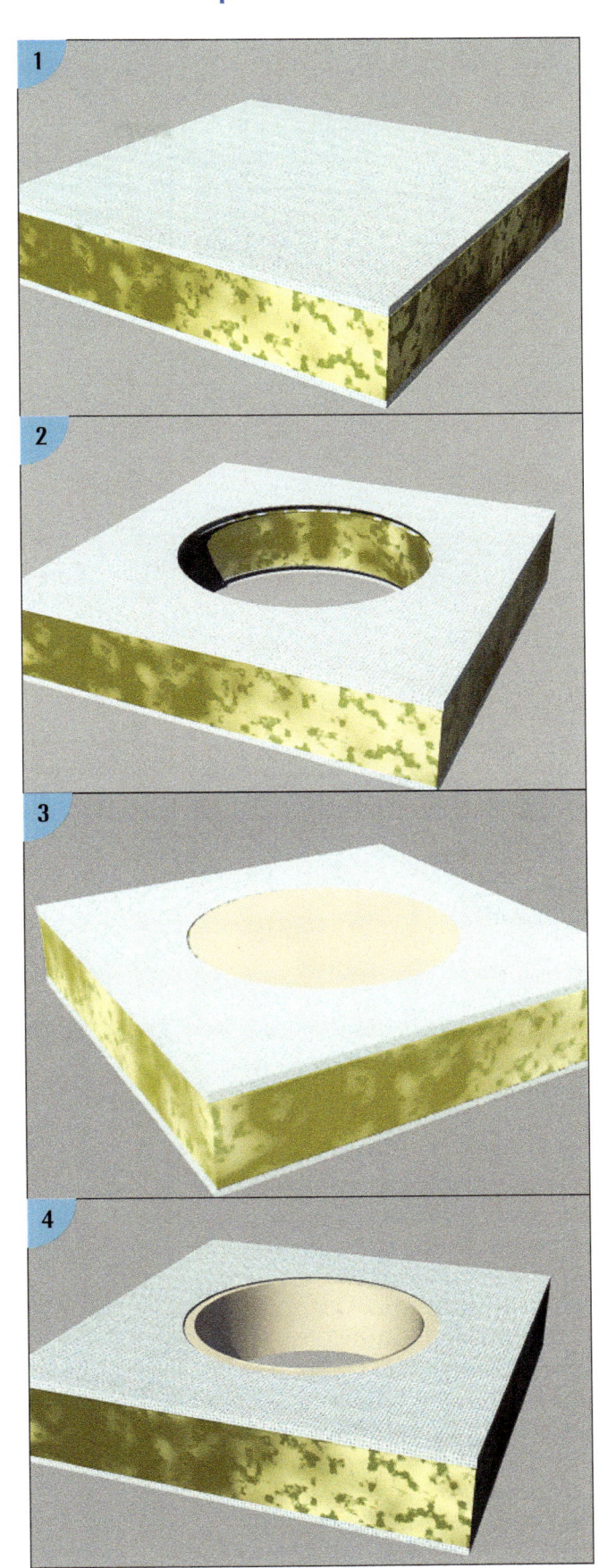

96 • MINOR STRUCTURAL REPAIRS

Repairs to a Cored Laminate

1

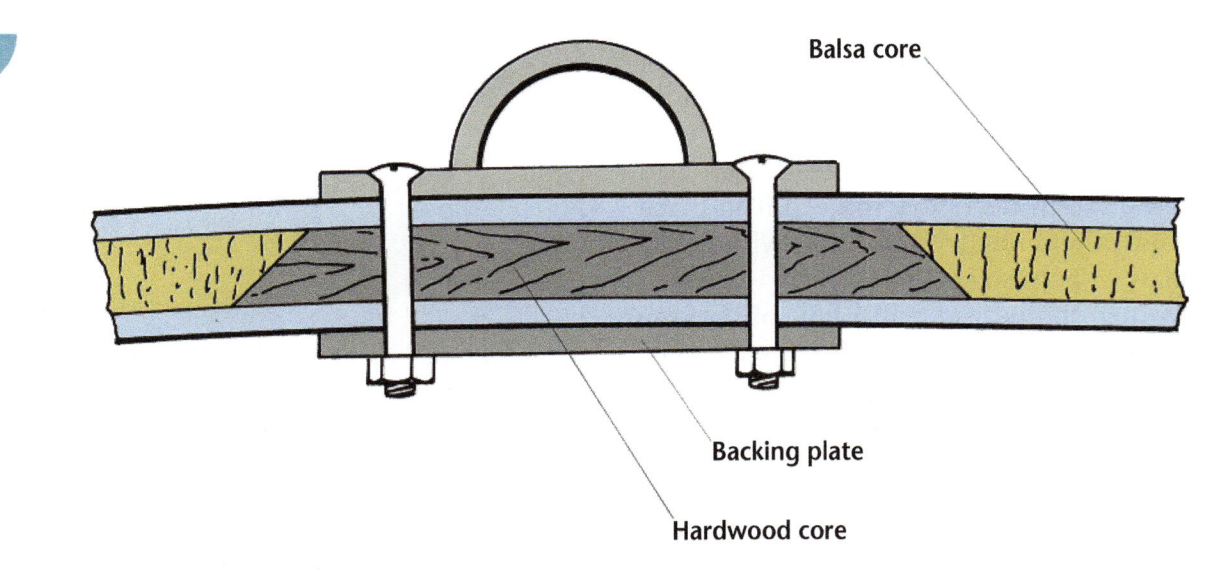

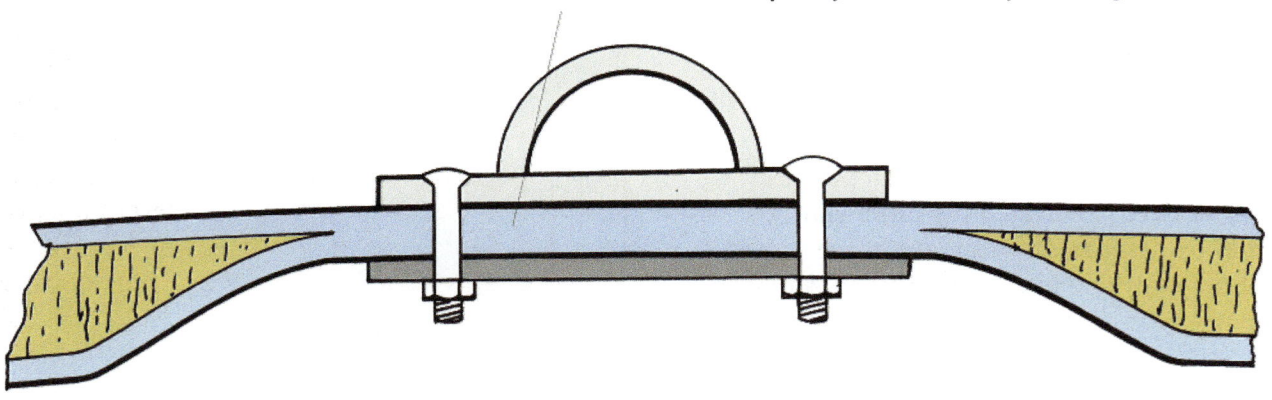

Balsa core

Backing plate

Hardwood core

Core removed completely and laminate joined together

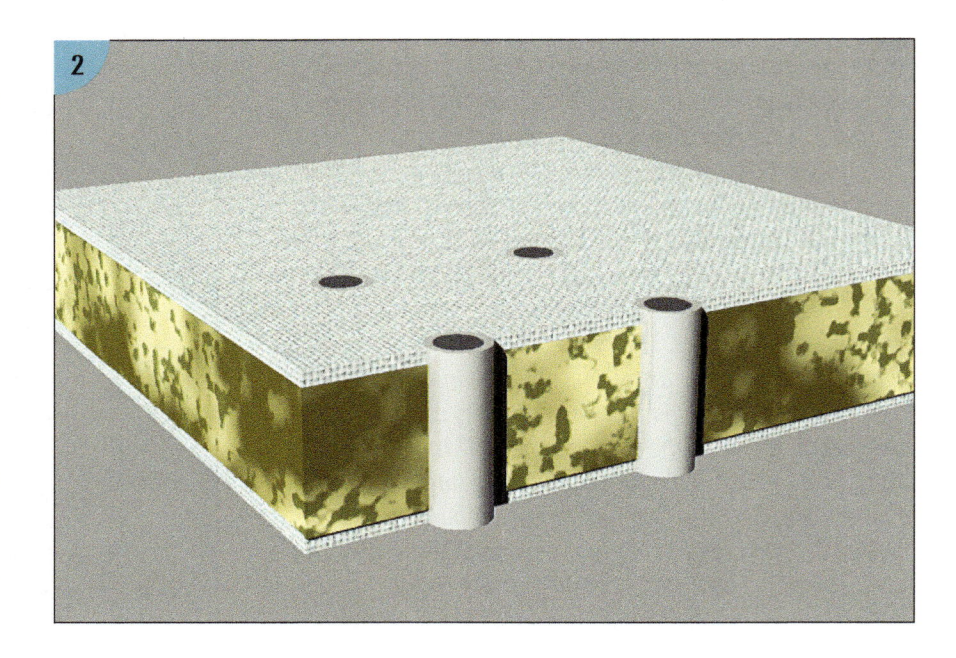

(1) *If you need to install a padeye, cleat, or other hardware that will exert a high load on the deck, you should replace the core with a piece of plywood or remove the core entirely. Both options are illustrated here. Note that the core is tapered where removed to prevent an abrupt transition that could lead to a laminate fracture.*
(2) *If you cannot remove the core or install a higher-density core material, your remaining option is to install compression tubes through the deck to absorb the loads and prevent the core from being crushed. The problem with compression tubes is that they have to be cut precisely to the right length.*

2

garbage bag will do) over a piece of plywood large enough to cover the hole. Wedge the plywood under the hole to prevent resin from simply dripping through it.

4. Mask off the area around the hole's exterior so that you won't make a mess that you'll need to clean up later. Remember to remove the masking tape while the resin is still soft, however. If you leave it until the resin has hardened, it may be difficult to remove.

5. Wearing latex gloves to make cleanup easier, mix a batch of epoxy or polyester resin. (I prefer epoxy for a job like this because it is easier to thicken and its odor bothers me less than that of polyester.)

6. Thicken the resin to the consistency of peanut butter. (If you are using WEST System epoxy, use colloidal silica; if you are using Epiglass epoxy, use Interlux's glue powder.) Wear a mask when adding the powder to the resin mixture, and mix it thoroughly.

7. Don't fill the entire hole in one shot. Epoxy and polyester resins are thermosetting and give off heat as they cure. If you try to fill the entire depth of a 3-inch-diameter (75 mm) hole in one shot, you could generate enough heat to ignite the core material. Simply smear the thickened epoxy around the edges of the core initially, and let it set. Keep filling with layers about ¼ inch (6 mm) thick until the hole is level with the deck.

8. If you are going to use a hole saw to cut a final hole of large diameter, make sure you've built up enough epoxy to give the saw some bite. Then you can cut the hole, install the hardware, and finish filling around the hardware. But if you will be using a drill bit to make a smaller hole, you might as well fill the hole completely before drilling the final, correctly sized hole.

9. After you have made the correctly sized hole, install the fitting, making sure to caulk around the fitting to avoid deck leaks. For smaller holes, I use a countersink bit to bevel the top of the hole. When the fitting is bedded, this small countersink retains a doughnut of caulking that remains flexible and stops water from getting into the hole.

If you are drilling fastener holes for the installation of hardware such as a padeye, stanchion, cleat, or winch that will put some strain on the deck, make sure that you also install a backing plate that is larger than the hole you drilled; otherwise, the padeye and the epoxy plug could pull right out of the deck. Ideally you should replace the foam or balsa core under the hardware with plywood, which is relatively immune to crushing, or omit the core under the hardware altogether. Plywood or solid-laminate core substitutions are generally incorporated when a deck is built, but you can retrofit a core substitution if you have access to the underside of the deck.

If substituting plywood core or a solid laminate under installed hardware is unfeasible or overly ambitious, a third option is to install the fasteners through spacers, or compression tubes, which are steel or aluminum cylinders cut to exactly the thickness of the deck to prevent the bolt tension from crushing the core, or to drill the holes oversize and install thickened epoxy plugs as described above. If you do not do this, you risk fracturing the outer laminates under the compressive load, which may let water into the core and cause it to degrade.

REPAIRING OR INSTALLING A BULKHEAD

Another common repair is rebonding a bulkhead to a hull. The bulkhead might be either fiberglass or wood, either of which, if not installed properly, can create a hard spot on the hull surface outside the bulkhead edge.

To eliminate potential hard spots, a bulkhead should be mounted on a foam cushion or with a fillet joint. Most boatbuilders use a fillet joint because it is easier and faster than installing a foam strip around the bulkhead's perimeter. The taper of the fillet joint allows the bulkhead and hull to flex and to transmit flat-panel loads more evenly through the area of transition.

98 • MINOR STRUCTURAL REPAIRS

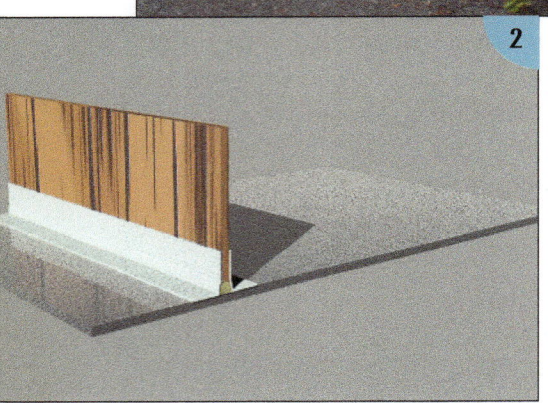

(1) *A hard spot on a hull is never more visible than when primer has been applied to the topsides and the hull has been sanded. The high spots lose their paint first during sanding. This hull shows three distinct lines over bulkhead edges. Looking along the side of a finished hull is another, more difficult way to detect a hard spot. A bulkhead should be mounted in the hull on a small pad of foam to prevent the formation of a hard spot on the hull surface.* (2) *Here you can see the tiny foam pad (Airex foam or similar) between a wooden bulkhead and the hull skin. The insert is then concealed by the tabbing, which this illustration also shows. When you are reattaching a bulkhead, however, you may not be able to insert foam around the bulkhead perimeter, in which case you should make epoxy fillet joints before tabbing the bulkhead to the hull.*

Making a Fillet Joint

To make a fillet joint, you will need a round-ended spatula. Most builders use the knowledge gained from experience to adapt the size of the fillet to the job. As a rule, however, the fillet radius should be at least three to four times the thickness of the material. For example, if you were to join two ¼-inch-thick (6 mm) sheets of fiberglass at right angles, the fillet radius should be ¾ to 1 inch (19 to 25 mm). To bond a ½-inch (12 mm) plywood bulkhead to a hull, you'd want a fillet radius of 1½ to 2 inches (38 to 50 mm). The fillet radius is determined by the width of the spatula end you apply it with.

Masking off the sides of the fillet before mixing epoxy gives a cleaner joint, so I first offer up the spatula to the job and mark where it touches the bulkhead and hull. I mask off the job along those offsets, which is easy when the joint is straight. The typical bulkhead-to-hull joint will

Repairing or Installing a Bulkhead • 99

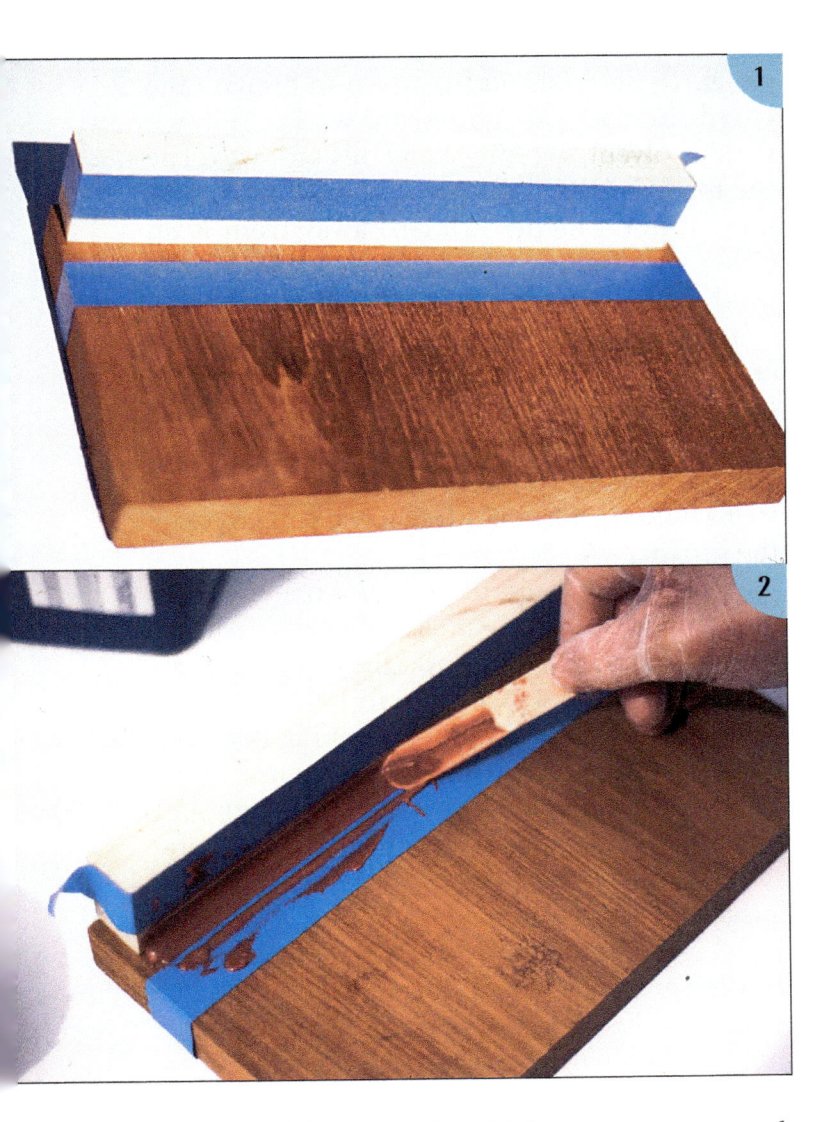

This fillet joint fastens two pieces of wood together, but you can also use a fillet to join a bulkhead to a hull or to join two panels of fiberglass. (1) First, determine the appropriate offset of the fillet edges on both surfaces, and mask those edges. (2, 3) Apply the fillet using a spatula of the chosen radius, and remove the tape before the epoxy is fully hardened. By virtue of its tapered edges, the fillet allows the parts to flex a little and the flexing loads to be disseminated around the corner. The radius of the fillet should be three to four times the thickness of the materials joined. When joining a bulkhead to a hull, you will cover the cured fillet with tabbing as described below.

be curved, however, in which case you can mask off both sides of the joint with wide masking tape, trace the offset lines along the masking tape, and then cut the masking tape to these curves with a razor knife or similar.

Mix epoxy in the conventional fashion, thickening with filler or glue powder to a peanut butter–like consistency, and lay the mixture into the joint. Run your spatula along the joint, maintaining contact with the hull and bulkhead to obtain a nice even finish. Try to get the fillet as smooth as possible, because once the epoxy has hardened, the only way to smooth it further is by sanding. I generally allow the mixture to set for a few minutes before peeling off the masking tape. If you leave the tape on until the epoxy has hardened completely, it will be glued in place and may never come off.

A good-quality finish joint made by the professionals at Goetz Custom Boats. They covered this fillet with carbon fiber tabbing rather than ordinary fiberglass, but the technique is the same.

Glassing a Plywood Bulkhead to a Hull

When a plywood bulkhead is glassed to a hull, it must first be carefully positioned. In original construction, if the hull is a single-skin laminate, the bulkhead is often positioned on a foam insert as described above. In repair work you are more likely to use epoxy fillets instead.

When glassing bulkheads in place, be sure to provide drain and limber holes as appropriate. If not, water will accumulate behind the tabbing and may eventually rot the bulkhead.

REINFORCING A FLAT PANEL

Flat fiberglass panels are easy to lay up and are often used as flat seats, bulkheads, deck sections, and in other areas where a flat panel may be needed. When making a repair to a flat bow area, you may need a large flat panel, for example. To make a flat panel, you need to work on a flat surface. A large pane of glass is ideal.

Flat fiberglass panels tend to vibrate, just as flat spans in a boat's topsides (often forward) may flex in waves when insufficiently supported by interior stringers and bulkheads. You can use a sandwich laminate to make the panel stiffer, but even that might not be enough to eliminate vibrations in a large flat panel. In this case, there are several ways to stiffen a panel.

A *stiffener* is simply a reinforcing member—a rib or stringer—added to the hidden side of a panel. In cross section the stiffener might be hat-shaped, semicircular, triangular, or rectangular, depending on what you use as a form to mold the fiberglass over. The form might be a split cardboard tube, a strip of plywood set on edge against the panel, or a length of half-round molding, split vinyl hose, or PVC pipe, etc. These days, stiffeners are increasingly likely to be cut from foam and glassed in place. It's a matter of convenience what material is used for the form the stiffener is shaped over, because the fiberglass reinforcement itself is what provides the stiffener's strength.

To glass a stiffener in place requires what is known as a secondary bond—that is, you must adhere fiberglass to an already cured fiberglass panel. To do this, you first need to prepare the cured surface by grinding and wiping it down with a solvent to remove any oils and wax. Lay the form for the stiffener on the job and mark lines about 4 inches (10 cm) away from it on either side. Remove the form, then grind some tooth into the work surface with an 80- or 100-grit disk. Then wipe down with a solvent such as DuPont's Prep-Sol or MAS Epoxies' Bio-Solv. (Acetone dries too fast for this purpose.) Wedge the form into place and tab it with 2-inch-wide (50 mm) strips of prewetted fiberglass. These strips hold the form in place while you laminate the stiffener over it.

Four or five strips of fiberglass material over the form constitutes a sufficient laminate. Cut the widest one so as to drape over the form and overlap the panel 3 to 4 inches (75 to 100 mm) either side of the form. Each of the remaining strips can be ¾ inch (19 mm) narrower than the next wider one. Opinion differs as to whether the widest or narrowest strip should be applied first, but I prefer to start with the narrowest strip—so that each successive strip forms a bond directly with the panel—and have always had good results this way. If using polyester resin you can build the laminate with mat plus cloth or roving, depending in part on what you have on hand. If using epoxy resin, you can build the laminate entirely of cloth if you so choose.

If you're using epoxy resin, coat the form and the surrounding surface of the panel with lightly thickened resin the consistency of maple syrup. When this has kicked but is still tacky, coat it again with more heavily thickened resin (the consistency of thick syrup), adding fillets where the form meets the panel. Now wet out your first layer of fiberglass, press it into the thickened epoxy, and roll it out until all the air bubbles have disappeared. Mix a new batch of resin (thickened as necessary to keep the resin in place while it hardens) and lay a second piece of prewetted fiberglass on top. The second piece should overlap the first by a small amount. Add two or three more layers in the same way, with each succeeding layer overlapping the previous one. After rolling the wet fiberglass to eliminate any air bubbles,

(1) *This floor is held in place temporarily by wooden L brackets glued to the bulkhead and the floor. They will be removed when the floor has been tabbed to the hull. Because this hull is carbon fiber, the tabbing will also be carbon fiber, but the technique is the same as it would be for fiberglass (or Kevlar, for that matter). The floor is carefully masked off and the area wiped down with a solvent to get good adhesion. The crew are working on the inside of an upside-down hull.*

(2) *The joint between this longitudinal and the hull has been given an epoxy fillet (white) and carefully masked off. The next step is to lay carbon fiber tabbing over the joint to ensure a good bond.* **(3)** *This joint is finished and the masking tape has been removed. The work is very clean and professional—you can barely see the carbon fiber tabbing against the carbon fiber hull—and illustrates the sort of standard you should aim for.*

Reinforcing a Flat Panel

102 • MINOR STRUCTURAL REPAIRS

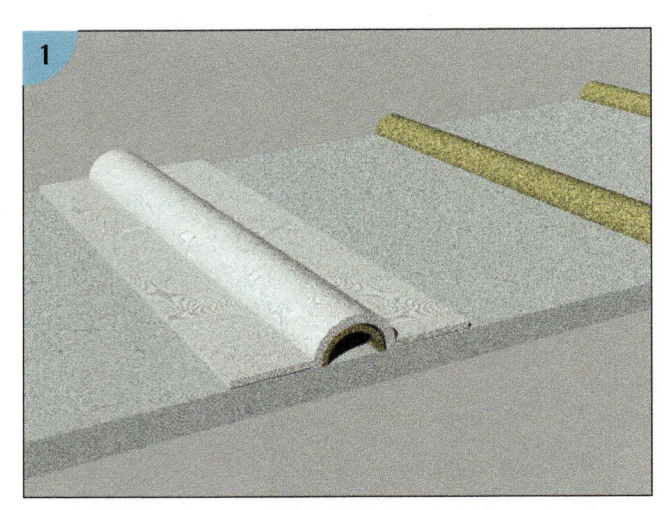

(1) *Using a stiffener to prevent flexing of a large flat panel. In this case the stiffener is formed over a half-round cardboard or light plastic tube. Though not shown here, you should taper the tabbing as described in the text. Adding fillets along the form edges will provide a smoother transition and a stronger result.*

(2) *Here a hat-shaped section of foam comprises the core.*

leave it to harden. Wetting out four or five layers of glass at once in a job of this size should not cause overheating.

REPLACING MISSING PARTS

Sometimes whole parts of a boat are destroyed. For example, a large chunk may be smashed in a collision, or an entire section may have to be cut away in pieces while you're making a major repair. One option in such cases is to have the original hull manufacturer make a new part that can be glassed into place. To avoid this expense, however, a second option is to make a splash and build the missing part yourself. In other words, you can make a mold around the same part on a sister boat (or on an adjacent portion of the subject boat) and use that mold to laminate a new part that is identical to the destroyed one. In boatbuilder terminology, you have "splashed" the part, using the sister ship as a plug.

To ensure that you don't ruin the sister ship, cover its hull with mold release wax and then put plastic over that. Creases left in your splash by the plastic won't matter, and this belt-and-suspenders approach ensures that the new splash and the sister ship don't stick together. Laminate your splash and stiffen it with plywood- or foam-cored ribs as necessary. When this sets up, peel off the splash, polish it or sand it smooth, coat it with mold release wax, and tape or screw it over the exterior of the damaged area to make a backing for the repair.

Even a hull section with a deep compound curvature can be splashed in this way, and of course the technique is easier if the part or surface being replaced is flat. With that overview in mind, let's look at the technique in a little more detail.

Making a Splash for a Repair

Suppose you have to make a new hatch cover to replace one that has been destroyed. If there is a similar-sized hatch cover on your boat, you can use it as your plug and make a splash from it. First, clean it thoroughly and repair any imperfections so that they will not be duplicated in the new cover you make. This may require filling screw holes or repairing scratches, dents, or dings. Wipe the part with a solvent to get it really clean, then polish it with mold release wax. If the texture of the part you will be making is not critical, you can skip the mold release wax and simply lay a piece of plastic over the original part. Then lay up the mold on the plastic. If the part is small, you can simply put it in a plastic garbage bag, though you

Replacing Missing Parts • 103

(1) This splash is a bow template used by the builder of a production boat to locate the bolt layout for the stemhead.
(2) The template next to the stemhead that was prepared from it.

should first test to see that your resin does not react with the bag. If you use a plastic bag or sheet, make sure that you have removed any creases in it before starting work.

Once the part is coated with mold release wax or covered in plastic, the next step is to spray or paint the work with gelcoat and leave the gelcoat to cure. This will provide a reasonably smooth mold surface. The following day you can start laminating by placing several layers of fiberglass on the work and wetting out each layer with resin. Roll everything well to eliminate voids. Gradually build up the layers of fiberglass until your laminate is the desired thickness. If you choose to reinforce the mold with stiffeners—a good idea for a mold of more than 1 square foot—you might want to add the stiffeners while the laminate is still tacky in order to reduce distortion as it cures.

When the new mold has set up hard, remove it from the original part that served as your plug and inspect it carefully. You may have to fill holes or cracks and correct distortions before you can proceed. Clean the work thoroughly, wipe it down with a solvent, and coat the inner surface with mold release wax. You now have a piece of tooling

(1) Another template made by a production builder.
(2) This one shows where the stern chock hole is to be cut. Any template, or splash, you might need to mold a missing piece could be fabricated in the same way.

104 • MINOR STRUCTURAL REPAIRS

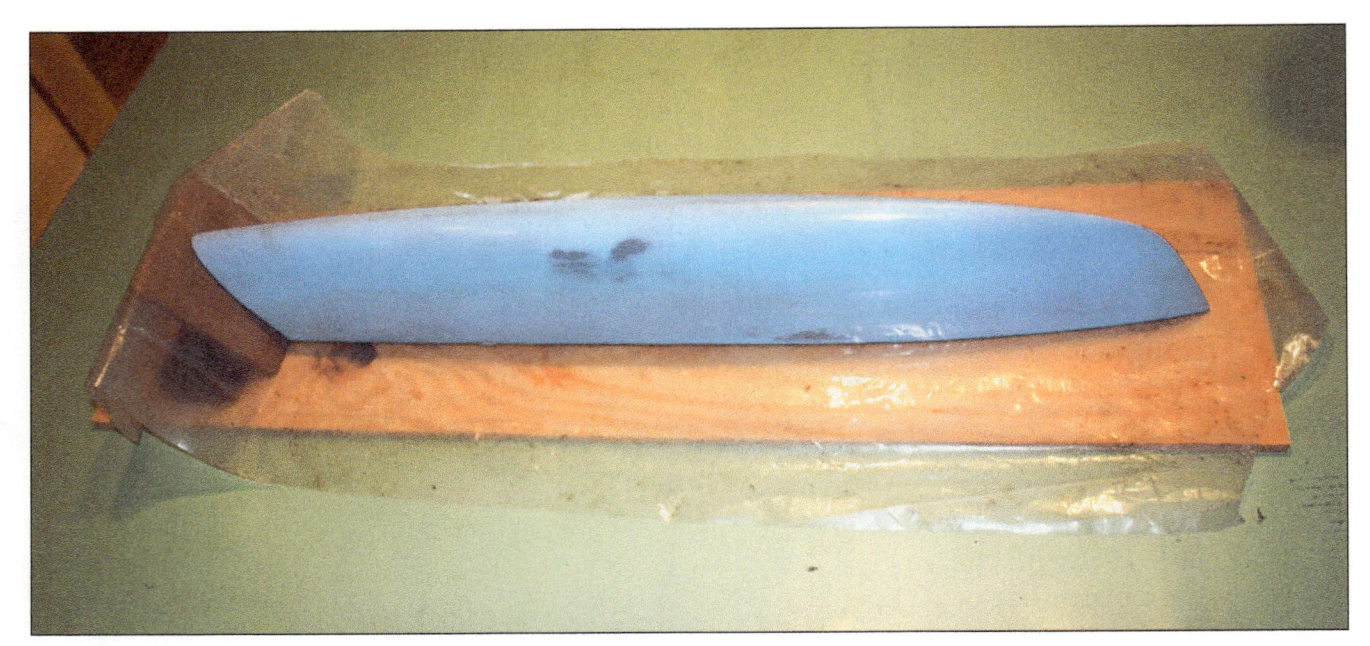

A plug can be made for a model hull, as shown here, just as it can be made for a full-sized hull. This plug has been coated with mold release wax and is sitting on a piece of plastic, ready for the mold laminate to be applied. Any fiberglass part can be molded over a plug like this.

that can, if necessary, last through a half-dozen projects before the heat of curing breaks it down.

Making a Plug

Occasions may arise when a piece from your own or someone else's boat is not available to make a mold for a missing part. In this case you will have to construct your own plug. As we saw in Chapter 1, a plug is a mock-up, usually made of wood, that is identical to the finished part, and a mold is the piece of tooling that is built over the plug and serves as the structure for building the finished part. You can make any number of identical finished parts from a single mold.

Since plugs are usually made from wood, you will need some woodworking skills to construct one. You can use a plug to make a mold for a part of any size from a winch base or hatch cover to a full hull.

The first step is to obtain a design drawing for the part in question. If you can't get this from the designer or builder, you'll have to develop it yourself. Think carefully about the shape, because this is trickier than you might think. Let's say that you are going to mold an icebox to be fitted with a lid and installed in a locker. If you make a conventional box the corners will be very sharp, so it will be difficult to mold fiberglass into and around them. Typically, sharp corners like this will end up resin-rich, with insufficient fiberglass reinforcement, or you may get voids under the gelcoat that will later chip and look unsightly. So you need to round off the corners to make the box easier to shape.

Nor is that the only complication. You also will have to get the finished fiberglass icebox off its plug, so you need to very slightly taper the sides of the box, making the bottom slightly narrower than the top. Most fabricators make this taper no more than about $3/16$ inch per foot, or about 16 mm per meter. This allows the box to slide off the plug easily.

When the plug is finished, it looks like an exact replica of the eventual icebox. In this case, since the interior surface of the icebox is the surface you want to be smooth and polished, you will mold the finished part over the plug. Note that while the inside of the box will be smooth, the outside of the finished box will be rough fiberglass. This doesn't matter, however, because it will be covered with insulating foam.

Alternatively, if you were making a dock box and desired a smooth surface on the outside of the finished box, you would build a female mold over the male plug, then laminate the finished box inside the female mold.

Now suppose you want to put an access hole in one side of the dock box with a boss (a raised lip) to take a hatch. This is more difficult than it seems. Because the box will have to slide out of the mold, the mold around the boss has to be made with a removable part. Typically that entire side of the mold is removable. This allows any seams to be in the corners, where they can easily be polished out. If you put a seam on a flat surface, it is a lot harder to polish out and hide.

When you make a two-part mold, the common practice is to put a flange on the plug where the two mold parts will join, and then to fiberglass each mold part up and over the flange. (This is shown in the photos of two halves of a boat mold in Chapter 1; see page 4.) The two molded parts are then trimmed, bolted together along their

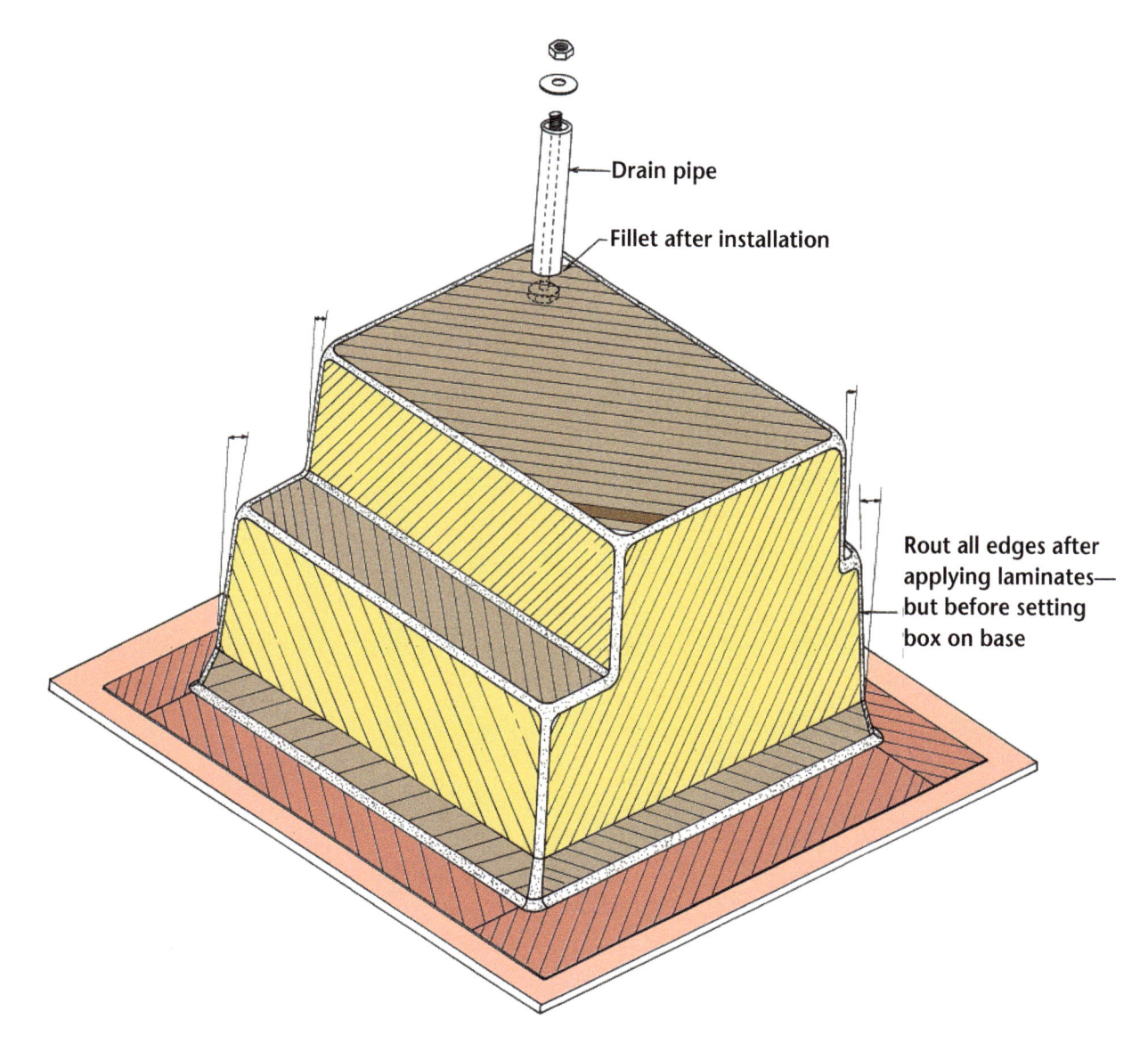

- Drain pipe
- Fillet after installation

Rout all edges after applying laminates— but before setting box on base

This drawing for an icebox plug shows how the box is tapered and the corners are rounded, not only to allow the finished icebox to be removed easily from the plug but also to prevent voids and resin richness in the corners of the molded part. The corner radius may be as small as ½ inch (12 mm) or as large as desired.

mating flanges, and then waxed to make them ready for use.

More-complex molds may be made in multiple parts, although fiberglass production builders try to reduce the number of seams that need to be polished out, because polishing is a time-consuming process. Often all the corners of a complex mold are rounded, or radiused, to allow the mold and the production parts to be released easily. This work is time-consuming and requires a lot of skill on the part of the craftsman.

Chapter 6: HULL, KEEL, AND RUDDER FAIRING

When a fiberglass boat comes out of its mold, the hull exterior is very smooth. From that point on, accumulating layers of bottom paint; the addition of depthsounder and speedometer transducers, water intake strainers, and other protuberances; and the accumulation of nicks, bumps, and marine growth all serve to decrease that smoothness.

A smooth underbody can save a lot of fuel on a powerboat or make a racing sailboat faster. At slow speeds, the major part of a boat's resistance to progress through the water is from frictional drag. In fact, when a sailboat is in light winds or a powerboat is at low throttle, hull friction accounts for about 60% to 90% of the resistance to forward motion. To minimize this frictional drag, you need to make your boat's bottom as smooth as possible. While doing so is not a "repair" in the technical sense of the word, it is a skill that is often called for when finishing repair jobs.

In this chapter we'll look at ways to make your boat's bottom very smooth. We'll also look at smoothing, or fairing, a sailboat's keel and rudder. These improvements can help you get where you want to go faster and/or with less fuel consumption.

FAIRING A HULL

Compounds used to make a hull smooth vary from the ubiquitous polyester autobody putty known as Bondo to a filled epoxy mixture. We touched on fairing compounds in Chapter 4. Awlgrip's Awlfair epoxy fairing compound, while wonderfully effective in the hands of a skilled worker, is only available to the professional market, and in any event is best used for the topsides of a boat since it is not impervious to water and should be covered with an epoxy barrier coat if used underwater. For underwater surfaces and for do-it-yourself applications, you should use an epoxy or polyester resin filled with an appropriate amount of powder to achieve the consistency of peanut butter. Depending on the filler used, you can fair such a mixture nicely, and it is not too hard to sand when cured. It is also waterproof. An epoxy-based fairing can be stronger, but polyester is much less expensive and makes an adequate fairing on a polyester-based hull or appendage. "Sandability"—the most critical feature of a fairing compound—is a function of the filler, not the resin. (See Chapter 3.)

Fairing in Below-the-Waterline Protuberances

The first job is to make sure that any protuberances on the hull bottom are faired in so that water flows around them with minimal drag. Take a look at the bottom of your boat. Maybe you have a bow thruster, a water intake, or a through-hull jutting out from the hull. Each of these causes turbulence and drag. Each serves to slow your boat and increases the cost of moving it through the water under power. If you cannot eliminate these items, you should at least smooth the area around them to minimize their interference with water flow. You can make the fairing out of solid resin if the protuberance is smaller than roughly 1 inch (25 mm) deep and 1 inch in diameter. If it is larger than this, make the fairing from foam covered with fiberglass.

Smoothing a Hull Surface

The next stage in fairing a hull is to make the entire skin as smooth as possible. Particular attention to fairing is needed anywhere a repair has been made. Often it is hard to see small bumps or depressions in repair work. The best test for high or low spots is to bend a flexible batten across the repair, but even then you may miss slight areas of unfairness until the job has been painted and small ripples show up.

When you find a low spot, wipe it down with solvent, sand it with 80- to 100-grit, wipe again, and apply a skim coat of fairing compound (either polyester or epoxy, as discussed above). Using your batten, "scrape" over the faired area to ensure that you have filled the hollow.

When you find a small hump or bump, sand it down if you can do so without damaging the gelcoat. In most cases, however, you'll need to build up the surrounding surface instead, so as not to damage the gelcoat.

Work over the entire hull, filling hollows until you can find no more under your batten. Then longboard or block sand the hull using 100-grit sandpaper. Next go back and refill any areas you may have sanded too enthusiastically, then sand again.

Following this fairing—especially on an older hull—you may be well advised to apply an epoxy barrier coat to the underbody so as to prevent future osmosis (see Chapter 8). Popular barrier coats include Interlux's Interprotect and WEST System's 105 Epoxy Resin, but other manufacturers offer similar products. Most can be applied either

Block sanding the side of a sailboat to get the hull and appendages as smooth as possible. The most critical portions are the forward third of the hull underbody, keel, and rudder. The goal is to keep water flow attached to the hull and foils as far aft as possible.

Fairing a Hull • 109

(1) Because this hole for a bow thruster is in the forward part of the hull, it causes major turbulence over the entire underbody. A retractable thruster would impose much less drag in the retracted position than this open-tunnel thruster. **(2)** A large depthsounder transducer protruding beneath the hull in this fashion is efficient but creates a lot of additional drag under the boat. Drag could be reduced by making the sounder flush with the hull or by building up a fairing piece around it. **(3)** This prominent water intake for the main engine of a powerboat would cause less turbulence if its back edge were faired into the hull. **(4)** This engine water intake is similar but has a small fairing piece on its trailing edge. The fairing strip would be more effective, however, if it were longer and more gradually smoothed into the hull. **(5)** These two through-hulls stand proud of the hull surface and will cause turbulence. Fairing them into the surrounding surface—or possibly replacing them with inserts that end flush with the hull—would reduce drag and make the hull more efficient.

110 • HULL, KEEL, AND RUDDER FAIRING

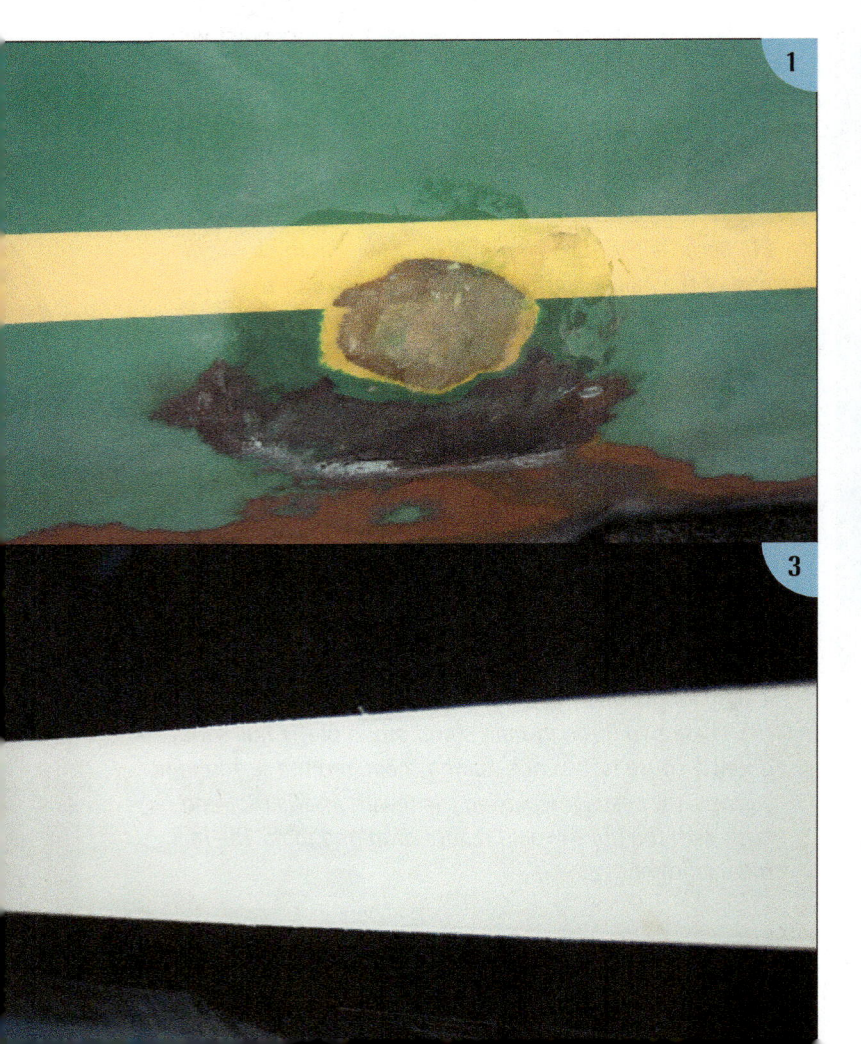

by spraying (at least four coats) or rolling (to a cumulative thickness of at least 10 mils). On a racing sailboat that will be dry-sailed, you can follow the barrier coat application with another round of sanding using 400- to 600-grit wet-or-dry paper to get an amazingly smooth bottom. On a boat that will receive bottom paint, however, you should follow the barrier coat with an application of a two-part epoxy primer, which is designed to prevent a reaction between the barrier coat and the bottom paint.

For a racing sailboat, my preferred bottom

As discussed in Chapter 3, preparing a filled resin is not difficult. Simply mix the hardener into the epoxy or the catalyst into the polyester, then add your chosen filler powder. Make your mixture the consistency of peanut butter to reduce the risk of sags.

(1) *This hull sustained a hole at the boottop. The repair looks fair prior to painting.* **(2)** *From up close, however, you can see some slight ripples in the surface of the boottop. To get it smooth, the owner would need to sand back the area, cover it with a skim coat of filled resin, allow it to cure, and then sand it using a longboard before recoating it with primer.* **(3)** *The finished and painted hull—the repair is barely visible.*

Fairing a Hull • 111

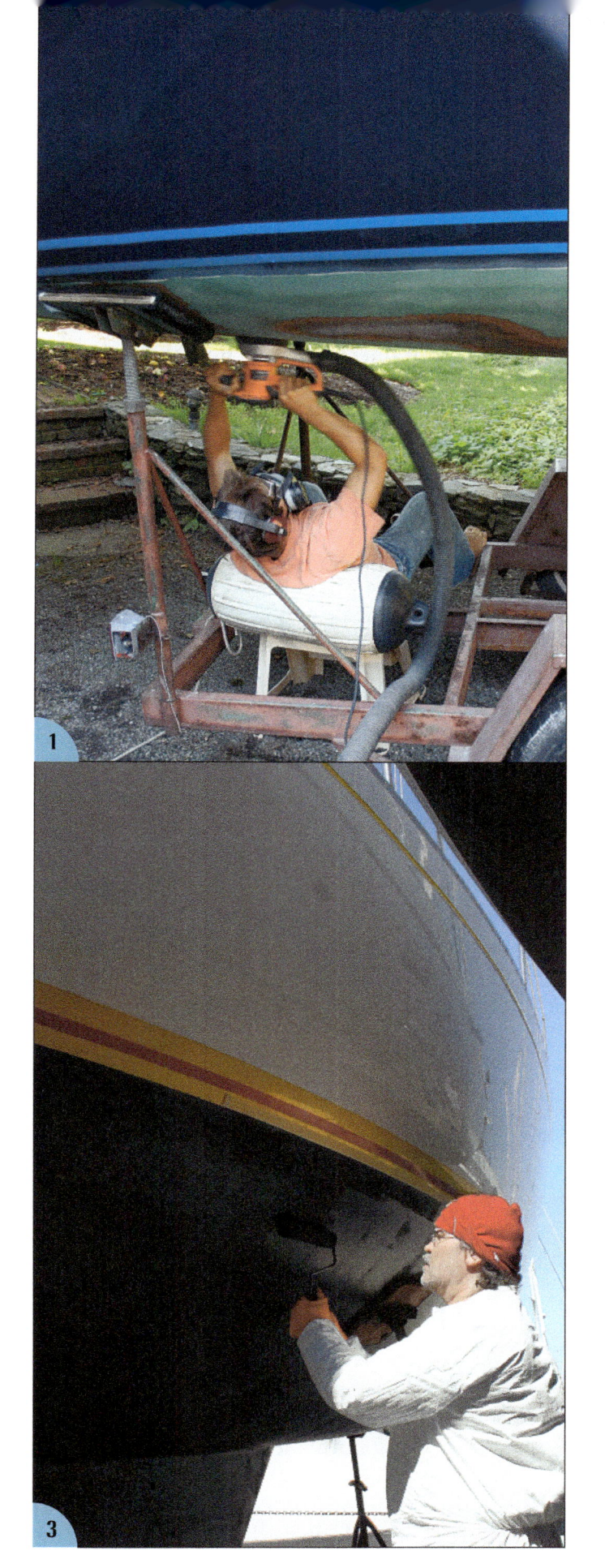

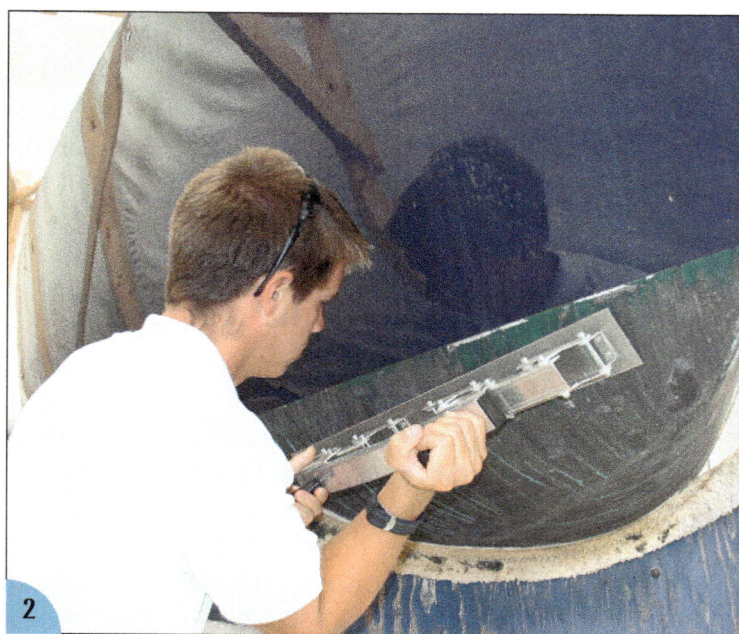

(1) Power sanding a bottom with a RIDGID 6-inch (15 cm) random orbit sander rigged to exhaust the dust into a RIDGID shop vac. This setup makes a messy job less messy. Here my son is using 120-grit to remove all bottom paint back to the gelcoat. (2) Here my other son is longboarding the hull to get it smooth after rotary sanding. (3) Applying the final black bottom paint with a sponge roller. The last job will be wet sanding the hull bottom with 400- to 600-grit wet-or-dry paper to get it absolutely smooth for racing.

paint is three to five coats of Interlux's Baltoplate (a racing bottom paint), sprayed on and sanded with 400- to 600-grit wet-or-dry paper. Applying several coats helps ensure that you don't sand through the paint layer when you are doing your final sanding.

When finish sanding a hull, use a longboard to get the bottom very smooth, and start at the front of the boat. The forward third of the underbody and of the keel and rudder must be sanded especially smooth for best performance in light winds. The farther aft you go, the less critical smoothness becomes (though it remains important), because the after half of the underbody (or the foil) operates in turbulent water no matter what you do. The job is messy and tedious, but the result is a remarkable improvement in boat speed.

FAIRING A KEEL

If you want to race a sailboat, you'll probably want to fair the keel sides and bottom to obtain optimum performance. This job is not difficult to do. It just takes time and a little care.

Before you start, you need to obtain measurements of the keel from the boat's designer or builder. This information will include at least three horizontal sections through the keel: the keel tip section (or for purposes of fairing the shape, 1 or 2 inches/25 to 50 mm above the tip), the midchord section, and the section at the root or top of the keel. These sections may be drawn out as in the accompanying illustration, or they may just be given in a table of offsets. Either way, you'll need to draw the full-size half-sections on light plywood or heavy cardboard. When you cut out a half-section, it leaves behind in your plywood or cardboard stock a curve that you can fit to your keel at the appropriate height to gauge its fairness.

Remember that the leading edge of a keel should be a parabola in cross section, not an oval or circle. A parabolic leading edge allows water to flow around the front of the keel without separating. It is almost impossible to sharpen a keel's trailing edge to a fine point (I know, I've tried), so the best thing to do is to make the trailing edge $\frac{1}{8}$ to $\frac{3}{16}$ inch (3 to 4 mm) thick, and flat.

Before you start fairing a keel, you must first remove old bottom paint, old fairing compound, and anything else that might affect the new keel shape. You may have to power-wash, sand, or grind the old material away. The goal is to clean the keel as well as you possibly can to ensure that the templates will fit properly. A single barnacle under a fairing template can ruin an entire job.

Armed with your fairing templates, you should mark the keel to show the height at which each template should be fitted. You might want to make marks on the centerline of the keel's leading and trailing edges at those heights to ensure that you can still find the marks after you start fairing. Some experts hammer a nail into the keel at each these points. Then, when the rest of the fairing is finished, they remove nails and also fair the nail holes before painting.

With everything marked out, offer up the templates to the keel and see where the high and low spots are. You may have to grind away a high spot or two to ensure that the keel template fits properly along its entire length. It should meet the centerline of both the leading and trailing edges; only when it does will you know that low spots really are low spots and not just artifacts of an improperly positioned template. Mark the low spots and the high spots in different colors. Then flip the template over and do the same thing on the other side of the keel.

Before you begin fairing, you'll need to remove any grease or grime on the keel surface in order to get good adhesion. This means putting on rubber gloves and wiping down the entire keel surface with a solvent. Then determine how much compound you'll need to apply in order to fair the hollows. A thin skim coat should cause very little problem. If you have to build up the fairing more than $\frac{1}{4}$ inch (about 6 mm), however, you will probably want to tack a $\frac{1}{4}$-inch-thick batten vertically in place to show you exactly how much you need to raise the keel surface. Use thin brads to fasten the batten to the lead. When applying fairing compound, fair to the top of the batten and leave the compound until it is almost hardened before removing the batten. Once the compound has hardened fully, clean up the ends left from pulling the batten away and fill the slot with new fairing compound. Leave it to set up before you start sanding.

Only mix your fairing compound when the surface is prepped and you have positioned any battens. Make sure the compound is designed for underwater use, because many are not. For fairing a keel, I prefer to use epoxy thickened to the consistency of really thick peanut butter and troweled into place. You can fair it with a thin batten to get it smooth. If you have to build up more than $\frac{1}{8}$ inch (3 mm), do so in several stages. Too thick a layer will sag before it has set up properly, and it also gets very hot as it kicks off. While heat is not a problem on a lead keel, it could be a problem if you are coating both a lead keel and a fiberglass stub.

Before your fairing compound has set up hard, check it vertically with a straightedge to en-

Keel Ratios and Measurements

The distance from the top of a keel to its bottom is known as its *span*.

The *keel chord* is the horizontal distance from the keel's leading edge to its trailing edge at any given depth along the span.

It is common to measure a keel with a *root chord* (the chord where the keel joins the hull), a *midchord*, and a *tip chord*. To get a keel absolutely fair you need to make a template for each chord. If the keel were very deep, you might add extra chord templates between the tip-, mid-, and root-chord locations.

The *sweepback angle* of a keel is calculated at 25% of the chord length aft of the leading edge.

A keel may be fitted with a bulb for added stability, or it may have some form of wing to reduce vortices coming off the tip and thus reduce drag, and also to create additional lift when the boat is heeled. Bulbs and wings do create more wetted surface and are slightly more difficult to fair.

The leading edge of a keel should be parabolic in cross section to allow water to flow across it. Virtually all keels sail at an angle of leeway that varies from 4 to as much as 12 degrees. This leeway angle determines the keel's *angle of attack* to the oncoming water flow and enables it to lift the boat to windward. Without this lift from a sailboat's underwater foils, the boat would be unable to sail to windward. A parabolic leading edge enables water flow to stay attached to the keel, which is vital to the creation of lift. The same is true of the rudder.

The *keel thickness ratio* is the ratio of the keel's thickness to its chord length anywhere along the span. It is around 10% for an average cruising sailboat keel. It can be as low as 6% for a high-performance keel, but such a keel tends to stall early. Rudders need a higher thickness ratio because they experience higher angles of attack when turned through angles of up to 30 degrees. A higher thickness ratio delays the onset of stalling over the rudder blade.

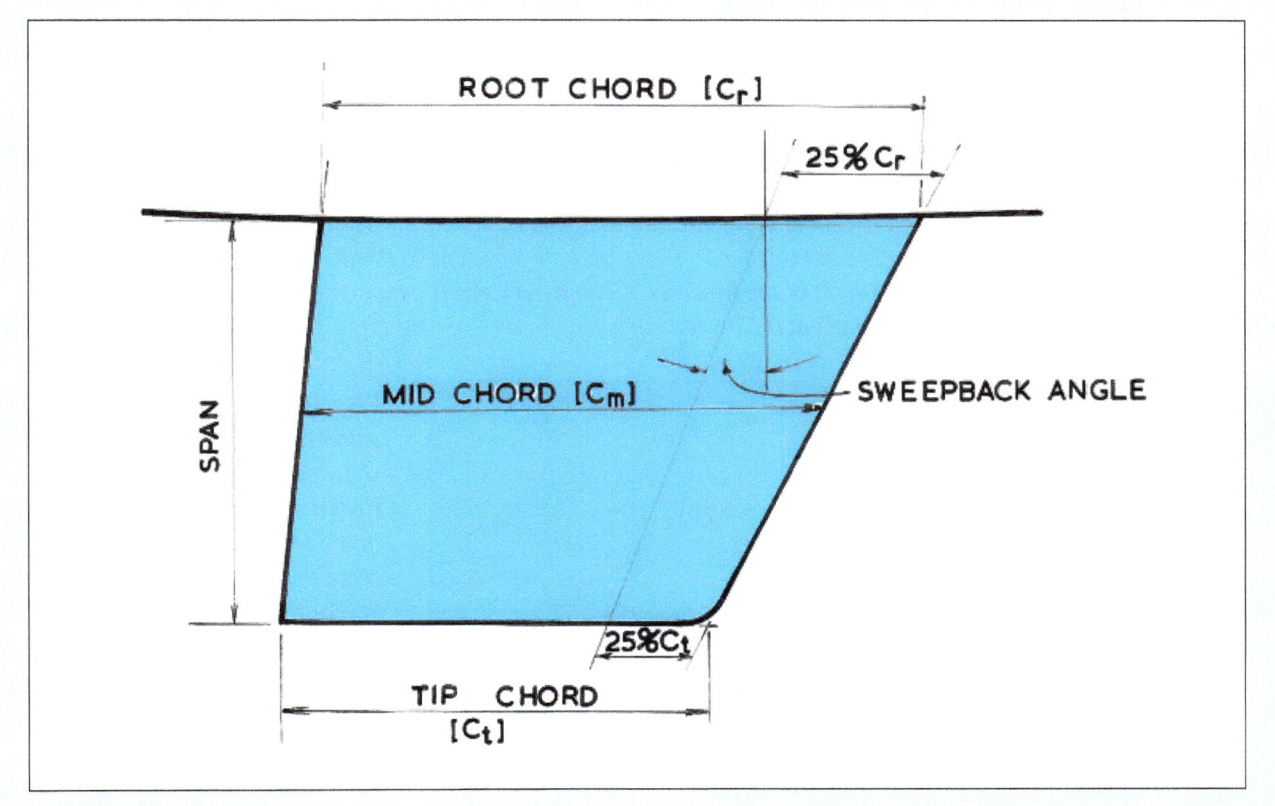

Keel measurements.

114 • **HULL, KEEL, AND RUDDER FAIRING**

Fairing a Keel

1

trailing edge

leading edge

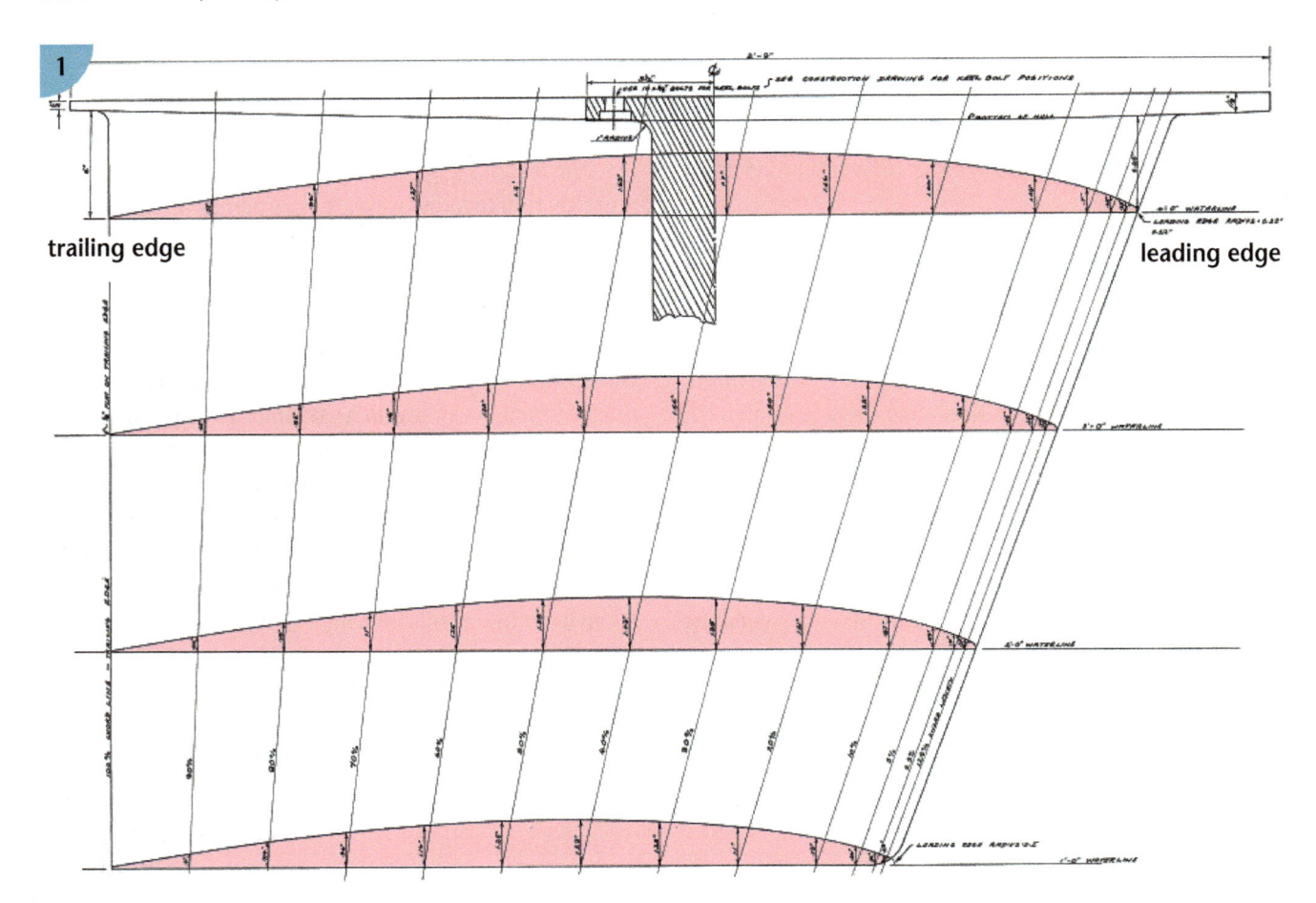

(1) *You can lay out keel half-sections full size on plywood or stiff cardboard stock as shown here. You need at least three half-sections; here we show four. Each chosen keel chord serves as a baseline and is divided into ten equal segments. The leading-edge segment is then further subdivided at 1.25%, 2.5%, and 5% of the chord length aft of the leading edge, and again (for the leading edge radius) at 0.02% of the chord length aft. Next measure the half-breadth offset as a perpendicular to each of the points you've just ticked off on each baseline, as shown in this drawing. Make sure that your perpendiculars are for half the keel thickness (from the fore-and-aft centerline to the port or starboard side), not for the entire thickness (from one side to the other).*

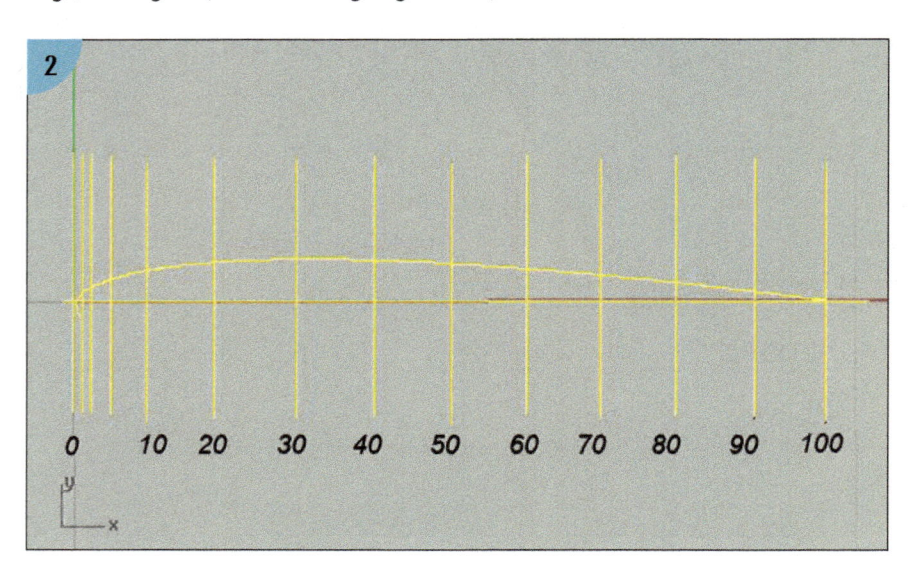

2

(2) *Use a flexible spline to draw a smooth curve through the offsets, as shown here, then cut it out. You can hold the concave curve left behind in the template stock when the half-breadth is cut out of it up against the keel at the appropriate chord height to evaluate fairness. You should use either thin plywood or heavy card stock for your template. You will be holding it up to the job many times, so you don't want it to be too heavy, but it must be strong enough to be used repeatedly without bending or breaking.*

Fairing a Rudder

root-chord template

midchord template

tip-chord template

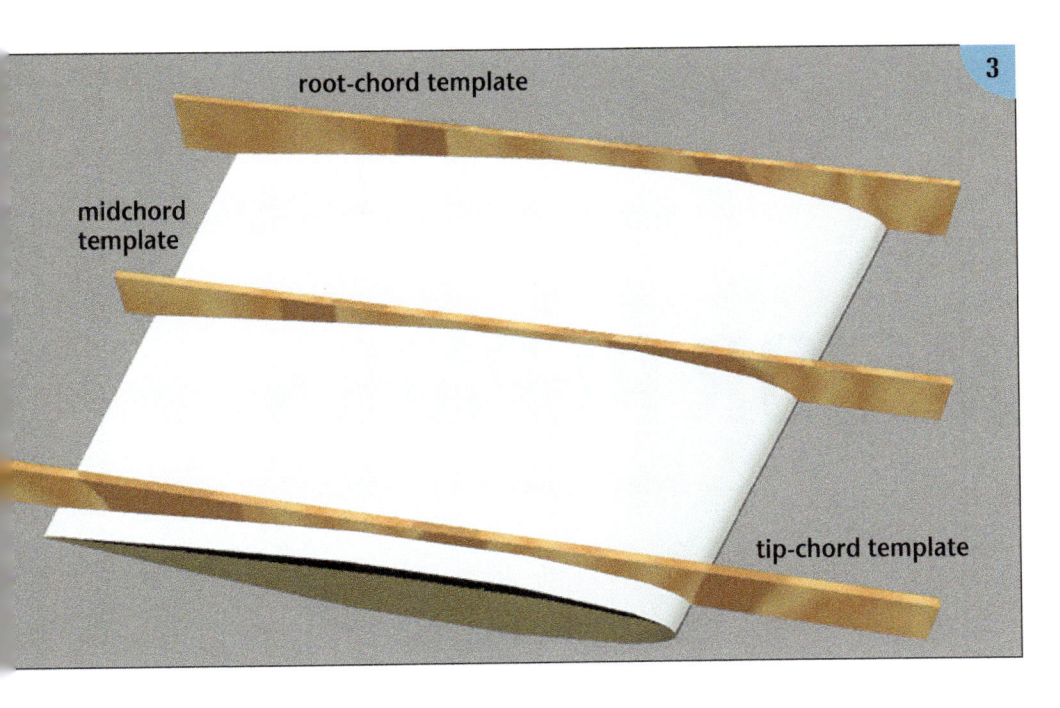

(3) *Offer the section templates up to the boat to see how well they fit the existing keel. You will need to mark your existing keel to locate the tip-, middle-, and root-chord locations so that you can be sure your keel is correctly shaped. With your templates held up to the job, mark high and low spots with differently colored crayons. If any high spots protrude outside the keel template, you may have to grind them down before you can determine the locations of low spots. Double-check these locations by placing a straightedge vertically against the keel. The straightedge should show highs and lows in the same places indicated by the templates.*

sure that it is not sagging and that you have not left hollows between the template heights. When the compound has hardened, check it again with the templates. Sand off any high spots and mark the low spots for filling. Repeat the fairing process and check yet another time with your templates, sanding high spots and filling low spots. Keep doing this until you have a perfectly smooth, fair keel.

The final step is to smooth the leading and trailing edges. The trailing edge is easy to fair. Simply use a straight length of wood covered with sandpaper, and sand vertically to ensure that the trailing edge makes nice, square corners with the sides of the keel. Fairing the leading edge is more difficult. You'll need to fair carefully to get an optimum parabolic shape. Sand with a flexible longboard in the horizontal and vertical directions to ensure that the keel is fair both vertically and horizontally. Remember that the first third of the keel is the most effective—and therefore the most critical—part. In light winds this area needs to be very, very smooth. Use 600-grit wet-or-dry paper for optimum racing smoothness.

FAIRING A RUDDER

Rudders also require smoothing to deliver optimum performance, although a smooth rudder is not quite as critical as a smooth keel. If your rudder has a constant section (and many do), you will need only one rudder template, but if the rudder is tapered, you may need to make three or more templates for different depths. Because a rudder is turned to sharper angles of attack than a keel, making the blade slightly fatter and a little more rounded will give you better steering ability while sacrificing very little boat speed. If you make the leading edge sharp, the water flow over the rudder blade will become turbulent a few degrees into a turn, and you may lose control of your boat.

Fairing can improve the performance of your boat and save fuel. It will also make a boat look more attractive when the time comes to sell it. Always make sure that any repairs you do are faired to invisibility.

Chapter 7 MAJOR REPAIRS

This chapter focuses on larger and more complex repairs than those covered in Chapter 5. Here we look at repairs that might normally be done by a boatyard, but which can also be accomplished by a patient and competent do-it-yourselfer. The projects in this chapter do not cover the entire gamut of fixes that might be called for on a fiberglass boat, but each one introduces you to important skills that can be applied to projects not specifically covered. In this way you will ac-

Procedure	Time
1. Assess the problem carefully and determine exactly what is required.	1–4 hours, depending on the nature of the damage
2. Remove the damaged material.	A few hours for a small repair; up to several days for a major one
3. Clean out the entire area by grinding it back. Also grind scarfs into any edges you are going to adhere fiberglass to.	1 hour to several days, depending on the extent of the repair
4. Prepare and dry-fit new materials, making sure that each part is correctly sized. Remember to allow for the thickness of the fiberglass laminate.	A few hours to cut and trim materials to patch a hole; several days or even weeks to build a major new part
5. Wipe the entire area clean with a solvent.	30 minutes
6. Fit the structural parts and wet them out with polyester or epoxy resin.	1–8 hours
7. After letting the resin cure for at least 24 hours, you may have to clean up the area with a little grinding or sanding to ensure that you can get a smooth finish.	1–3 hours
8. Finish off the area with reinforcement and resin.	A few minutes to a few days, depending on the complexity of the job
9. Fair and smooth the repair.	Usually at least 2 days to as much as 2 weeks
10. Spray or brush-paint the job.	1–4 hours

quire the knowledge needed to evaluate almost any fiberglass repair and determine whether you have the ability—or the time and desire—to tackle it.

Do not be intimidated by a project that seems overwhelming at first glance. Most large repairs can be broken down into smaller steps that are not so daunting. What you need is the stick-to-itiveness to stay with the job over a long period of time. By breaking the work down into manageable steps, a do-it-yourselfer can accomplish even very large repairs.

A word of warning, however: Don't set unrealistic goals. If you are not sure at the outset what a project calls for, don't assume that you will be able to figure it out as you go along. If in doubt, seek advice before proceeding. This will help you avoid costly mistakes. Also, don't underestimate the time needed to complete a major repair. Inexperienced do-it-yourselfers often assume that they can complete a fairly large project over a single weekend. In many cases, just allowing fiberglass laminate to harden can take more than a day. Keep your goals in proportion to your abilities and your available time.

Although each of the repairs in this chapter differs from the others, they all have certain standard procedures in common. This is true of virtually any fiberglass repair that you might undertake. The table shows a ten-step guideline for organizing any fiberglass repair project. Each step includes a rough estimate of the time required to complete it.

PROJECT 1

MAKING AN ENGINE-WELL GUARD TO KEEP WATER OUT

Our first project is not actually a repair but rather a modification to an existing boat. This is an important modification, however, because it can make a boat a lot safer. After I made this alteration to my center-console powerboat, a surveyor who saw it commented that a well guard like this for an outboard engine could prevent a lot of boats from sinking.

Many small outboard-powered boats have a cutout in the transom to allow the outboard motor to reach the water. The problem with this arrangement is that the cutout also allows water to flow in when the boat comes off a plane, when it backs down, or when it is overtaken by a following sea. Water flooding through the outboard well is one of the most common causes of small-boat

(1) *The cutout transom in my project boat. This outboard has a 20-inch shaft. When the boat is coming off a plane or backing down, water can flood the cockpit. I first raised the engine to its maximum position and measured carefully around it.* (2) *This photo was shot when I had fitted but not yet trimmed the well guard.*

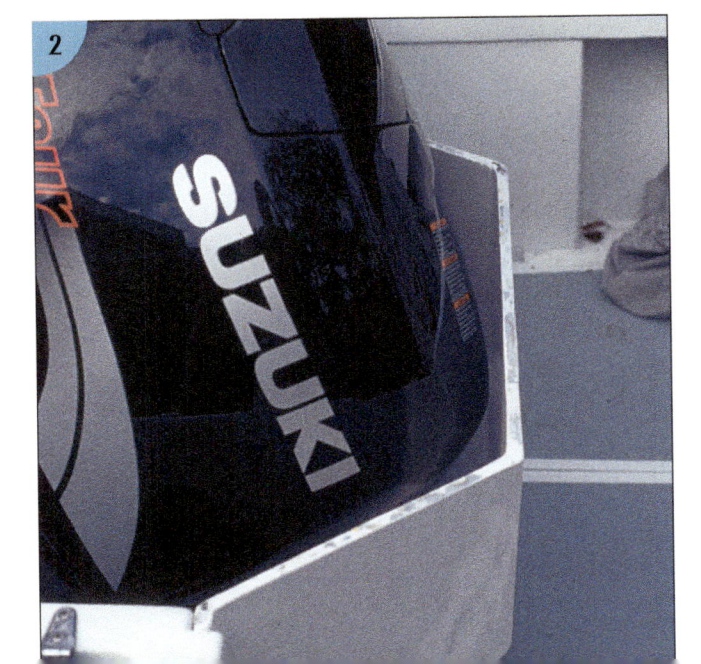

118 • MAJOR REPAIRS

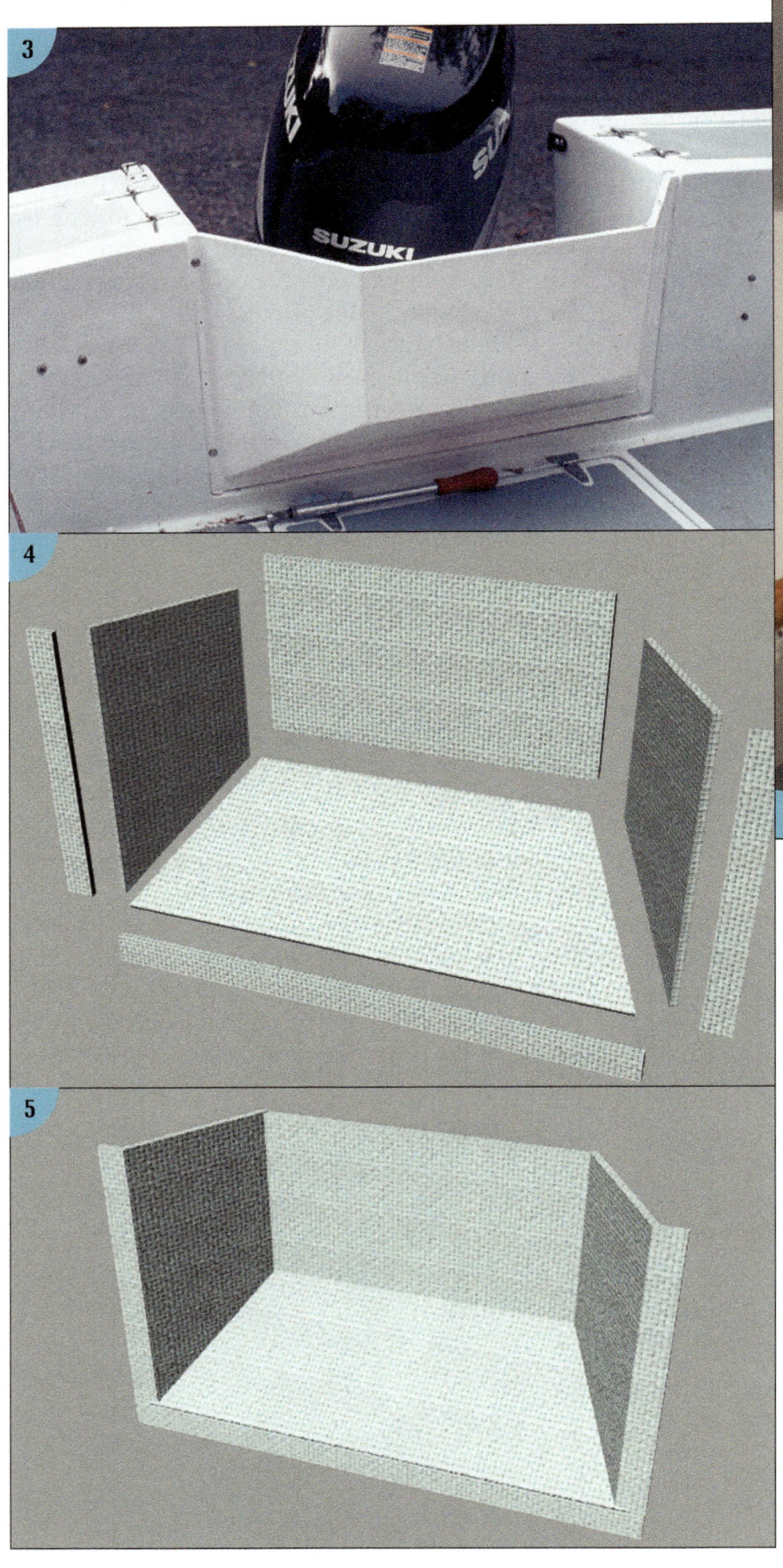

Making an Engine-well Guard

(3) I also took measurements with the engine lowered to make certain that nothing would jam or distort when the engine was put to use. (4) This exploded view of the enclosure shows its components. I built the well guard from ½-inch (12 mm) plywood and assembled it by taping the seams together over a temporary frame. (5) When I had taped the entire assembly together, I covered it with two layers of 6-ounce fiberglass cloth (both inside and out) epoxied into place. After the epoxy set up, I faired the job with a thin skim coat of thickened epoxy to provide a smooth finish. I then sanded and painted the surface. (6) I finished the job with teak trim around the top to match the rest of the boat. We also fitted a rod rack on the front to hold extra fishing poles when we were heading to and from the fishing grounds.

sinkings. If that water finds its way into a locker or the bilges, or if it simply floods the cockpit faster than the cockpit drains can get rid of it, the boat is in trouble. Once the cockpit drains are below the waterline, it becomes next to impossible to get the water out. The solution is to isolate the engine well from the rest of the boat with a well guard that rises to the height of the surrounding rail or to the top of the freeboard.

To make my well guard, I put the engine in its maximum raised position and carefully measured around it to determine the clearance needed. The boatbuilder—apparently with the possibility of a well-guard retrofit in mind—had incorporated a 1-inch-by-½-inch (25 mm by 12 mm) rabbet in the transom cutout perimeter, so it was natural to have the ends and bottom edge of the guard land there. Using my measurements, I cut the well-guard pieces from ½-inch (12 mm) marine-grade plywood and screwed them to a temporary frame to hold them in place for fiberglassing. I then coated the outer seams with slightly thickened epoxy, placed a single layer of 3-inch-wide (75 mm) 6-ounce fiberglass tape over the still-wet resin, and wet out the tape with epoxy using a short-haired paintbrush as described elsewhere. I rolled the wet tape to eliminate air bubbles, then allowed it to harden. I then removed the well guard from its framework and taped the inside seams using the same method.

When the tape had set up, I covered the entire box, inside and out, with two layers of 6-ounce cloth using the same laminating method as for the seam tape. The cloth left a fairly rough finish, which I smoothed with a layer of thickened epoxy (see page 51 for more on thickening agents) applied using a wide spatula. I then sanded this fairing coat, primed the well guard, and then painted it the same color (Interlux's Perfection white) as the cockpit interior.

Next, I dry-fitted the guard into place and made a few adjustments to ensure a good fit. I then caulked the rabbet around the transom cutout perimeter, inserted the guard, and screwed it to the rabbet using 1-inch (25 mm) #8 stainless steel Phillips-head screws. To finish the job, I installed a small piece of varnished teak trim around the top of the guard.

The entire project required one full weekend plus three more days spread over a three-week period to allow for curing and drying times. Cutting out the wood and making the temporary frame took most of the first Saturday, with curing time for the seam tape extending through Saturday night. I covered the outside of the guard with fiberglass on Sunday and left it to cure. Returning to the project at midweek, I turned it over and coated the inside surfaces with fiberglass. The following Saturday I applied a fairing layer of thickened epoxy on the inside and outside surfaces, then left this to harden for a week. I then sanded and primed it, let the undercoat dry for another week, then sanded that and applied the topcoat in one morning. Trimming the guard to fit and screwing it into place took about 2 hours, and adding the teak trim took another 2 hours.

PROJECT 2

REPLACING ROTTEN FLOORS

When my son bought a J/24 in poor condition, we knew a reconstruction project would be needed before he could campaign the boat. The first job was to restore the floors under the cabin sole. In early J/24s the keel sump beneath the floors was filled with resin and vermiculite. Given that vermiculite is used in gardening to lighten the weight of the growing medium and to absorb water, using it in boats sounds like a bad idea and indeed it proved to be so. Virtually every J/24 built with vermiculite sump filler has since had it removed, and this boat was no exception. But in this case the job had been done poorly. It looked as if the vermiculite in the sump well had been replaced with a water-absorbent, non-closed-cell foam, which had since turned to gunk. Fiberglass edges had been left rough, and above the sump, the rotted

(continued on page 122)

120 • **MAJOR REPAIRS**

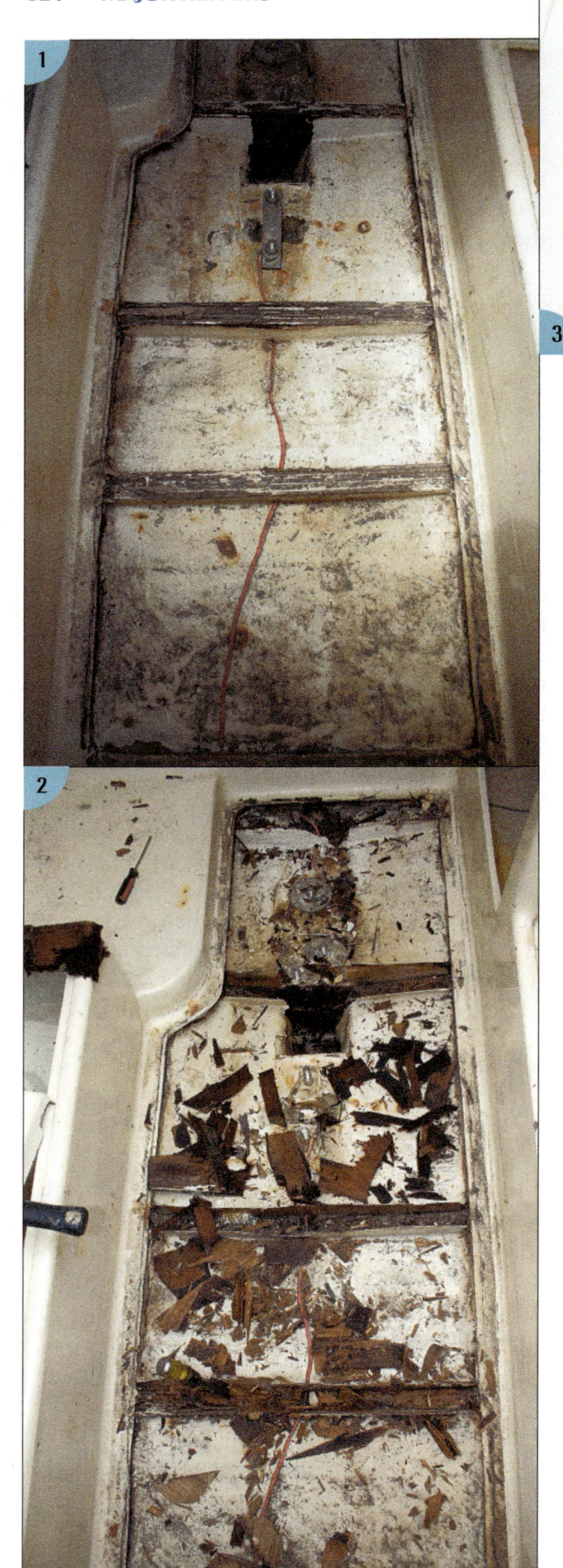

Replacing Rotten Floors

(1) The floors in the J/24 before we started work. As you can see, they were quite rotten and were easy to strip out. In places the entire fiberglass laminate simply pulled off the hull. **(2)** Removing the floors was easy. Smacking them with a hammer destroyed most of the wood, so it was just a matter of pulling the pieces out. **(3)** At this stage, rotten floors littered the cabin sole because the wood fell apart during removal. The entire removal took about 2 hours. **(4)** The floors have been completely removed, and we've dug the waterlogged filler out of the keel sump, exposing the keel bolts. You can see how the fiberglass simply peeled up from the hull. Grinding back the area to provide a good clean surface for new material took about an hour.

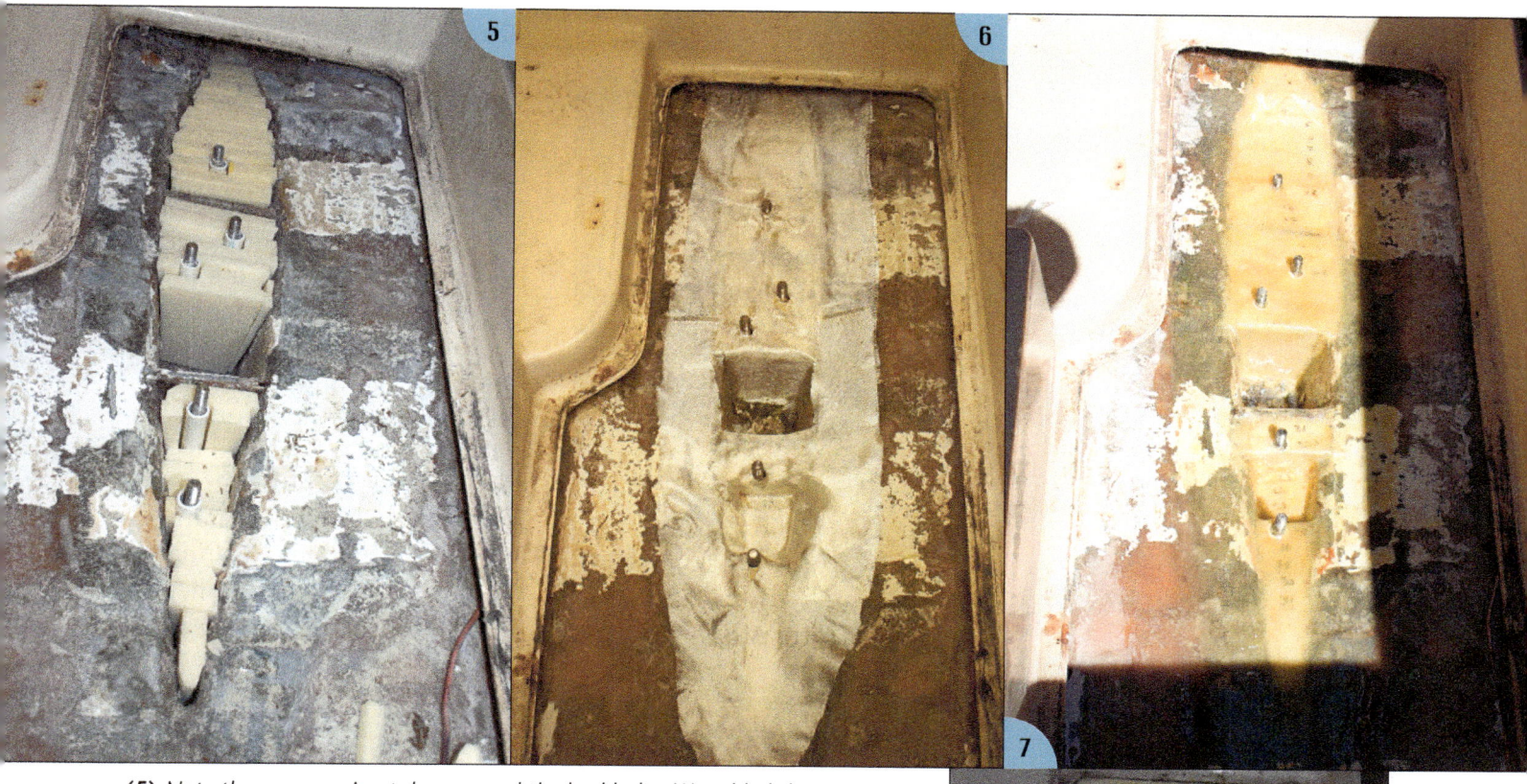

(5) *Note the compression tubes around the keel bolts. We added these to provide a firm seat for the washers and nuts and to prevent the bolts from pulling down through the new keel-sump filler we were about to add. We selected a high-density closed-cell foam as the new keel-sump filler. Sizing, cutting, and dry-fitting the foam took most of a day. Then we numbered each piece, removed it, and wiped everything down with a solvent to make sure it was clean. In this photo the filler pieces have been numbered but not yet epoxied into place. We smeared Epiglass epoxy, thickened to a peanut butter–like consistency, around the bottom and edges of each foam piece. The process was rather like laying bricks with mortar. We then filled all remaining voids from the top with runny, unthickened epoxy. The entire structure was then left to set up. To prevent any moisture ingress into voids that might remain in the foam, we glassed over the top of the foam, leaving a recess for the lifting strap and a small sump for any water that might get inside the hull.* **(6)** *We've cut the glass and are about to epoxy it into place.*
(7) *Despite the sun shining directly through the companionway, you can see that the bilge and keel area have now been glassed over.* **(8)** *The next job was to build new floors. We made the forms from the same high-density foam used in the keel sump, shaping and cutting each one to make a good dry fit, then covering them with fiberglass before setting them into the hull. We remembered to cut limber holes in each floor before installing it. Fitting the floors in place took most of a day. We taped each one in place using masking tape to hold it, then covered each one with two precut layers of 6-ounce cloth, and we removed the masking tape as we worked. The entire job of floor cutting, trimming, and glassing took almost two days to complete. After the job had set up hard, we spent another 2 hours or so "touching up" with a grinder to remove sharp edges before painting out the area.*

Replacing Rotten Floors

(9) We glassed the floors in place and painted out the entire area with Interlux Epoxy Primekote. The keel bolts fashioned for the lifting sling well are visible here.
(10) A flange on the keel bolt washer is intended to protect the glasswork in the lifting sling area.

(11) The final job was to cut a teak-and-holly sole from plywood and place it on the new floor bearers. We screwed the sole to the old fiberglass liner around the edges. Measuring and cutting the sole took several hours. We coated it with Ultimate Sole, a high-gloss, varnish-style finish with low skid properties (www.ultimatesole.com). This product looks just like varnish but is much less slippery when wet. Compare this to photo 3 on page 21—it is the same boat.

floors had been replaced with non-marine-grade plywood, which had rotted almost completely away in its turn. So our first job was to remove the rotted floors and the gunk in the keel sump. This job took several hours of chipping with a long-handled cold chisel. Eventually the entire bilge was clean and the floors were ground flush.

To prevent the floors from rotting again, we decided to use marine-grade high-density foam for the keel-sump filler and also as forms over which to laminate the floors, as described in Chapter 5. On a J/24 the stainless steel keel bolts stick up into the keel sump. We could have removed the bolts from the keel and then shortened and rethreaded them, but this seemed like a time-consuming, expensive job. So we opted instead to fill the keel sump with pieces of 1-inch (25 mm) foam bedded in a resin mix.

We shaped the foam pieces carefully to fit the sump, and we put compression tubing around each keel bolt to ensure that it could not pull through the foam. We left two small wells in the filled sump: one to function as an actual sump (i.e., a low spot in the bilge to collect bilge water) and the other as an attachment point for the keel lifting strap. We then made new keel bolt washers to suit the new floor arrangement. Because the washers overlapped slightly and I wanted to protect the edges of the sump we'd made for the lifting sling, these washers were fabricated from aluminum. This work took about 4 to 6 hours.

Project 3

REPLACING A WATER-DAMAGED DECK CORE

One of the more common forms of damage boatowners encounter is a balsa deck core that has been penetrated by water and has become sodden, delaminated, or even rotten through the affected sections. The usual cause is the many holes that are drilled into decks for fasteners to hold cleats, winches, blocks, and other gear. Any such hole is a potential conduit for moisture penetration. As discussed in Chapter 5 and elsewhere in this book, any hole drilled into a cored laminate should be drilled oversize, filled with thickened epoxy, and then redrilled to the size of the fastener. This seals the otherwise exposed core edges from moisture penetration. Once water gets in, core saturation and core-to-skin delamination can follow—and if the core is made of balsa, it can start to rot.

On some boats the entire deck core needs replacing, and the owner must decide whether to make the repair or scrap the boat. That decision depends on all sorts of highly individual variables. The repair *can* be done, but only you can determine whether doing it makes sense. Fortunately, the rotted section of balsa core in the deck of the J/24 my son acquired was relatively small, so the decision was easy to make. I decided to do the job with polyester resin, since a deck flexes and polyester is slightly more flexible when cured than epoxy. I figured an epoxy repair might eventually crack, and any strength advantage epoxy might confer would not in this case justify its greater expense. Having chosen polyester, I elected to do the work outside, mostly because I dislike the smell of styrene and wanted to ventilate it quickly.

The first task in a core replacement—as in almost any fiberglass repair—is to identify the extent of the problem. The most common way to do this is to pass a moisture meter over the deck to see how far the core moisture extends. You can also tap the deck with a plastic mallet or screwdriver handle: a dull thunk indicates wet or rotted core, whereas a clear, sharp rap indicates core in good condition with a solid core-to-skin bond.

(1) *Here I have cut out the outer skin, chipped away the wet core, and exposed the inner skin. The darker area of the inner skin was covered by rotted core. When making this type of repair, it is always best to cut back until you reach good, dry core.* **(2)** *Pieces of rotted core are still clinging to the outer skin. The outer skin came up easily where the core was rotted but was much harder to remove where the core was good—another clue to the extent of the rot.*

Replacing a Water-Damaged Deck Core

(3) I have vacuumed clean the entire repair area. This marks the end of the destruction phase and the beginning of the reconstruction. **(4)** Laying the balsa core into the hole. Before I laid the new core, I coated the entire hole with a heavy layer of resin. Then I pressed the core into the resin. I used shims of balsa core to fill a few small voids around the edges of the new core. I wanted a "wall" of resin around the new core so that any water left in the old core could not migrate into the new material. **(5)** I then coated the top surface of the new balsa with unthickened polyester resin to ensure that the top laminate adhered tightly to it. **(6)** Laying the first layer of 24-ounce woven roving over the balsa. I will then saturate it with resin and roll it to ensure that no voids remain. I preceded and followed this layer with 1½-ounce CSM to fill voids and to enhance adhesion between the core and skin and between the two layers of woven roving. I then added the second layer of 24-ounce roving and two layers of 6-ounce cloth to leave a smooth finish on the job. **(7)** The job has been laminated and is now curing. When the resin has set up completely, I will smooth the edges with a grinder and coat the repair with a thin layer of thickened polyester resin to get a smooth finish. Then I'll cover it with gelcoat to match the rest of the deck before repainting the entire deck with Interdeck nonskid.

But a wet core isn't necessarily rotted. It may just need drying out. To find out how much rot has taken place, you may have to do what I did—keep cutting or making test bores until you reach un-rotted core.

To cut the deck open, set the blade depth of a circular saw or a Sawzall to cut the upper skin but not the inner skin. On this deck I used a circular saw set to a 3/8-inch (9 mm) depth. I first cut out a small square to assess the problem. That test piece revealed that the core was indeed rotten, so I gradually enlarged the hole until I reached dry wood, which was easily discernible by its much lighter color. I then left the job for a couple of days to allow any remaining wetness in the unremoved core to wick out and dry.

The next step was to cut replacement core to fit into the hole. The piece I cut wasn't quite a tight enough fit at the edges, so I made a few thin shims of balsa to slide in around the perimeter to fill remaining voids. Using what I had on hand, I also cut two pieces of 24-ounce woven roving, two pieces of 1½-ounce chopped strand mat (CSM), and two pieces of 6-ounce fiberglass cloth to comprise the new outer skin.

After cutting out and dry-fitting the pieces of the repair, I mixed a batch of polyester resin using a small amount of MEKP catalyst to obtain a longer pot life. I coated the entire surface of the exposed inner skin and the edges of the hole with a heavy coat of resin, then pressed the new balsa core down into it, inserting balsa shims around the edges as necessary.

Next I coated the upper surface of the new balsa with unthickened resin and laid down a layer of CSM followed by a layer of 24-ounce woven roving. I wet out these two layers thoroughly, removing all air bubbles, and then added the second layer of CSM and the second layer of woven roving. After wetting out and rolling these, I laid down the two layers of 6-ounce cloth and rolled out the entire laminate to ensure that no air bubbles remained. I was able to laminate this entire schedule in one go without generating enough heat to distort the laminate.

After the laminate had hardened, I ground back the edges to obtain a smooth transition from the repair to the surrounding deck. Because the repair hadn't quite built up enough to be flush with the surrounding deck, I added one more layer of fiberglass cloth cut to fit the remaining dimple. I then faired the entire repaired area with thickened polyester resin. Then I sanded the area smooth, covered it with a layer of gelcoat to match the repair with the surrounding deck, and finally repainted the entire deck with nonskid paint.

Project 4

REPAIRING A ROTTEN TRANSOM

Many older powerboats have transoms of encapsulated plywood. The fiberglass skins on these transoms, however, can sometimes lose their watertightness. An outboard engine mount that is through-bolted without proper caulking around the bolt holes; an insufficiently sealed stern-drive transom cutout; leaks around fasteners for swim ladders, depthsounder transducers, or other accessories; or cracks in the transom laminate caused by engine strain will allow water in, eventually causing the plywood to rot. We've found four boats with well-rotted plywood transoms in the last two years and expect that there are many others out there whose owners do not yet know they have a problem.

Repairing a rotted transom is not very difficult, but it is time-consuming. The old rotten wood must be removed completely, then a new core must be installed. Here we look at two ways of doing this work, the first of which involves installing a new plywood core.

The example shown in the photos is on the transom of my own Seacraft, built in 1985. This transom's plywood core was completely rotten except at the upper corners. Consequently, we had to entirely remove the original core and epoxy new marine-grade plywood into the void. We needed three people to install the new core in the short time available before the epoxy kicked off.

A second method of transom repair uses Seacast permanent, pourable foam as the core material. According to its manufacturer Invision Boatworks (www.invisionboatworks.com), Seacast foam is three times stronger than marine plywood and weighs only 40 to 42 pounds per cubic foot. It is water-resistant, has superior screw-holding capacity, and can be sanded like wood.

Method A: Fitting a New Plywood Core

No matter what method you choose to replace the core in a rotted transom, you must decide how you are going to access the old, rotten plywood. There are three possible approaches: removing the transom cap, re-

(1) I cut away the outer skin of this Seacraft transom inside a line I drew 3 inches (75 mm) inboard of the transom perimeter. This allowed me to grind back the remaining flange without having to go around the transom corners. If the work had gone around the corners, I would have had to repaint the entire hull. Here I'm using a hammer and chisel to remove the core residue from inside the flange. It took quite a while to remove the residue from the entire perimeter flange.
(2) Here is the part of the transom's outer skin that I cut away in two stages. At first I didn't think the top of the transom would be rotted, but when I found that the rot had spread upward, I had to cut away more of the outer skin to gain access to the entire rotten mess. I saved these pieces of outer skin and reinstalled them later, over the new core. (3) The damaged core as I removed it. The core was so rotten that much of it pulled away easily from the inner skin. It was made of two pieces of ¾-inch (19 mm) plywood that did not appear to be marine grade and were not glued together.

(4) *This is what remained of the transom after I removed the rotted core.*

moving the inner fiberglass skin, or removing the outer skin. You should select the approach that is easiest given the particulars of the job at hand. (See the sidebar for further details on the factors that bear on this decision.) When repairing the transom of my Seacraft, I chose to remove the outer skin.

Removing the Old Transom

To remove one of the fiberglass skins covering the core of an old transom, mark off where you are going to make your cuts. When replacing the transom on my Seacraft, I used a permanent marker to draw a line around the outer skin of the transom about 3

Reducing Your Paintwork in a Transom Repair

If your boat has no lockers on the inboard side of the transom, you can work from that side in order to preserve the boat's exterior finish. But if circumstances force you to access a rotted core through the outer skin, you can still reduce your exterior refinishing work by making your cuts about 3 inches (75 mm) in from the transom perimeter. Then, when the rebuild job is finished, you need only apply your new exterior topcoat to the transom edges. Even if the new topcoat doesn't quite match the rest of the topsides, the difference will be unnoticeable around the transom corners.

If, on the other hand, you are planning to repaint the entire boat, you can cut around the corners of the transom in order to remove it. This will make it easier to remove and replace the transom core, but when you install the new outer skin, it will have to wrap around the corners, so you will have to fair and finish both the transom and the sides of the hull.

inches (75 mm) in from the perimeter. Then I cut along the line with a circular saw, with its blade depth set so as not to reach the inner skin. I then peeled off the outer skin, using a crowbar as required. (Try to remove this in one piece so you can reinstall it later.) Be sure to remove all the rotten plywood you find underneath; this may involve sawing, chiseling, and prying. It took me an entire day to dig out all the rotten wood from the perimeter flange by patiently chiseling it away.

Making a Template

Once all the old wood is removed, your next job is to make a replacement core the same size as the original one. To match the size, you'll need to make a template from heavy cardboard—a large refrigerator box obtained from an appliance store will do nicely. Be sure to measure and cut the template carefully for a good fit. You can also use the template to decide exactly where to section the transom, if needed.

Preparing the Transom Pieces

Most plywood transom cores are 1½ inches (38 mm) thick, and the Seacraft transom was no exception. I constructed the new transom core from two layers of ¾-inch (19 mm) marine-grade plywood. Because of the outer-skin flange left behind when I removed the Seacraft's rotten transom, I was unable to drop in each layer as a single piece. Instead, I had to cut both layers into three sections. The outer layer consisted of a single piece from the boat bottom up to the well cutout, with a smaller piece outboard of the cutout on either side. For the inner layer, I made vertical cuts from each bottom corner of the transom cutout to the bottom of the boat, again creating three parts. Then I staggered the joints between sections from one layer to the other, which is what you should do for maximum strength.

I installed each layer separately in a dry run to make sure everything fit well. When assembling the pieces of a new transom, it is essential that they go together quickly and easily, or the epoxy might set up before the job is done.

After you have dry-fitted and removed the parts, you should seal them completely by rolling them with unthickened epoxy mixed with fast hardener. A low-viscosity epoxy will easily penetrate the wood to seal it tightly. This prevents water from penetrating the plywood after it is installed, and it also primes the plywood, making it easier to apply a second layer of epoxy when the time comes.

Grinding Back

The next job is probably the most unpleasant one. You need to grind scarfs into all the fiberglass edges. For my Seacraft, that meant grinding a scarf into the flange around the entire transom perimeter, as well as scarfs in the pieces of the outer skin that I had removed and intended to reinstall.

First, put plastic sheeting under everything to contain the debris you will create while grinding. Next, protect yourself with a barrier coat of skin cream, a Tyvek suit, boots, rubber gloves, a respirator, and tight-fitting goggles. Then start grinding, making sure you grind back to a scarf width of at least 3 inches (75 mm), or nine to twelve times the skin thickness. This will give plenty of width for adhesion of the new epoxy-fiberglass laminations you'll lay down. On the Seacraft, grinding these scarfs took about 2 hours of miserable toil, and the cleanup took another hour.

Installing the New Plywood Core

You are now ready to install the plywood. When doing this job, you must work quickly before the epoxy has a chance to set up. (I gathered a crew of three for this phase of the work.) Make up an epoxy mixture consisting of resin, hardener, glue powder, and filler powder to the consistency of peanut butter, and fill an empty caulking tube with it. Squirt this mixture into the flange perimeter (i.e., against the outer edge of the hull) to ensure that there are no air pockets in the transom. The Seacraft required a particularly generous application of this mixture around the cockpit drains to ensure that no voids were left there. We then coated the middle section of the inner layer of plywood with a fresh coat of the thickened epoxy, put it into place, and then drove

Project 4 • 129

(1) I used cardboard templates to outline and cut the new transom core from marine-grade plywood. Two layers of ¾-inch (19 mm) plywood created a core 1½ inches (38 mm) thick. Because of the leftover transom flange, I could not cut these layers as single pieces but instead I had to install them in sections. I cut the inner layer into three parts by continuing the outboard well corners downward vertically. I cut the outer layer into three pieces by continuing the bottom of the transom well cutout horizontally across the transom. To ensure that water could not penetrate the plywood, I coated each piece with epoxy before installing it in the transom. The three pieces on top in this view are the sections of the outer layer.

(2) Here I'm holding one of the transom pieces up to the job. I made the semicircular cutout in the corner to clear the cockpit drain through-hull that you can see in the corner of the transom. In the original transom core each of these cutouts had no fiberglass at all over them, and the resultant exposed plywood edges were good places for water to start rotting the wood. I will fill the space between the cutout and the drain with thickened epoxy.

(3, 4) Before coating the plywood with epoxy, dry-fit the pieces to ensure that everything fits properly.

Repairing a Rotten Transom

stainless steel screws through the inner skin to hold it tightly in place against the skin while the epoxy hardened. (Later we filled these screw holes with epoxy.) Working quickly, we coated the two outboard sections of the inner layer with epoxy and pushed them into position. We then caulked the seams between the three panels with epoxy before screwing the outboard panels to the inner fiberglass skin. With that, we had the three-part inner layer of plywood in place across the entire transom.

The next step was to coat the two upper panels of the outer layer (i.e., the panels to port and starboard of the outboard well) with the thickened epoxy and push them into place. A single screw sufficed to hold each of these small, fairly flat panels in place while the epoxy hardened. The final piece of the outer layer was the full-width piece at the bottom of the transom. This needed some force—in the form of multiple fasteners—to get it into place. We screwed all the transom pieces together with 1¼-inch (32 mm) stainless steel screws through the inner skin, placed every 6 to 8 inches (15 to 20 cm). These screws can be removed after the entire job has set up. Fresh epoxy should then be squirted into each screw hole to ensure that the transom is fully watertight.

Finishing the Fiberglass Work

Finally, you can reinstall the removed section or sections of the outer fiberglass skin. You should grind scarfs into these edges, too, to create a tapered shelf for the new fiberglass to adhere to. Coat the inner face of the outer skin with epoxy,

(1) We sealed the wood pieces with a coat of unthickened epoxy resin, and then immediately installed them. Bedding and installing both layers of core and reinstalling the outer skin took us about 2 hours to complete, working fast. We used a slow-cure hardener to give ourselves time for the job. (2) Here the inner layer of core is in position and we've back-screwed it to the inner skin to hold it tightly in position while the epoxy hardens. The outer layer of core is next, and then we'll reinstall the outer skin, a section of which is visible at bottom.

Project 4 • 131

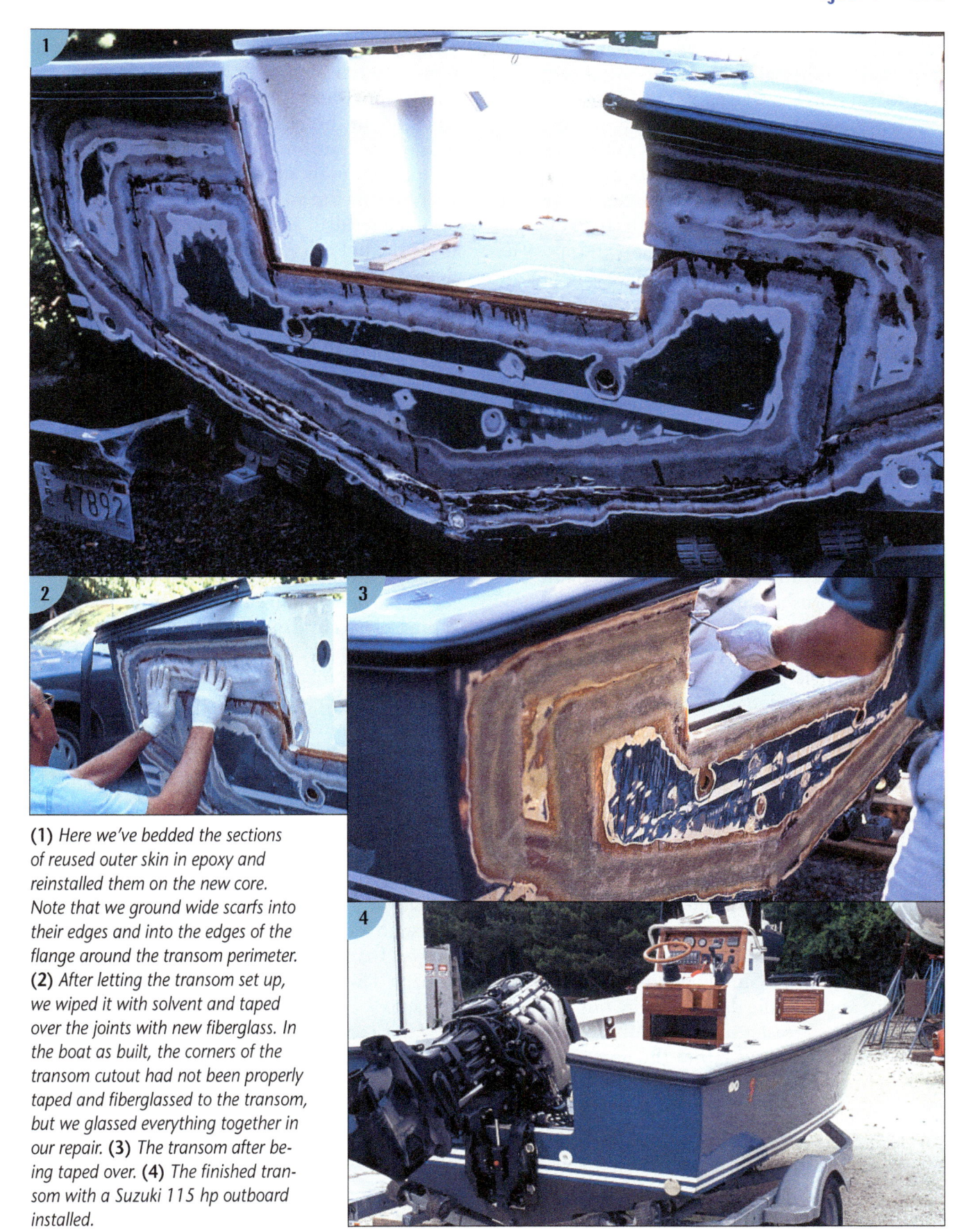

(1) Here we've bedded the sections of reused outer skin in epoxy and reinstalled them on the new core. Note that we ground wide scarfs into their edges and into the edges of the flange around the transom perimeter. (2) After letting the transom set up, we wiped it with solvent and taped over the joints with new fiberglass. In the boat as built, the corners of the transom cutout had not been properly taped and fiberglassed to the transom, but we glassed everything together in our repair. (3) The transom after being taped over. (4) The finished transom with a Suzuki 115 hp outboard installed.

Repairing a Rotten Transom

and clamp it into place. Insert a dozen or so screws to hold the skin tightly to the plywood until the entire transom has set up.

Once everything has hardened, remove the screws, clean up epoxy drips and spills by grinding them away, and apply fiberglass strips over the joints. Start with 3-inch-wide (75 mm) strips and build up to the full scarf width with strips of 1708 or the equivalent. Leave the fiberglass and epoxy to set up hard, and then grind the surface to a smooth finish. Once the transom is smooth, you can fair it using either a mixture of epoxy and fairing powder or Awlgrip's Awlfair, which is a professional fairing compound (note—it is difficult to obtain).

To paint the transom, mask off the area and undercoat it with Awlgrip's Awlprime or Interlux's Epoxy Primekote (if you plan on painting with Interlux's Perfection two-part polyurethane). Then sand it back using 320-grit wet-or-dry sandpaper. Finally, paint it again with two coats of either Awlgrip (if you are using a paint sprayer) or Interlux's Perfection (if you prefer to roll on the paint and tip it with a brush, as described in Chapter 9).

Note: I prefer the higher gloss, better hardness, and longer life of a two-part polyurethane, but Interlux's single-part Brightside urethane, or the equivalent from another paint manufacturer, will also give good results. For more on finish choices, see Chapter 9.

Method B: Using Seacast Foam to Repair a Transom

When using Seacast foam to repair a rotted transom, the cap-removal method of accessing the old core is often the easiest approach to take, because the fiberglass skins form a perfect pocket to accept this pourable foam. Simply remove the top of the transom and pull the damaged core out through the top. (This is easier said than done, of course.) If you instead remove either the inner or outer skin in order to reach the core, you must then replace that skin to form a pocket before you can pour the foam.

In the example shown in the photos, the cap-removal method is being used. The cap of aluminum or other material is removed first. Then, using a handheld cutting wheel, cuts are made across the transom on the inside surface just below the top, where the seams meet. These cuts are repeated on the outside surface and across the ends of the transom. Once all the cuts are made, the top section should lift off in one piece.

With the top edge of the core exposed, use a wood auger drill bit to drill holes down into it. Space the holes across the top of the transom, as closely together as possible, in order to break up most of the original core. Seacast recommends working a chain saw very carefully into the transom, essentially turning the rotted wood into mulch. Before you do this, however, make sure there are no bolts remaining in the transom. Remove any large chunks by hand and vacuum out the splinters with a wet-or-dry vacuum. Try to get at least 90% of the wood out of the transom.

When you have removed the wood from the pocket, wipe down the inner faces of the inner and outer fiberglass skins with a rag wetted with isopropyl alcohol, or as a second-best choice, with acetone. Now you are ready to pour the foam. Taping plastic around the edges of the transom opening will make cleanup easier.

Mix the contents of the Seacast can well. Then add all the BPO (benzoyl peroxide) catalyst supplied by the manufacturer and stir again until the mixture is a uniform color. Finally, add the ground fiberglass reinforcement (also supplied by the manufacturer) and mix well a third time.

Now pour the Seacast foam into the transom pocket until it is full. Using a rubber mallet, tap lightly on the exterior fiberglass skin to settle the mixture and ensure a complete fill. Cap the transom with a length of fiberglass tape tucked into the wet foam so that it forms an upside-down U shape. Then lay a thin coat of Seacast foam over the tape.

After the foam at the top of the transom has cured, sand the job and place a piece of fiberglass tape wetted out with catalyzed resin over the outside of both fiberglass skins. Allow the resin to set up. Finish the transom top with fairing compound, and you are ready to sand and paint it. Wait three to five days to drill holes for drain tubes and engine mounting bolts.

Project 4 • 133

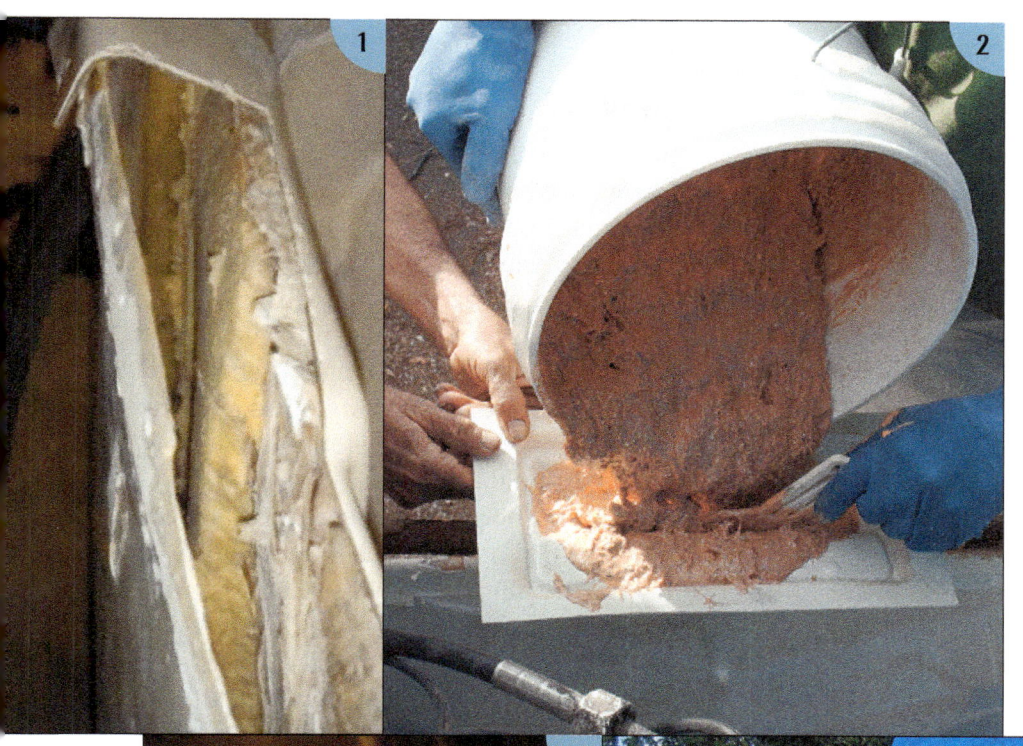

(1) Cut the transom open at the top and drill down into it to remove the old core. Seacast recommends using a chain saw to chew up the wood. With the old core cut up, use a shop vacuum to remove the remains. That will leave a pocket between the two fiberglass skins, like the one shown here. (2, 3) Mix the Seacast foam according to the manufacturer's instructions and pour it into the pocket. Tap the transom with a rubber mallet to ensure that there are no voids in the foam. (4) The transom has been taped and enclosed. All that is needed now is a minor amount of fairing and painting. (5) Here is the finished transom, ready for an outboard engine installation. (Courtesy Seacast)

Repairing a Rotten Transom

134 • MAJOR REPAIRS

PROJECT 5

REPAIRING MAJOR GROUNDING DAMAGE

The sailboat shown in the accompanying photos was damaged when it went aground and was repaired at the Jamestown Boat Yard in Jamestown, Rhode Island. It illustrates just how extensive grounding damage can be, not only in the area where the impact occurred but in other parts of the boat as well. Much of the interior furniture was soaked with water when the boat was holed, and most of the onboard equipment had to be replaced. In addition, the teak deck was damaged by rocks and had to be replaced. Note that this is a single-skin hull. We look at damage to a cored hull in Project #7.

A repair likes this one requires considerable effort. First, all the ruined equipment and furniture must be removed. This job usually necessitates the services of a skilled craftsman to ensure that undamaged parts are removed in a way that will enable them to be reused. Only when the gear and furniture have been removed can the full extent of the damage be assessed.

The next step was to cut away the damaged part of the hull to a perimeter of undamaged laminate. Then scarfs were ground into the edges of the cutout both inside and outside the hull so that the patch would form a strong bond and an invisible transition with the interior and exterior surfaces of the original laminate.

At this point in the project, the yard had three options: 1) It could ask the original manufacturer to lay up the damaged part in the original hull mold to ensure a perfect match. 2) It could take a splash off the hull of an identical boat—as described in Chapter 5—and use that as a backing when relaminating the damaged area. 3) Or it could place strips of wood covered with plastic

(1) The grounding damage on this boat runs along the starboard side of the hull, but the major damage occurred near the transom where the boat lay on the rocks. The hull there was completely stove in, and the laminate had to be cut away completely. **(2)** The rudder was also extensively damaged, and the stock was bent. **(3)** The cutaway portion of the hull shows how much of it was damaged. The yard had to cut deep into the transom and remove part of the deck.

Project 5 • 135

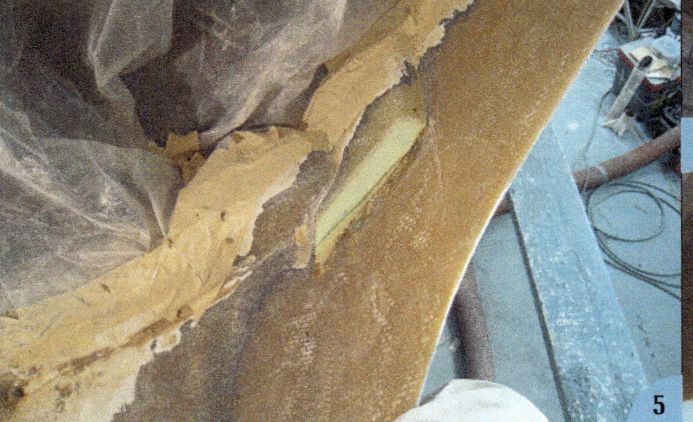

(4, 5, 6, 7) These photos taken from inside the hull show how much of the stern and transom was cut away. Note that edges of the cutaway section have been ground back into scarfs several inches wide.

(8) After cutting back the hull and grinding scarfs into the edges of the opening, the yard fastened several layers of thin plywood over the hole to allow new laminate to be glassed up from the inside. Laminating that repair in the confined space between the hull side and the cockpit tub must have been an unpleasant job.

(9) The cutaway portion of the transom had to be laid up again using the same technique as on the hull side, leaving this small hole (between the top of the swept-back transom and the aft rim of the cockpit coaming above it) to be finished.

Repairing Major Grounding Damage

136 • MAJOR REPAIRS

or mold release wax over the damaged section—again as described in Chapter 5—and laminate against the wood from the inside. Then, when the inside part of the laminate hardened, the mold or backing could be removed and the outer layers of the repair could be laminated to get a smooth exterior finish. As you can see from the photos, the yard placed plywood on the outside of the hull and laid up the first few layers of fiberglass against it from the inside out. If the repair work had not been completed within a fixed budget, the insurance company might have declared the boat a total loss.

Once the damaged area has been laminated, finish work can start. This includes fairing the hull smooth, rebuilding and replacing damaged furniture, and replacing any wiring, plumbing, or hydraulic systems that had to be removed from the damaged area. Often this part of the repair takes longer than the laminating.

(10) *The same part of the hull viewed from inside the boat. The job was more complex than usual because it included the transom as well as part of the cockpit, requiring an extensive coaming rebuild and a difficult transition between coaming and transom.* **(11)** *Note how the surrounding area was masked off to protect undamaged parts during the repair.* **(12, 13)** *The coaming during the rebuilding.*

Project 5 • 137

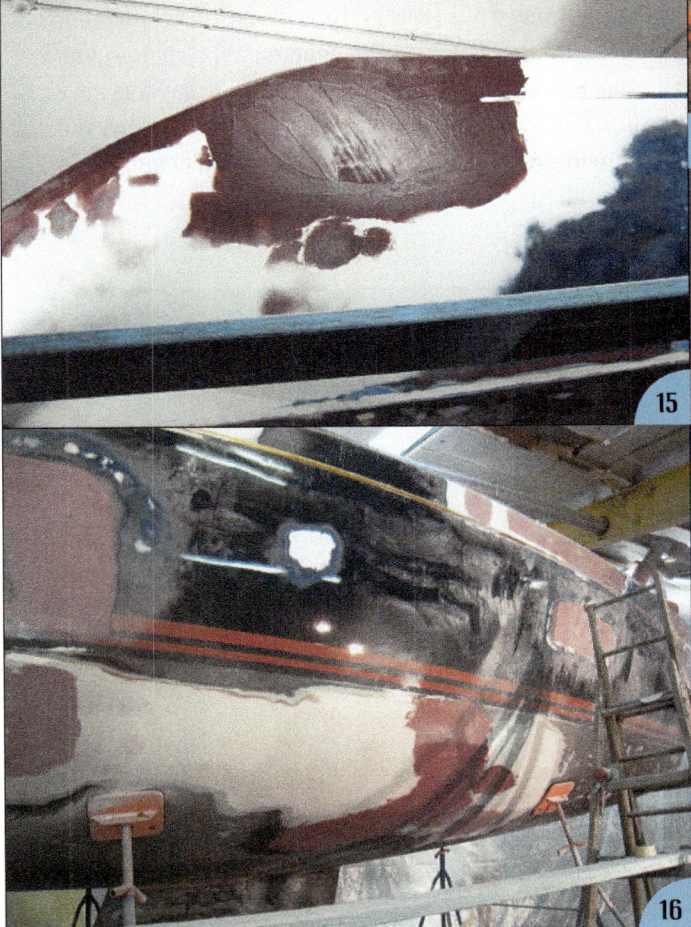

(14) Here the repair of the hole in the starboard side aft is laminated but not yet faired and painted. (15) The fairing is underway. (16, 17) There were additional areas of damage farther forward on the starboard side, but none of these completely penetrated the hull. These repairs required grinding back the damaged fiberglass to expose solid laminate, then laminating and fairing patches over that. With no backing required and no difficult transitions to make, these patches were much easier to make. (18, 19) The bent rudderstock was difficult to straighten, but hydraulics can do a lot, even when they are attached to the yard crane. (20) The yacht in the paint bay, ready to be painted.

Repairing Major Grounding Damage

Do-It-Yourself Vacuum Bagging

A hand layup repair done by a do-it-yourselfer could wind up with as much as 20% voids. Each void weakens the laminate and has the potential to form a location around which the laminate can start to come apart.

To increase the fiberglass-to-resin ratio and get a stronger final job with almost no voids, use vacuum bagging: cover the repair with plastic film and use a vacuum under the film to remove all the air. Resin then flows into any voids, and the laminate is sucked down onto the job to form a stronger, tighter, void-free repair.

You can easily vacuum bag a job. WEST System markets an entire kit for less than $100 that contains all the parts for a simple vacuum-bagging job. I recommend this kit for any beginner. The instructions are clear and concise, and you will get a stronger job.

A couple of caveats are in order, however. If you do not have any experience with vacuum bagging, you need to be especially sure that your parts are laid down in the order described in the instructions, that you apply the perforated film (Peel Ply) and the bleeder cloth properly, and that you seal the impermeable vacuum-bag material properly. Most first-time vacuum baggers have problems getting a good seal. At the other extreme, you should avoid sucking a vacuum too long, or you could suck all the resin out of the repair!

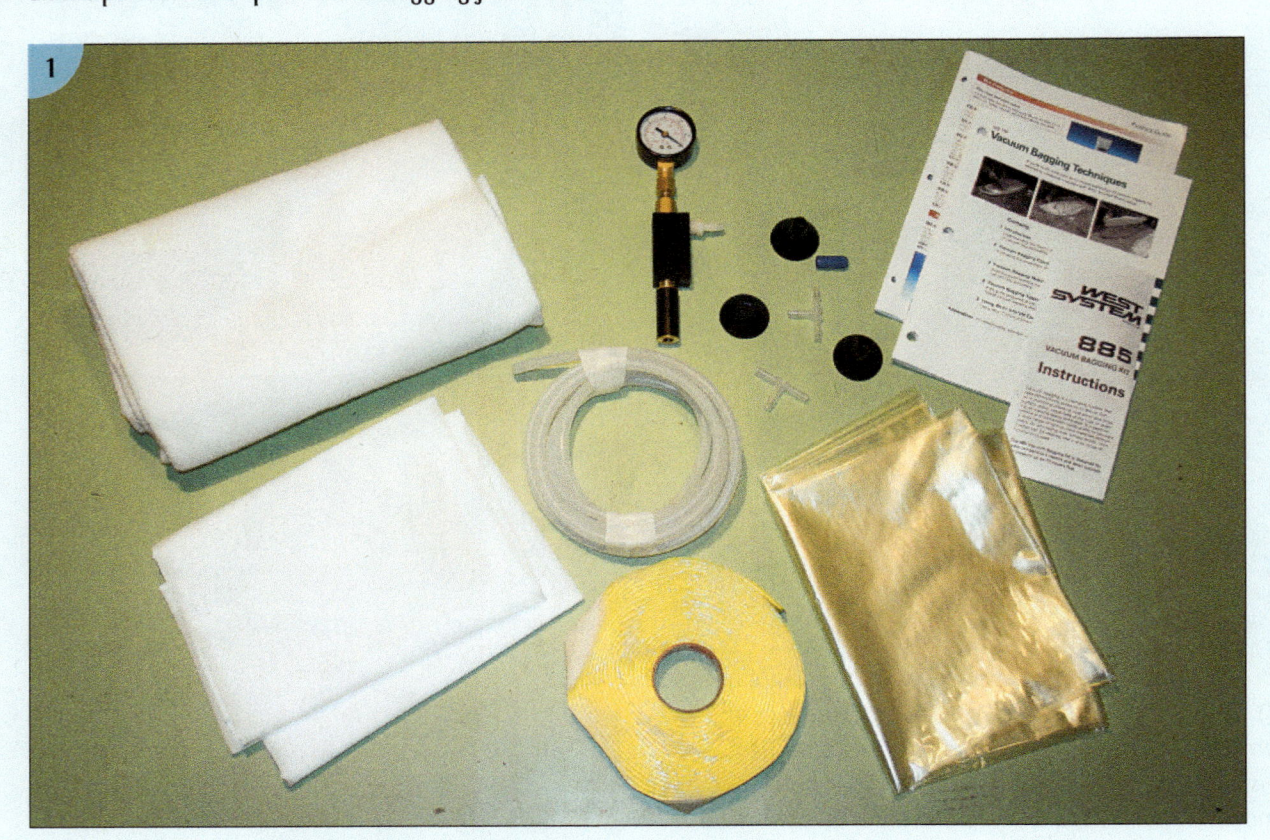

(1) We used the WEST System vacuum-bag kit to repair a wakeboard that had been damaged when the operator landed after flying off a large wave. The basic kit is shown here. At the top left is the bleeder, or breather, cloth, with the release fabric underneath it. At the middle top is the gauge that shows how high a vacuum has been drawn. This is connected to the valve that allows an air compressor to use the venturi effect to draw air out of the laminate. To its right are the suction cups and T connectors. The kit includes the manuals shown at right and a coil of pressure hose as well as a coil of sealing mastic, shown at bottom. At bottom right is the impermeable vacuum-bag material.

Project 5 • 139

(2) All the parts have been cut and are ready for the vacuum bagging to begin. On the left you can see the perforated film (often called Peel Ply, a manufacturer's trademarked name) and the breather cloth. On the right, on the other side of the damaged area, are the foam core and two layers of fiberglass cloth.

(3) Here we're coating the gap with epoxy to ensure that the foam is glued to the original surface. Note the yellow, double-sided mastic sealant to hold the cloth in place. In retrospect we felt that we would have made a better job had we put the entire board (rather than just the repair area) in a vacuum bag.

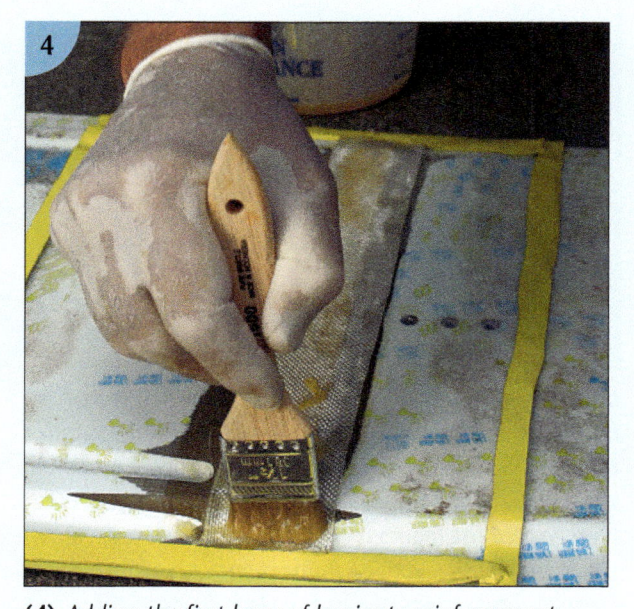

(5) Installing the perforated cloth and the breather fabric over the freshly epoxied job.

(4) Adding the first layer of laminate reinforcement.

(6) Pressing the vacuum-sealer material into place. We created a vacuum using our air compressor through the venturi vacuum generator supplied with the kit. The gauge shows how much vacuum we are drawing.

Repairing Major Grounding Damage

Project 6

REPLACING A FOREDECK HATCH

This is another project from my son's J/24 rebuild. In common with all J/24s built prior to 1980, our boat had a fiberglass forehatch, which we decided to replace with something nicer. Our choice was between a Lewmar 60 and a Lewmar 70. Boats prior to 1980 need the Lewmar 70, while newer boats need the Lewmar 60, which is slightly smaller. To bring our boat up to current norms, we chose the Lewmar 60. This necessitated extensive changes to the foredeck to fit the boss to the smaller hatch.

The first job was to construct a mold for the foredeck surrounding the hatch opening. We made it from a flat piece of 3/16-inch (4 mm) plywood, curved over two 2 x 8s that we cut to match the existing deck camber (as ascertained from cardboard templates). In the middle of the plywood we placed a square of plywood to represent the Lewmar 60 hatch opening. Around the exterior of the hatch-opening square we laid 3/8-inch (9 mm) balsa, the core material used throughout the J/24 deck, and over this core we laid an outer skin of 1½-ounce CSM, 24-ounce woven roving, and another layer of 1½-ounce CSM. We fitted a foam core for the new bossing on top of the fiberglass around the wooden hatch-opening square and covered it and the rest of the new part with two layers of 6-ounce cloth wet out with polyester resin.

Turning our attention to the existing deck, we cut away the outer skin as close as possible outside the original hatch boss. This left the inner skin protruding about 3 inches (75 mm) inside the freshly cut perimeter of the opening in the outer skin, so as to provide a shelf to support the new deck mold we were about to install. We removed the balsa core from this shelf.

Then we lowered the new hatch boss into place to dry-fit it. The fit was satisfactory, so we coated the upper surface of the existing inner skin with slightly thickened polyester and glued the hatch boss into place. After the polyester glue

(1) The plywood mold for the new deck section sits on 2 x 8s that replicate the deck camber. The wooden frame standing on a square of plywood in the center of the mold marks the outside perimeter of the opening for the new Lewmar 60 hatch. The foam core for the new hatch boss will butt up against the outside of this wooden frame. **(2)** Here we're laminating the new deck section over the mold. We placed a sheet of plastic over the plywood mold to stop the resin from sticking to it, then laid down the 3/8-inch (9 mm) balsa core. (We butted this deck core against the wooden frame you see in photo 1.) On top of the balsa we laminated an outer skin of 1½-ounce CSM followed by 24-ounce woven roving and another layer of 1½-ounce CSM. We then erected the foam core for the new hatch boss against the outside of the wooden frame, removed the frame, and laminated two layers of 6-ounce cloth over the entire part, encapsulating the foam boss core.

Project 6 • 141

(3) We marked the cut lines around the old foredeck hatch as close as possible to the existing hatch boss. Since the replacement hatch will be smaller, not larger, there is no sense making the opening any larger than necessary. We used a circular saw riding on the edge of the boss to make the cut. **(4)** Here we're ready to fit the new section of foredeck with its hatch boss into the hole in the deck. The old hatch cover is under the new boss. Note how the inner skin extends about 3 inches (75 mm) inside the outer skin around the entire perimeter of the cutout. To achieve this, we set the blade depth at about 1/8 inch (3 mm) when cutting away the outer skin, then pried it away from the core material. We then trimmed the inner skin only slightly around the old hatch opening, leaving a shelf as a landing for the new boss.

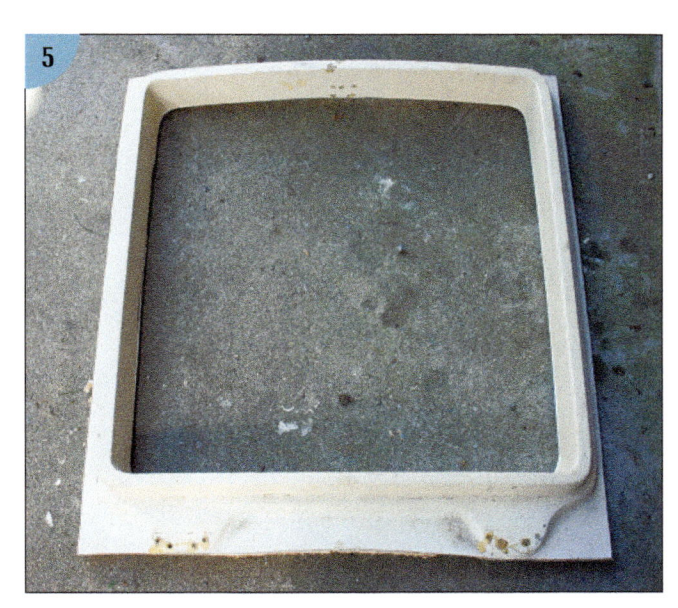

(5) The bossing for the old hatch was removed and discarded. **(6)** We dry-fitted the new foredeck section and hatch boss, weighting it as necessary until its camber matched the surrounding deck. We then removed it, smeared thickened polyester resin on the upper surface of the protruding inner skin, and lowered the new boss into this bedding compound to glue it into place.

Replacing a Foredeck Hatch

had set up, we ground back the surrounding deck laminate inside and outside and laminated new fiberglass into place to seal the joint between the new and old deck sections, covering the entire hatch opening inside and out with two layers of 6-ounce fiberglass. We then faired the hatch bossing and the inside portion of the deckhead with thickened polyester, and when that had hardened, we sanded it back and checked that the hatch boss was perfectly flat in all directions (unless the boss is perfectly flat, it will leak). To finish the job, we undercoated the installed part with Interlux's Epoxy Primekote, sanded it, and applied a topcoat of Interlux's white Perfection over the boss and outward onto the deck to overlap the surrounding nonskid. When the Perfection had dried, we masked off the deck and painted nonskid over the entire deck.

(7) We then laid up two layers of 6-ounce cloth over the exterior joint, up over the boss, and down through the hatch opening and over the deck underside to lap the existing inner skin, into which we had ground a scarf. When the fiberglass had set up we sanded the entire area smooth and faired it into the surrounding deck. This shows the laminate before it was coated with fairing and sanded smooth.

(8) The new hatch sitting on the new boss, ready to be bolted down—which will happen after we've sanded and painted the area around the hatch. At this stage the deck is still slightly flexible, but when the hatch is bolted in place it will help stiffen the deck. It is very important to get the top surface of the hatch boss flat and level. If the boss is not level, it will distort the hatch rim and cause a leak.

(9) The finished installation after we painted it with Interlux's white Perfection and Interlux's gray Interdeck.

PROJECT 7

REPAIRING DAMAGE TO A CORED HULL

As an example of this sort of repair, the photos show a 41-footer that went aground in a storm and was beaten up on the rocks. The boat suffered extensive damage to its keel and the forward portion of its hull underbody. The owner was lucky that the balsa-cored hull prevented the rocks from punching through the laminate and making a hole large enough to sink the boat. He was lucky, too, in that a surveyor detected no damage to interior reinforcements or furniture. Repairs were made at Conanicut Marine in Jamestown, Rhode Island, by Mo Mancini and Mike Irvine, who graciously allowed me to take photographs as they were working.

The first tasks were to drill a few holes in the cored hull to determine the extent of the damage, and to use a moisture meter to ascertain if water

(continued on page 146)

(1) *The boat has been hauled after grounding on rocks, and here we're looking up at damage in the bow area. Impact damage has penetrated the outer laminate and into the core, which has been exposed in places.*

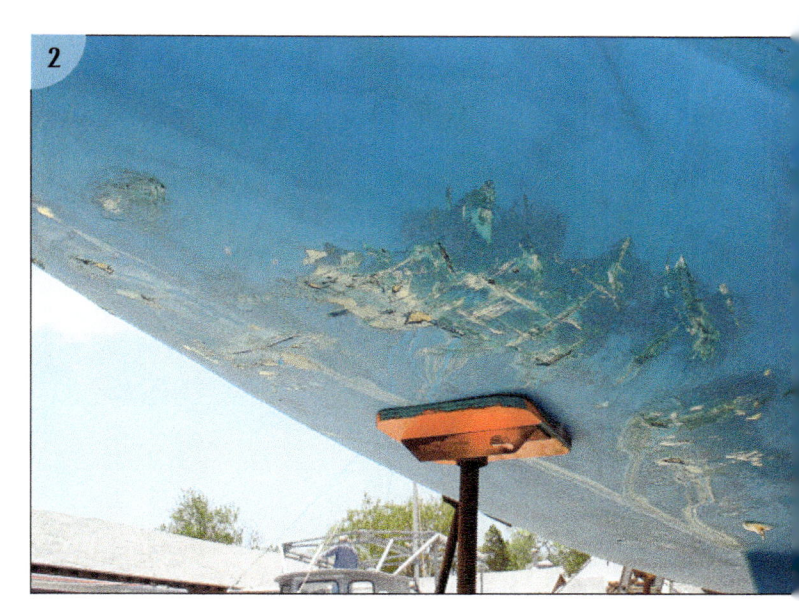

(2) *A view of the damage a little farther aft. The rocks punched into the hull in several places, fracturing the outer laminate.*

(3) *The keel has also received its share of damage. Note the upturned tip on the keel bulb.*

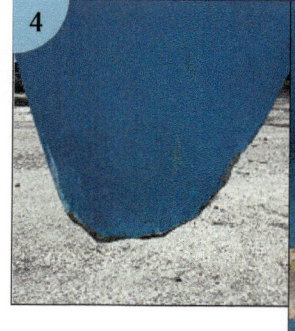

144 • **MAJOR REPAIRS**

Repairing Damage to a Cored Hull

(4) The end of the rudder blade was also extensively damaged and needed to be checked to ensure that water had not penetrated the core. **(5)** All the pounding fractured the filler from the hull-to-keel joint and the top of the keel, leaving a bare area exposed. This kind of impact damage called for an inspection of the interior to see if any furniture had been displaced or if floors or longitudinals had been fractured. Fortunately in this case, a surveyor found no interior damage.

(6) The first step in the repair job was to cut away much of the damaged area to get an idea of its extent. Here Mo and Mike have made the first cut on either side of the hull, revealing that more of the outer laminate needs to be removed along the centerline. After removing the damaged outer laminate and repairing the small punctures in the inner skin, they could start patching the balsa core.

(7, 8) They coated the inner skin and each piece of replacement core with resin.

Project 7 • 145

(9) *Then they pressed the new core into place and clamped it until the resin hardened.* (10) *The finished core patch.*

146 • MAJOR REPAIRS

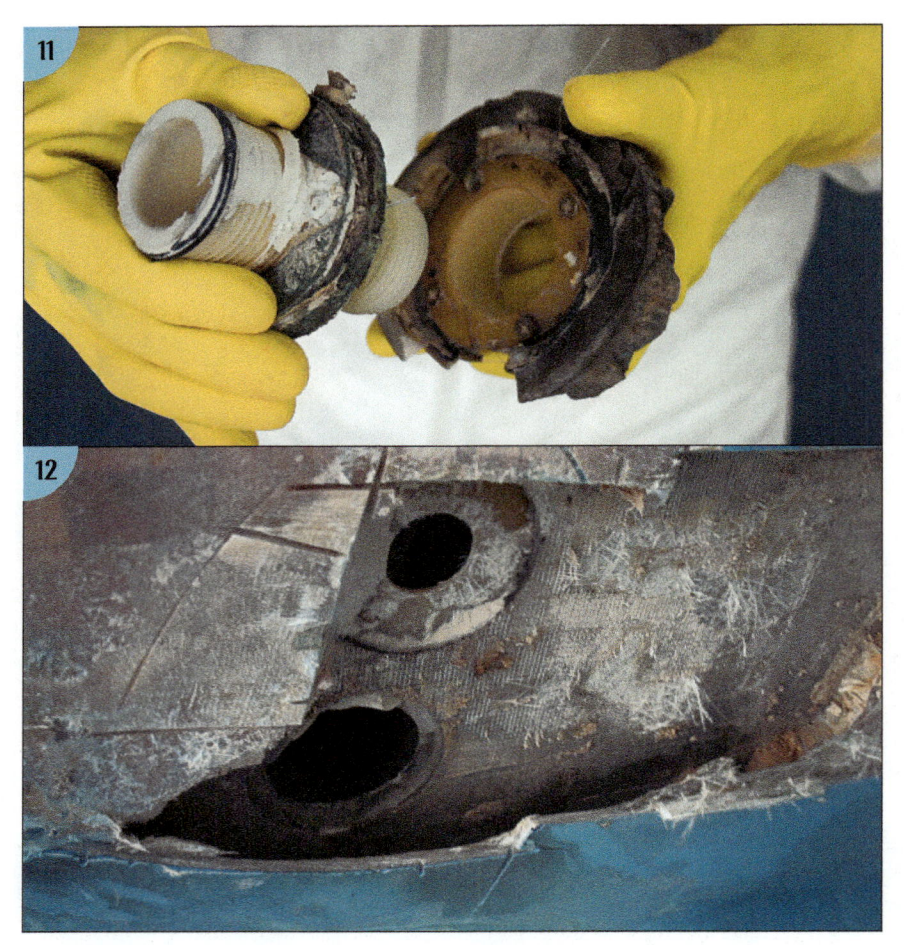

During hull repair, they removed the speedometer through-hull and found that the core around it had rotted. **(11)** *When the instrument had been installed, some material had been squirted into the void, but this material had merely hardened to a rocklike consistency and allowed water to seep into the core, requiring the removal and replacement of an additional core section.* **(12)** *With the new core in place, they began laminating the new fiberglass.*

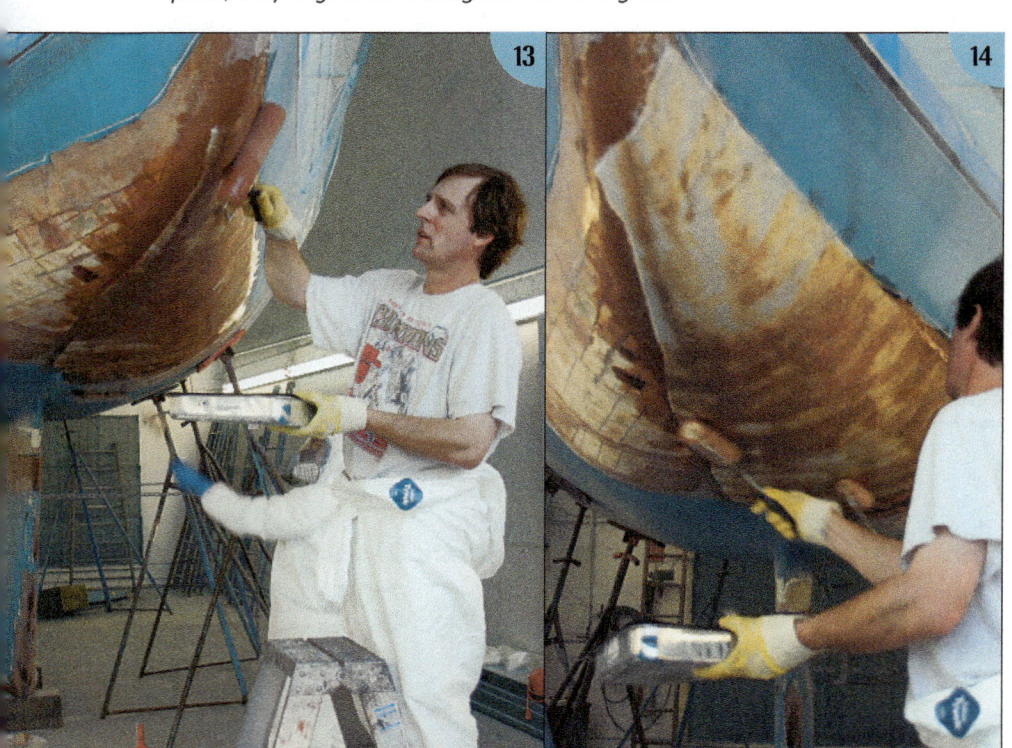

had penetrated the balsa core. The test holes penetrated the outer skin and the core, but not the inner skin. As the damaged and wet core material was cut away, we found that previous water penetration around a speedometer transducer had rotted the balsa core there, increasing the area of core that Mo and Mike needed to remove.

With the core removed, Mo and Mike repaired a few quarter-sized punctures in the inner skin where the rocks had punched all the way through. Next they coated the inner skin and the replacement balsa core with unthickened polyester resin, and then they pressed the two together and clamped them. After the resin had hardened, they laid up an outer skin over the balsa and rolled it out carefully to remove air bubbles. They did not vacuum bag the hull because the original laminate had been hand laid, and the surveyor felt that vacuum bagging the repair would not provide any advantages.

When the outer skin had hardened, they faired it with fairing compound and longboarded the surface to obtain a nice, smooth finish. Then they primed the hull underbody with Epoxy Primekote and finished it off with new bottom paint.

While this work was being done, repairs were made to the *(continued on page 149)*

(13, 14) *They rolled resin onto the new core, followed by a layer of fiberglass.*

Project 7 • 147

(15) More layers followed, and they rolled each one carefully to eliminate air pockets.

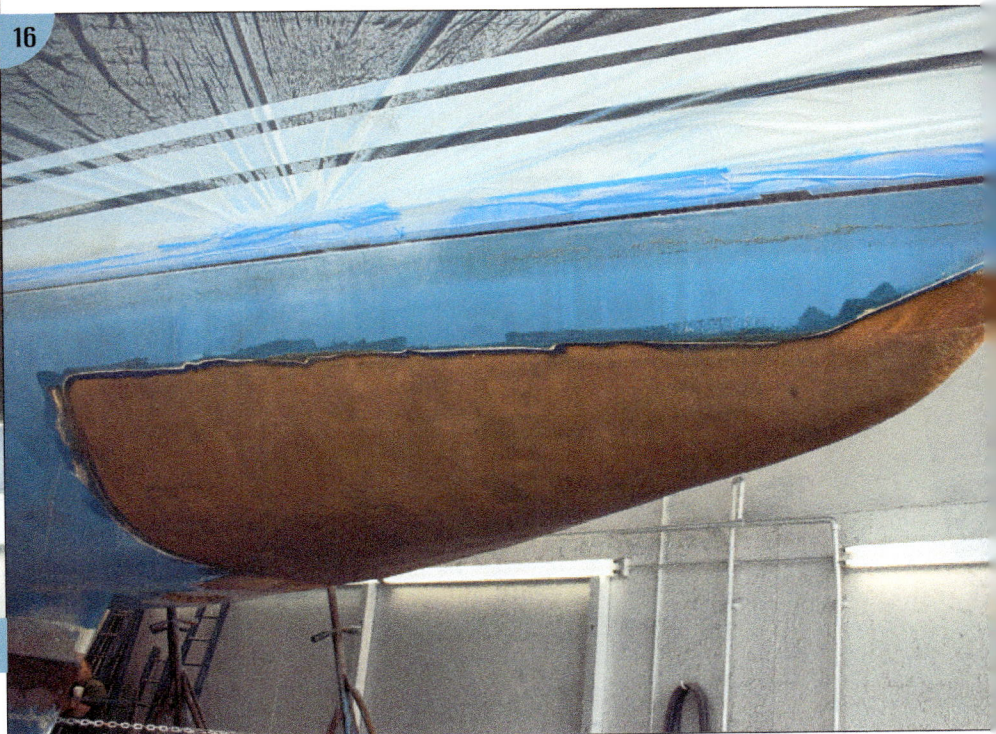

(16) After curing at 80°F, the repair was ready for fairing and finishing.

(17) They smoothed the hull with fairing compound, which shows as a gray layer.

Repairing Damage to a Cored Hull

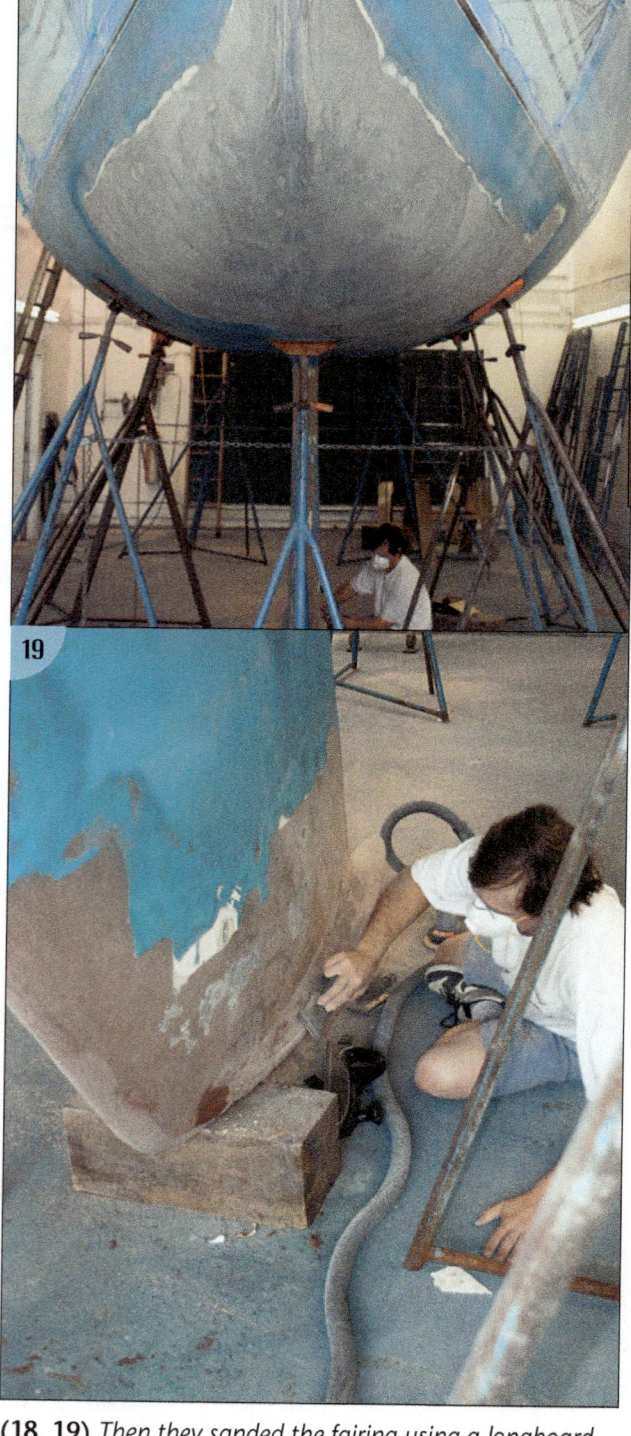

148 • MAJOR REPAIRS

Repairing Damage to a Cored Hull

(20) *They also refaired the top of the keel to its original contours, and refilled and refaired the hull-to-keel joint.*

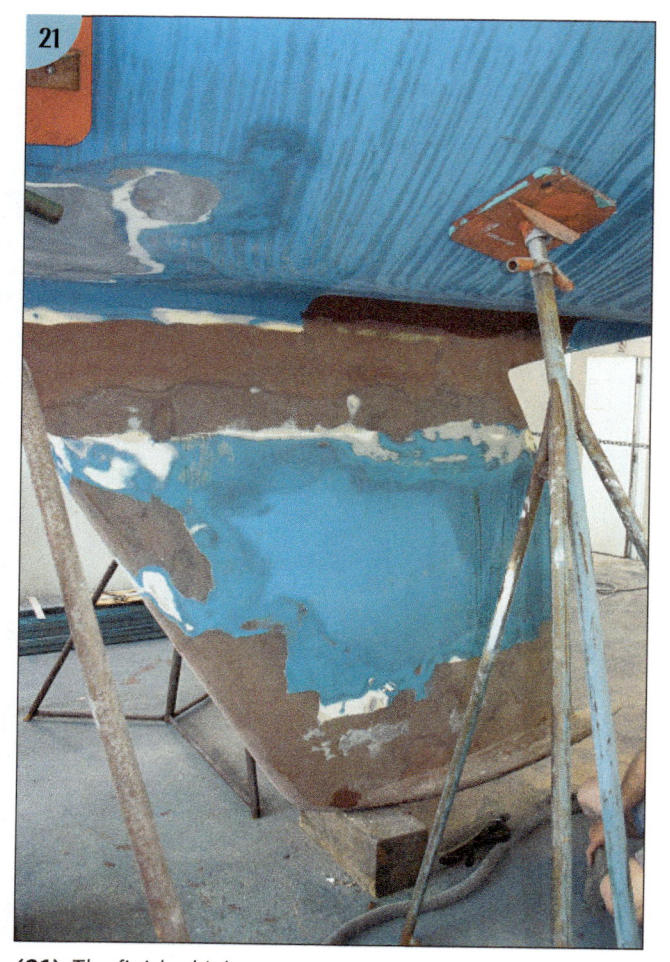

(18, 19) *Then they sanded the fairing using a longboard with progressively finer grits. While the hull repair was curing, they turned to the keel, first straightening its tip and then using fairing compound to smooth out the imperfections.*

(21) *The finished job.*

rudder and the keel, which had absorbed the worst of the damage. The workers drilled test holes in the rudder to assess the extent of water penetration into the core, then they laid up and vacuum bagged a new laminate to ensure that it would adhere to the blade properly.

The tip of the lead keel needed straightening, but that was nothing that a hammer couldn't solve. They also checked the keel to make sure that no damage had occurred where the keel bolts went through the laminate at the top of the keel. Finally, they faired the keel with fairing compound, using the techniques described in Chapter 6. The entire job, including hull, keel, and rudder repairs, took the two professionals roughly four weeks of work.

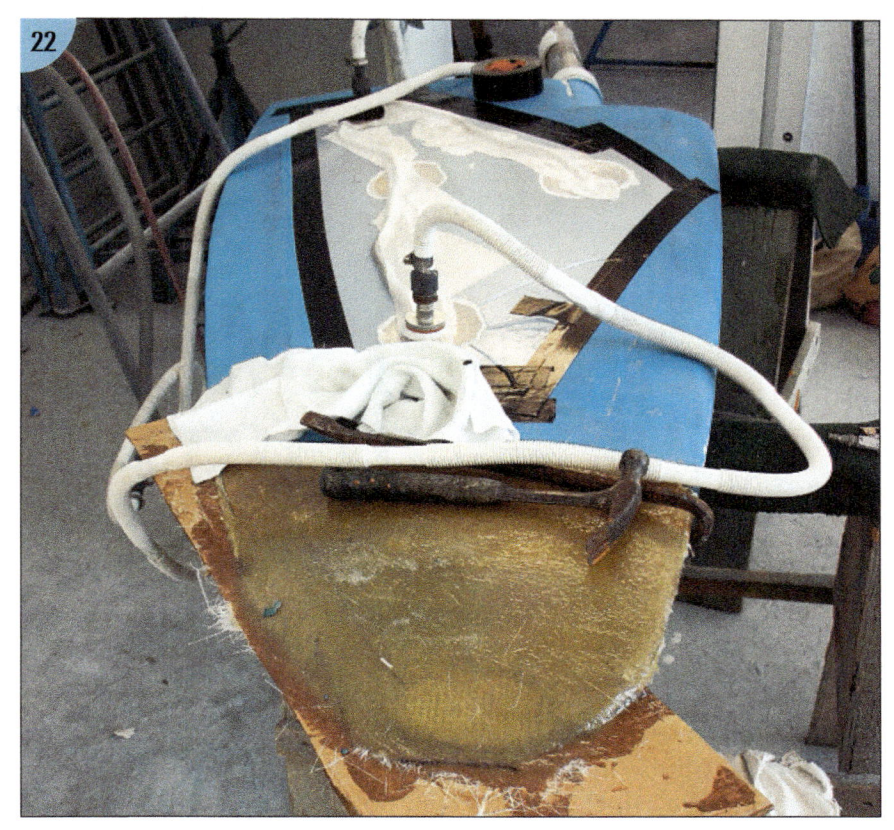

(22) *Here they are vacuum bagging the rudder repair to make sure that the laminate is strong in this crucial part of the boat.*

(23) *Here is the finished hull, ready to go back into the water.*

Chapter 8 OSMOSIS AND BLISTER REPAIR

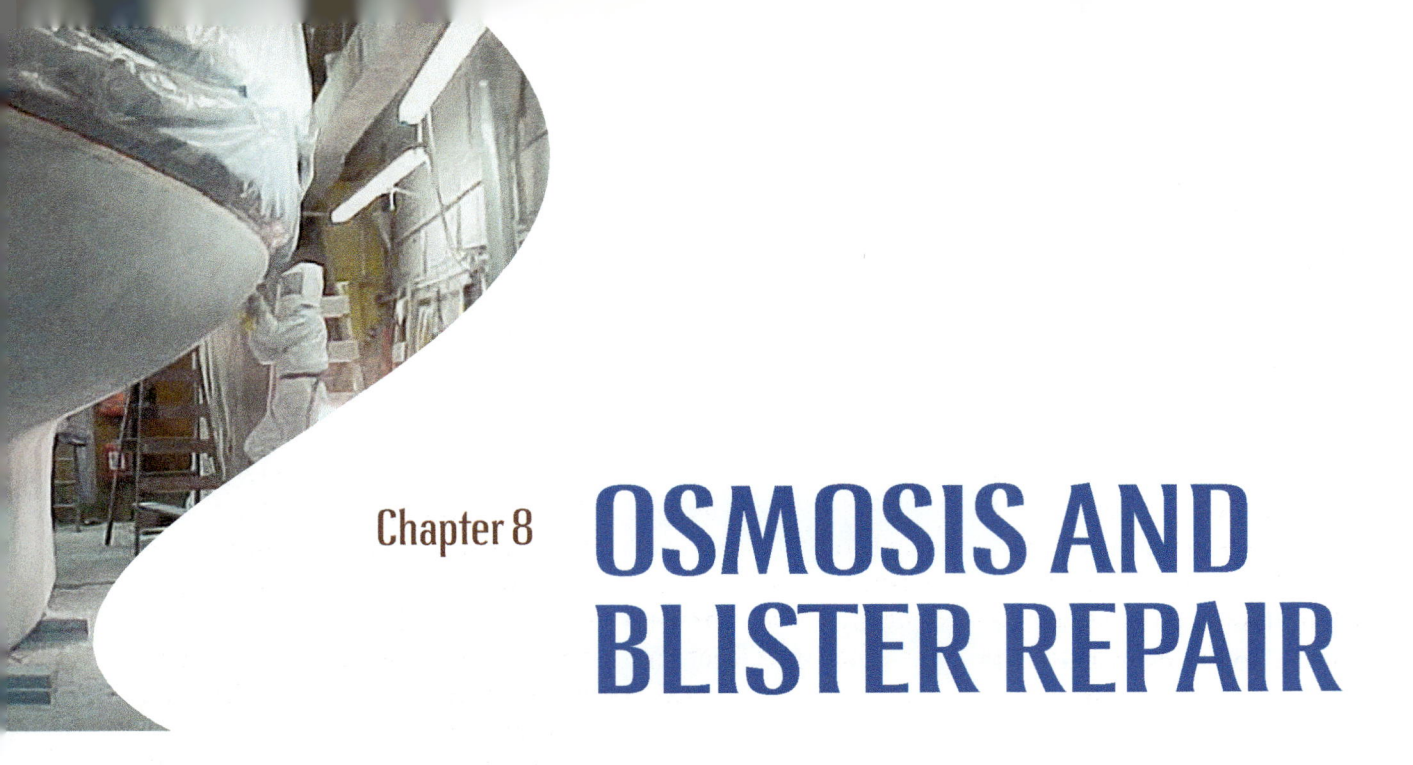

As mentioned in Chapters 1 and 2, blisters can appear on the bottoms of fiberglass boats, especially those that have been left in the water for a period of time. The affected boats have a porous gelcoat that allows minute amounts of water to seep through via osmosis. The boats also have small voids in the hull laminate, typically in the layer of chopped strand mat (CSM) that backs the gelcoat to prevent print-through of the woven roving beneath it. When moisture permeates the gelcoat and enters one of these voids, the styrene in the polyester resin reacts with the water molecules, forming a bubble in the gelcoat. The bubble, in turn, creates a larger void, which absorbs more moisture, and so on, until the blistering can become pronounced.

If you spot blisters on the hull of your boat when it has been hauled out, circle each spot with a felt-tip pen and wait a few days to see what happens to them. Often they will disappear as the hull dries out. Try puncturing one of the blisters to see if any liquid seeps out of it. (Note: You should wear eye protection when you do this, because the liquid in the blister may shoot out under pressure, and it can be nasty stuff. You do not want it in your eyes.) If the punctured blister emits a liquid that smells like vinegar, your boat may have a progressive gelcoat blistering rash, or *osmosis*—as opposed to isolated blisters—and you should call a surveyor to get an expert opinion on what to do about it.

A surveyor will assess how much moisture the hull has absorbed by using a moisture meter. If the hull is cored, he may also want to remove a few 1-inch-diameter (25 mm) core samples with a hole saw.

If the core is dry, and the surveyor concludes that the problem is confined to the surface layers of the outer skin, you can close up the holes and repair them as described in Chapter 5. If the core is wet, however, the problem is more extensive, and the surveyor may want to make more holes to determine exactly how much of the core is affected.

DIY BLISTER REPAIR

Many boatowners repair blisters as they arise. Whether or not this is sensible is a matter of debate, but it really depends on whether the first blisters you see are followed by many others. In the opinion of most professionals, a few blisters are usually followed by more blisters, and repairing them one by one is a losing situation. As one repair is made, another may open up. The boatowner will spend every spring repairing blisters before he or she can paint the boat's bottom.

Having said that, the easiest way to repair a blister is to grind it out with an angle grinder. If the blister is small you might prefer to grind it out with a Dremel tool, but in any case it is best to remove the laminate around the entire bubble at least down to the first layer of woven roving. This will give you a 2- to 3-inch-diameter (50 to 75 mm) circle of ground-off laminate that can be repaired as described in Chapter 5.

If you find blisters and are lucky enough to store your boat over the winter in a dry boatshed, you might want to try to dry the hull—by putting a dehumidifier inside the boat and another in the boatshed—to see if you can get the laminate dry. (It can take up to a year to get a laminate totally dry.) Aim for a moisture content of below 3% as read from a moisture meter.

If you can get a low moisture content in the laminate, you should remove all the bottom paint and coat the hull bottom with an epoxy barrier coat before recoating it with bottom paint. The process is described later in this chapter in the Protecting against Osmosis section.

Unfortunately, there is no way to predict blistering or to know what boats are most vulnerable. It has been found, however, that boats that stay afloat in warm waters for more than two years at a stretch tend toward worse osmosis problems than boats that are sailed in cool waters and hauled every winter. Note, too, that osmosis does not affect boats sailed in fresh water.

PROFESSIONAL BLISTER REPAIR

A variety of methods have been proposed to get rid of blistering. They range from grinding and filling individual blisters to sandblasting or shotblasting the hull. Unfortunately, most reports suggest that none of these approaches is adequate over the long run to address a serious case of boat pox. The limitations of grinding and filling individual blisters are mentioned above. Sandblasting or shotblasting the hull is not a good solution either, because you can damage the laminate by hammering at it with tiny grains of sand or shot. Most professionals believe that the only way to eliminate osmotic blistering is to remove the entire gelcoat and at least the first layer of CSM beneath it, where the chemical reaction might occur. Unfortunately, this is expensive, and even that may not cure the problem. If moisture has penetrated the outer skin and into the core of a sandwich hull, you may have to remove the wet core as well, making the job very expensive.

So what is the best way to remedy blistering? Unfortunately, the only way to both remove it and prevent its return is to eliminate the porous gelcoat and the area where voids can form—that is, the CSM behind the gelcoat. This requires using a boatyard's planer/peeler machine, an expensive tool that must be operated by a trained professional. It removes the major causes of the problem in one swoop—or in a series of swoops down the underwater portion of the hull. If you try to do the "peeling" work yourself using a grinder, there is a good chance that either you will not grind enough or you will grind too much, and will have to do the job all over again in a year or so, when more blisters start appearing.

Once a hull has been professionally peeled, it should be left to dry out. The amount of drying needed can be determined by a moisture meter. Dehumidifiers and/or infrared heaters enhance the speed and extent of drying.

Another method of drying a hull that has been used with some success is the HotVac system developed in England and now owned by the UK company Gelplane International (www.gelplane.co.uk). This system employs hot pads fitted to the hull that heat to around 185°F to 200°F (85°C to 95°C). Water vapor is drawn out of the hull with a vacuum, reducing the remaining moisture content to virtually undetectable levels. The system also vaporizes and removes any styrene and glycol left in the hull. The drying process takes one to two weeks rather than the six to eight weeks that might normally be required.

With the gelcoat and CSM layer removed and the boat dried out, the next step is to apply new laminate using either a vinylester or an epoxy resin. Vinylester and epoxy resins are almost com-

152 • OSMOSIS AND BLISTER REPAIR

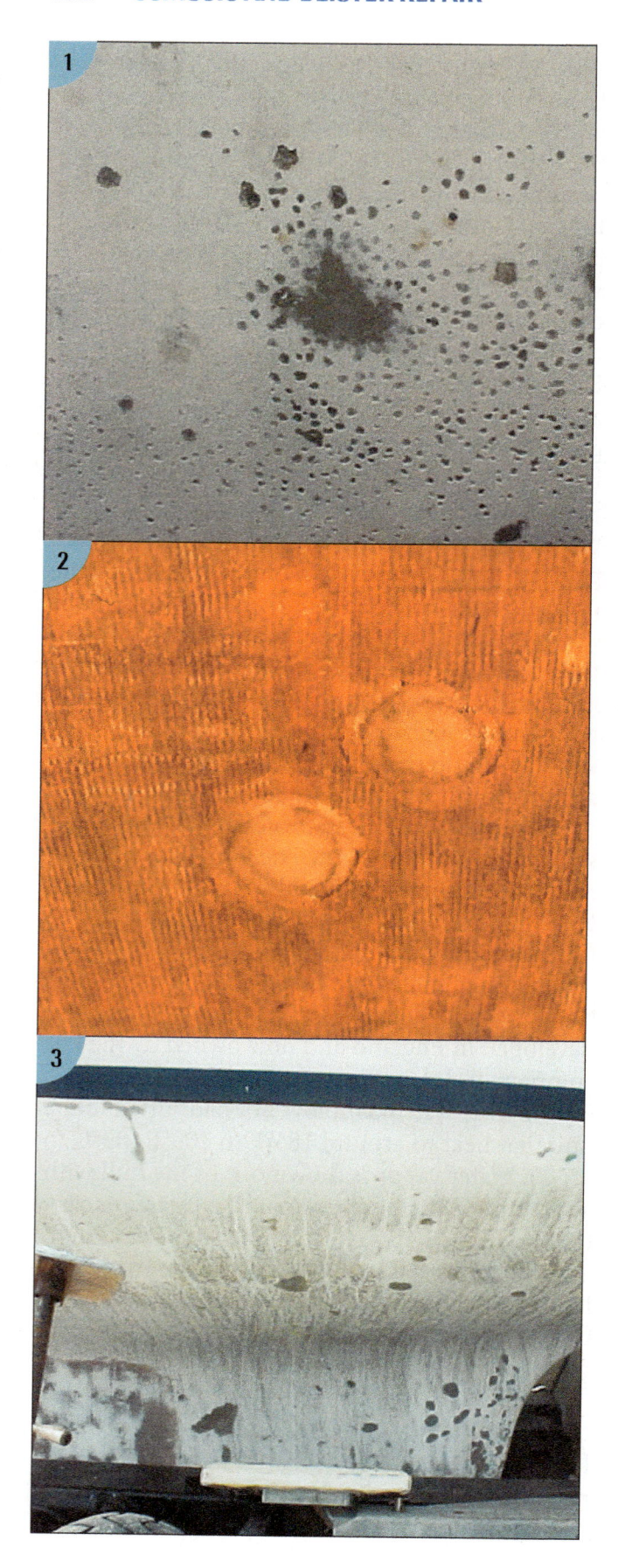

(1) *These representative examples of osmotic blistering caused by water penetration into the outer laminate of a hull include blisters after a hull has been peeled, water penetration via blisters into a peeled hull's core* **(2)**, *which will need to be dried out or replaced, and other examples of blisters* **(3, 4, 5, 6)**. *(All images courtesy Jamestown Boat Yard.)*

Professional Blister Repair • 153

(1) A peeling machine at work in the Jamestown (Rhode Island) Boat Yard. This machine has a small rotary planing head about 3 inches (75 mm) across. It can be set to a predetermined depth, and as it moves down the hull, it peels away both the gelcoat and the underlying layer of CSM. If the hull has a core that has been penetrated with moisture, a second peel is usually done to remove the entire outer laminate.

(2) The peeled chips are collected in the tube attached to the peeler head and go directly into the trash.

(3) After a hull has been peeled, a worker finishes the job by grinding off areas the peeler head can't reach.

pletely nonporous and do not allow moisture to get back into the hull. Because the new laminate is below the waterline where print-through is not visible, a coarse woven roving can be used to build up laminate thickness fast. Some boatyards try to eliminate troublesome voids in the laminate by vacuum bagging it. This is by far the best way to solve void problems and has been highly successful on many boats.

After the new laminate is in place, the hull is sanded smooth and a new vinylester gelcoat is sprayed on. If the hull is not sanded smooth, the new gelcoat can vary in thickness, causing problems later when a thin part allows moisture to penetrate. To be absolutely certain than no moisture can get into the hull, an epoxy barrier coat such as Interlux's Interprotect can be added.

154 • OSMOSIS AND BLISTER REPAIR

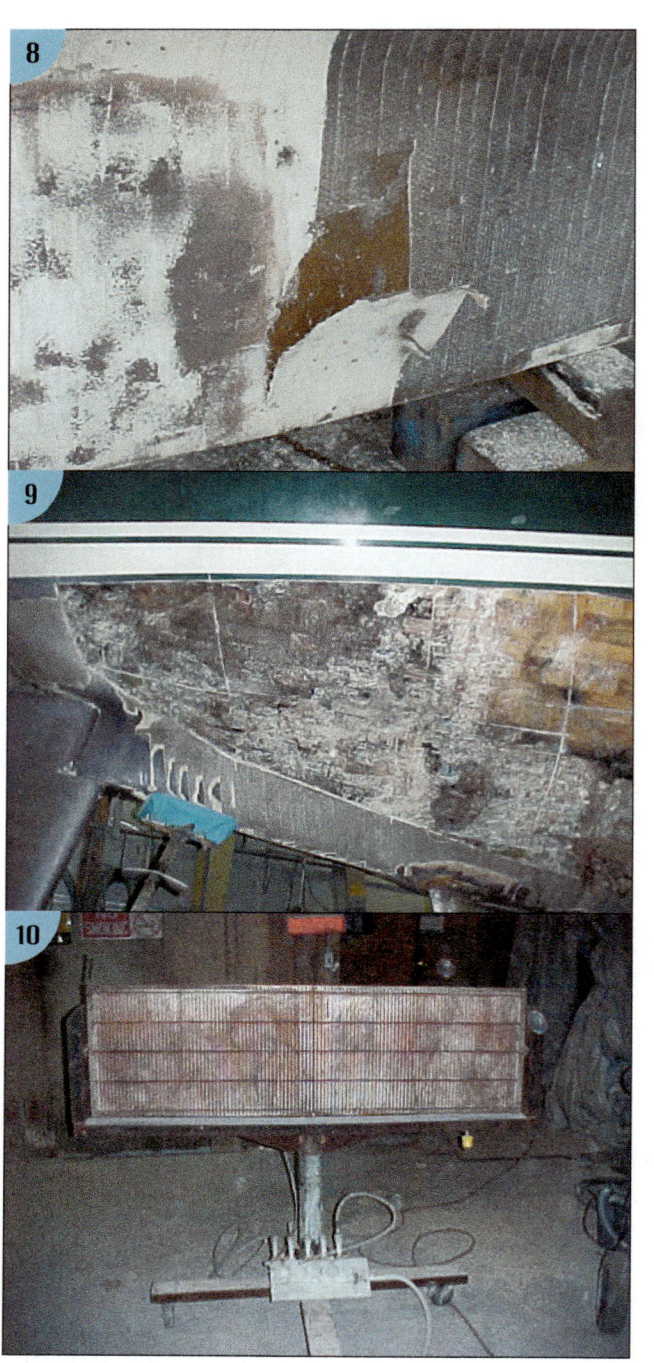

Professional Blister Repair

(4) A hull being peeled, exposing blister craters. (5) The laminate has been fully peeled, but moisture is still present in the cored hull. (6) A second peel exposes wet core, which will have to be replaced. (7) Moisture levels in the core are carefully measured to ensure that the core is dry enough for a new outer skin. (8) The peeling of this keel has exposed areas of delamination. (9) This hull has been peeled to its core, which is in very poor condition and will need to be replaced. After being peeled, a hull needs to dry out. (10) Powerful heaters like this infrared one help the process along.

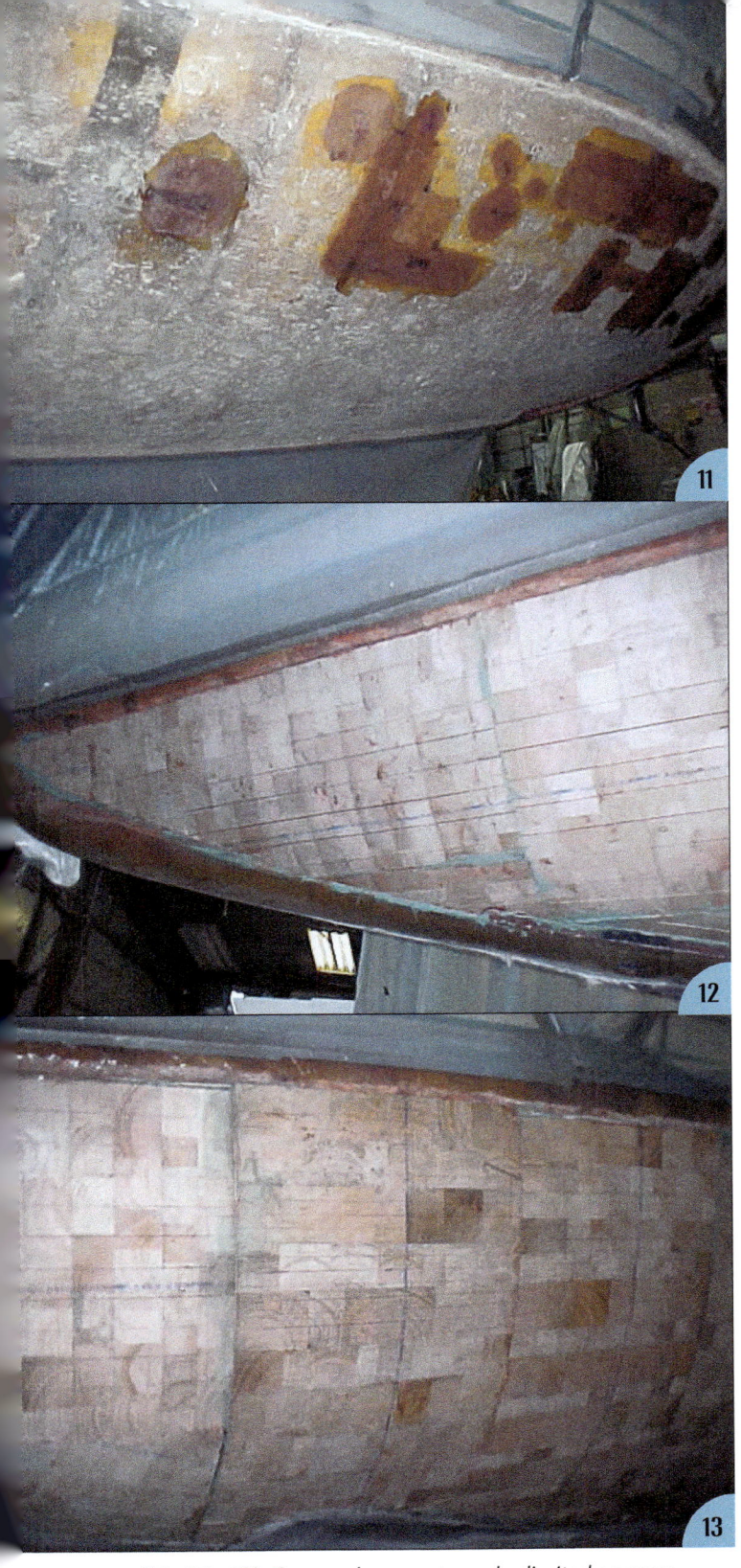

Professional Blister Repair • 155

(11, 12, 13) Core replacement can be limited or more general, depending on the need. (14) Vacuum bagging a replacement core in place to eliminate voids. With a hand layup you can expect about 15% to 20% voids in a laminate, but vacuum bagging can reduce the void content to under 2%, which reduces the potential for renewed hull blistering down the road. (15) Testing the vacuum sealing bag for leaks.

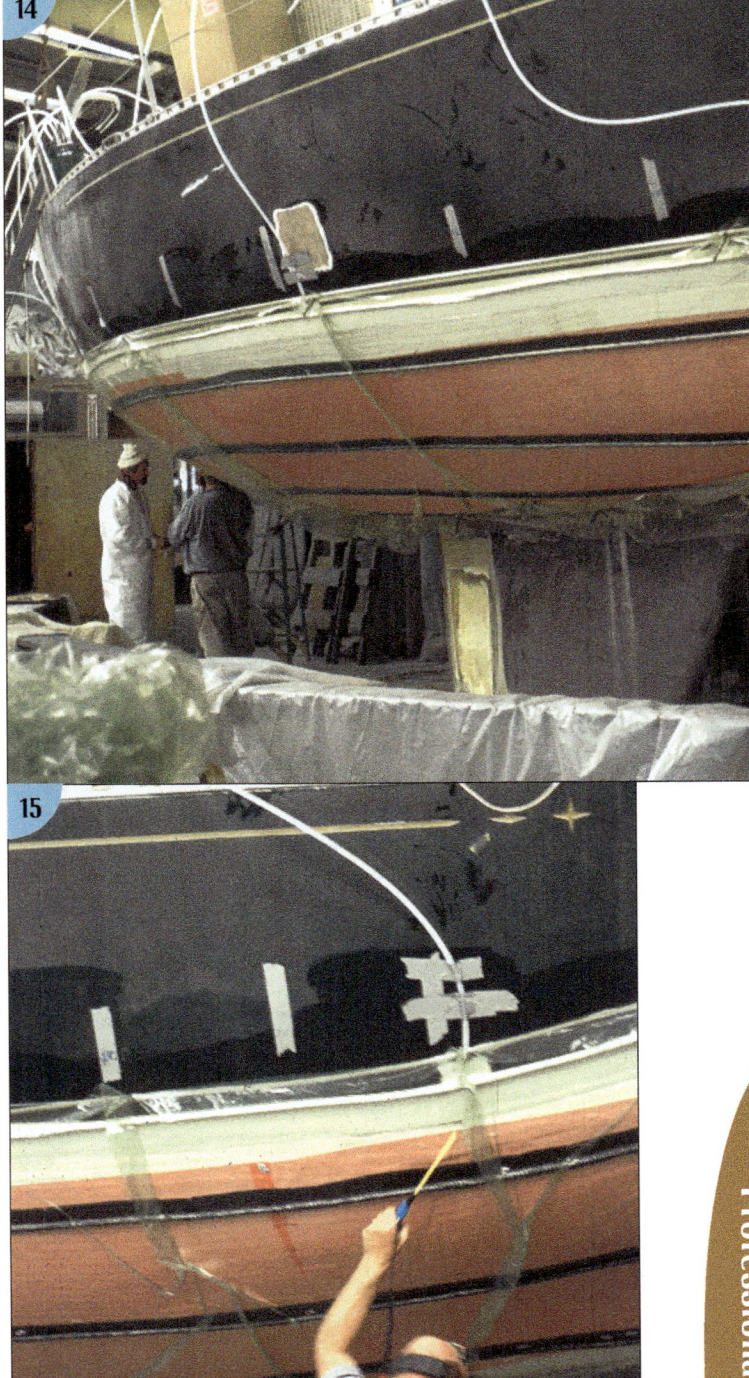

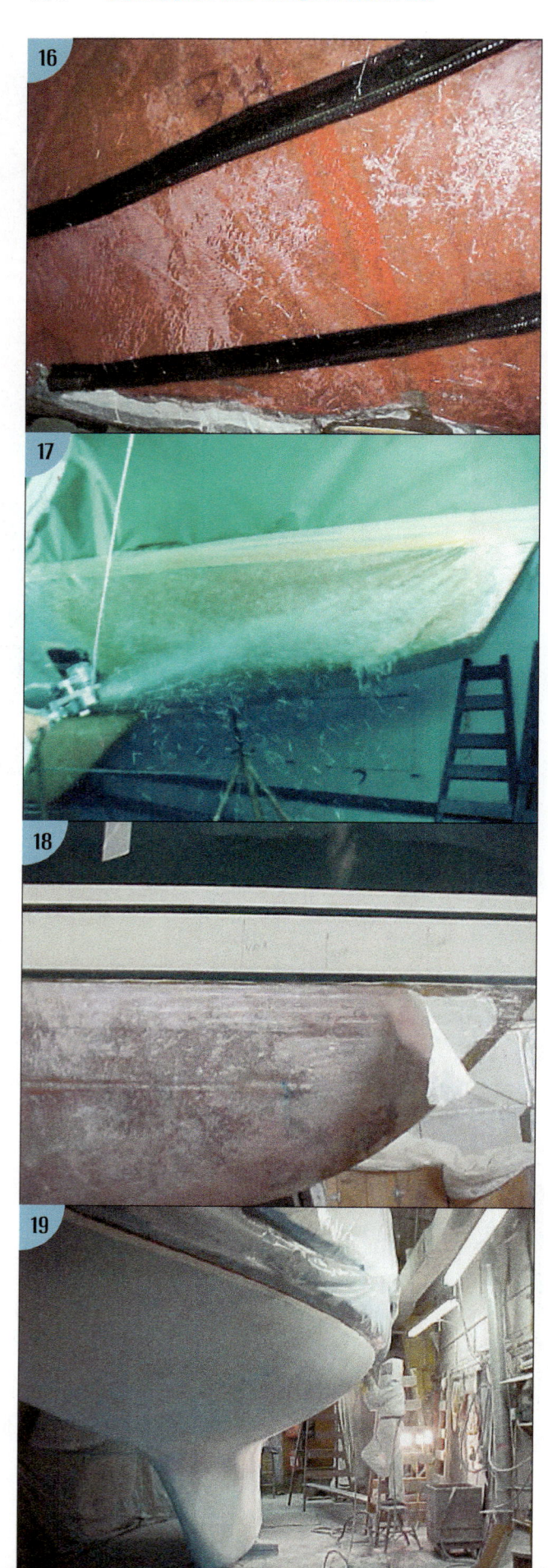

(16) *The vacuum bag in place with the vacuum lines running along the hull underbody. With the new core in place, the hull laminate is laid up using woven roving and CSM.* **(17)** *A worker sprays CSM on the core.* **(18)** *The outer skin laminate is laid up over the chopped strand and will then be vacuum bagged.* **(19)** *A worker sands the newly laminated hull.*

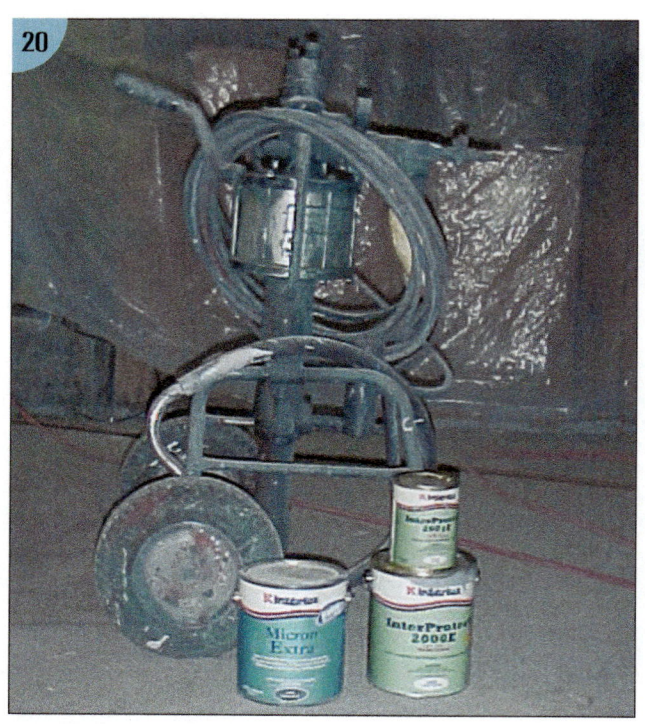

(20) *The exterior of the hull underbody is given a barrier coat of Interprotect epoxy resin to provide an additional guard against water penetration.*

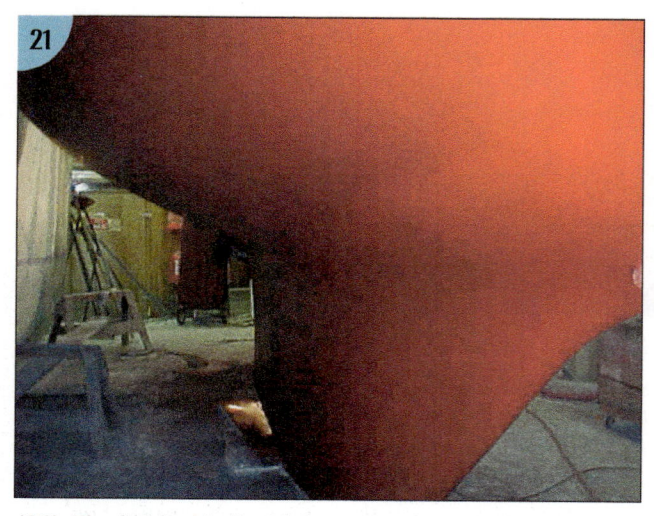

(21) *The finished hull with bottom paint. It looks as if nothing has happened—except that the boatowner left a large chunk of money at the boatyard.*

BLISTERING CAUSED BY VALIANT'S FIRE-RETARDANT RESIN

A particular kind of blistering has formed on many Valiant 32s and 40s built between 1975 and 1981 by the Uniflite Corporation of Bellingham, Washington. (After 1984 the Valiant line was built by Valiant Yachts in Gordonville, Texas, and none of the Gordonville boats have this problem. In fact they have a stellar reputation for solid construction.) The cause seems to involve the use of a fire-retardant resin that apparently reacts adversely with another resin used in construction and slowly works its way out of the laminate, producing huge blisters on the surface of the hull and deck. Most of these blisters are far larger than those caused by osmotic blistering. To cure the problem, the entire hull and deck must be professionally peeled and then replaced.

Some owners have tried to avoid this expensive solution by using a Dremel tool to puncture each blister, and then they grind the areas back and resurface them. This method has worked to some extent, but it still leaves fire-retardant resin in the hull to creep out and cause more blistering.

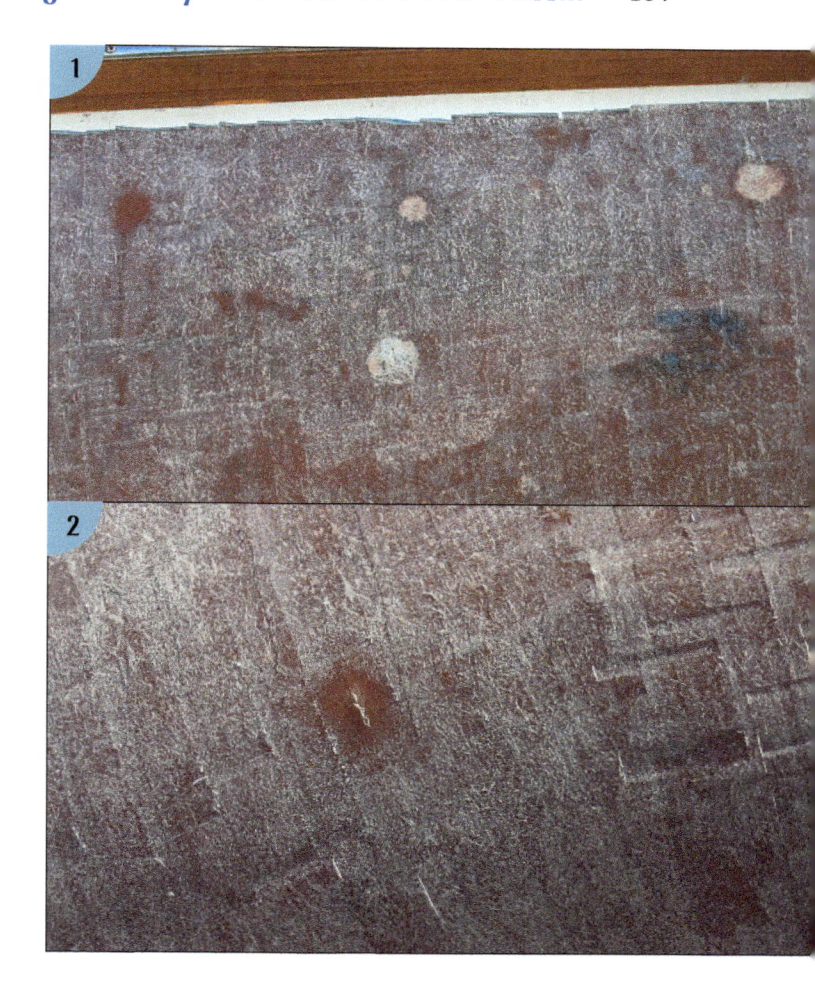

(1, 2) A blistered Valiant 40 hull after a professional peeling. (3) The extent of the work on the topsides.

PROTECTING AGAINST OSMOSIS

To protect against osmosis, you can recoat your hull bottom to stop seawater from migrating into the laminate. Currently, one of the two best ways to do this is to use a vinylester gelcoat, a practice many boatbuilders have now adopted. Lacking that, the second type of protective coating for a hull bottom is an epoxy barrier coat, which is designed specifically to guard against osmosis. Although the full extent of the protection thus achieved cannot really be known, both approaches have performed well on a number of boats over several years. For example, we applied Interlux's Interprotect epoxy barrier coat to the Jamestown (Rhode Island) Fire Department's fire and rescue boat several years ago, and the coating has held up very nicely even though the boat is used year-round in all kinds of weather. (A comparison of boatbuilding materials is not the object of this book, but it's worth pointing out that a similar vessel owned by the town but made of aluminum corroded within two years.)

To apply an epoxy barrier coat to your boat, you must first strip off the bottom paint. Place a plastic sheet under the boat to catch the debris, and remove the old paint chemically or by sanding it off. With the bottom paint removed, check for blisters. If any are present, pop them and then wash the boat with fresh water to remove any of the vinegar-like compound that may be contained inside them. To grind and fill any substantial blister craters, proceed as outlined earlier in this chapter.

Allow the hull to dry out for as long as possible before continuing with the work. In some cases this may be as long as six months or more. If you plan on proceeding without drying the boat, "paint" each blister site and its surrounding area with Interlux's Watertite Epoxy Filler YAV135 and sand with 80- to 100-grit paper before applying the Interprotect barrier coat. It is a good idea to have a surveyor check the boat with a moisture meter. You may get a recurrence of blisters if you apply a barrier coat over a wet hull.

With the hull dry and stripped back to the gelcoat, the next step is to wipe the hull clean with Interlux's Solvent Wash 202. (These instructions are centered around Interlux products because I have used them personally, but Pettit, WEST System, MAS, System Three, and several other epoxy suppliers also offer products for this purpose.) After wiping the hull down, sand it with 80- or 100-grit sandpaper to provide good tooth for the epoxy.

Mix Interprotect in a 3:1 ratio of resin to hardener, and allow it to sit for 20 minutes before rolling it on. You will need to apply at least four layers of Interprotect to build up the desired thickness (about 10 mils). Allow the resin to cure (about 4 hours) after each layer, and sand with 80- to 100-grit paper before applying the next layer.

On a new boat that has come right from the factory, the hull underbody only needs be wiped down with a solvent wash (such as Interlux's Solvent Wash 202) before the barrier coat is applied.

Rolling Interprotect onto a hull. Interprotect is an epoxy resin that helps keep water from infiltrating into the fiberglass hull skin through the gelcoat.

Chapter 9 FINISHING YOUR REPAIR WORK

A skilled paint job can make a boat look like it is worth thousands of dollars more than it actually is. But to get a perfect finish on a fiberglass boat takes a lot of work. Think of the topsides: There is more sanding than you can imagine, followed by careful priming, additional sanding, an undercoating or two, still more sanding, and finally the application of a smooth, high-gloss topcoat. And when the topsides are done, you should also tackle the deck—a project rendered still more finicky by the need to remove and reinstall deck gear, toerails, and other parts of the boat.

With enough care and perseverance in all of these tasks, you can achieve a boatyard-quality finish, but don't rule out the possibility of getting some help. One cost-effective way of ensuring great results is to do all the prep work yourself but use a professional painter to spray on the final coats. The preparation is far more time-consuming than the final painting.

Whatever route you take in search of that perfect finish, you need to be well informed about three things: (1) safety, (2) sanding, and (3) marine paints and how to apply them. In this final chapter we look at each of these. We have touched on all these subjects in earlier chapters in conjunction with specific projects, so some of the material in this chapter will be familiar to you. But we offer more detail here and gather all aspects of fiberglass finishing in one place. (See also the Chapter 6 discussion of fairing your repair prior to finishing.)

SAFETY

Protecting your lungs is probably the most important part of sanding and painting. You need to wear a dust mask at the very least, and a respirator offers much better protection. If you plan to use spray paint or a paint that contains isocyanates, wearing a respirator with filter cartridges made for this purpose is a must. Otherwise you may seriously damage your lungs.

You should also wear eye protection when sanding, because sanding is a dusty, dirty job that creates airborne particles even when the sander is attached to a vacuum bag. I like to wear a Tyvek suit as well to help keep the sanding dust out of my clothes. Even so, I often need to clean off my clothing with pressurized air after the sanding is done. I use gloves, too, although they do make my hands sweat, which opens pores and allows dust to get into them. For this reason I dry my hands regularly while sanding, and I use a barrier cream to help keep residues off my skin.

160 • FINISHING YOUR REPAIR WORK

Preparing a hull before painting is critical. This hull is being faired with thickened epoxy prior to sanding and priming (1, 2).

SANDING

Sanding is the most critical work you will do to finish a repair on your boat. You need to use paper of the right grit and apply the right amount of pressure for the right amount of time—and at the right speed when you are using a mechanical sander. If you do not sand properly, your efforts may end up doing more harm than good to the look of the finished job.

Selecting a Sandpaper Grit

The proper sandpaper grit depends upon the nature of the work you are doing. There is rough sanding, there is finish sanding, and there are gradations in between. Suppose, for example, that you have just laid down a new laminate using a finishing polyester resin for the last layer. As explained in Chapter 3, this resin contains a wax that rises to the surface of the freshly applied resin to shield it from the air and encourage the resin to cure. Similarly, if you laminate with an epoxy resin, it will form what is known as an amine blush on the laminate surface. The wax or blush needs to be removed before any paint is applied. This entails wiping down the surface with a solvent, then sanding it with a grit of about 100, the idea being to scratch enough tooth into the laminate surface that finishing fillers or a paint layer can adhere easily to it.

For sanding new epoxy surfaces or surfaces with fillers that are otherwise uncoated, AkzoNobel, the company that owns both Awlgrip and Interlux (International Paint outside the U.S.), recommends using a much coarser grade of sandpaper than I would normally use. It suggests a 40-grit paper for a first pass, followed by an epoxy filler and then another sanding with 80- to 120-grit.

If you are simply going to paint your boat's faded gelcoat, AkzoNobel recommends starting with 180-grit. This, too, is coarser than many painters normally use. Most painters recommend using 220- to 320 grit sandpaper to scratch up a gelcoat layer.

The accompanying table won't steer you wrong.

You should also be aware that in Europe, abrasive papers are graded according to a scale established by FEPA (Federation of European Producers of Abrasives), while in America a scale developed by UAMA (United Abrasives Manufacturers' Association) is used. The grit ranges for the two are slightly different, but not much. More information about sanding and painting can be found at Interlux's website, www.yachtpaint.com/usa.

Dry Versus Wet-or-Dry Sanding

Preferences vary regarding dry or wet-or-dry sanding, too. AkzoNobel suggests that dry sanding is better—as long as certain conditions are met—because it enables better contact between the paper and the job, easier recognition of sanded and unsanded areas, and less time spent washing away residues. It also eliminates the risk of applying paint to a damp surface or washing residues into winch grease or other such potentially harmful places.

On the other hand, dry sanding creates dust

Grit	Project
80–120	To prepare a surface for application of fairing compound
120–220	To smooth a faired surface and prepare it for a primer coat
220–320	Between primer coats or between the primer and the first layer of topcoat
320–400	Prior to the final topcoat
400–600	To burnish a racing-smooth finish onto a painted or unpainted hull underbody

Doing a final sanding of primed topsides with a wood block and 400-grit sandpaper. The hull has already been machine sanded with 320-grit. Once this sanding is done, the topsides will be ready for the polyurethane topcoat.

and can clog sandpaper more quickly than wet sanding. I prefer to sand wet because it is less work to move the sandpaper and the sandpaper clogs a lot less.

Be sure that any paint or filler that is about to

Sanding

An assortment of sanders. From left to right in the top row are a 6-inch RIDGID random orbit sander, a 5-inch Bosch random orbit sander, and a less expensive Black and Decker rotary sander. (This machine cost me about one-third as much as the Bosch and the RIDGID and works about one-fifth as well. I can almost stop the sander by pushing down on it.) The quarter-sheet Porter-Cable palm sander is a nice machine when used, as intended, only for finish sanding, as is the Makita palm sander at far right. Beneath the sanders are two longboards, a plastic one from West Marine and an alloy one from Flexicat Tools. After you have finished sanding, use a high-pressure air hose to remove all the dust from the machine. This will prevent dust from settling in the bearings and eventually clogging the machine.

be sanded is perfectly cured. Epoxies and polyesters need at least 24 hours of curing before sanding, even more on cooler days. Allowing a repair to cure for two or three days is even better.

Selecting a Sander

Unless a job is very small, most do-it-yourselfers use electrically powered sanders on their boats. Make sure the machine you use can vacuum dust away from the job. The most common cause of sandpaper breaking down is not that the grit has been abraded away by overuse, but rather that the sanding dust is not removed fast enough and ends up clogging the paper. I have used a 5-inch (13 cm) random orbit sander from Bosch and a 6-inch (15 cm) random orbit sander from RIDGID for a number of years. The filter box attached to the Bosch machine was not very good, however, so I removed it and now attach the suction hose from my shop vacuum to the sander. This means attaching a round hose to a square fitting, which is a hassle. The RIDGID sander, on the other hand, has a round fitting that perfectly fits the RIDGID shop vac. When the sander and shop vac are used in combination, the job is almost free of sanding dust and residues.

A random orbit sander is ideal for finishing

Sanding • 163

(1) My RIDGID 6-inch random orbit sander attached to the RIDGID shop vac. This method may look a little ungainly, but it keeps the job free of sanding dust and residues. You do, however, need to make sure the holes in the sanding disks align with the holes in the sanding pad. (2) Notice how little dust is generated around the sander in use. Even so, the operator is wearing a respirator and eye and ear protection.

repairs. Unlike a conventional orbital sander, which simply spins the sanding disk, a random orbit sander simultaneously spins the disk and moves it along an elliptical path. As a result of this combined action, the sanding disk is constantly varying its movement on the job, and this helps avoid leaving swirl marks behind. If you wish, your final finishing can be done with a vibrating hand, or palm, finish sander. This kind of sander is good for light sanding work, which is useful if you want to avoid the tedium of a lot of hand sanding. In my experience, however, a vibrating sander is not very helpful for coarse sanding.

I've found that inexpensive sanders tend to wear or burn

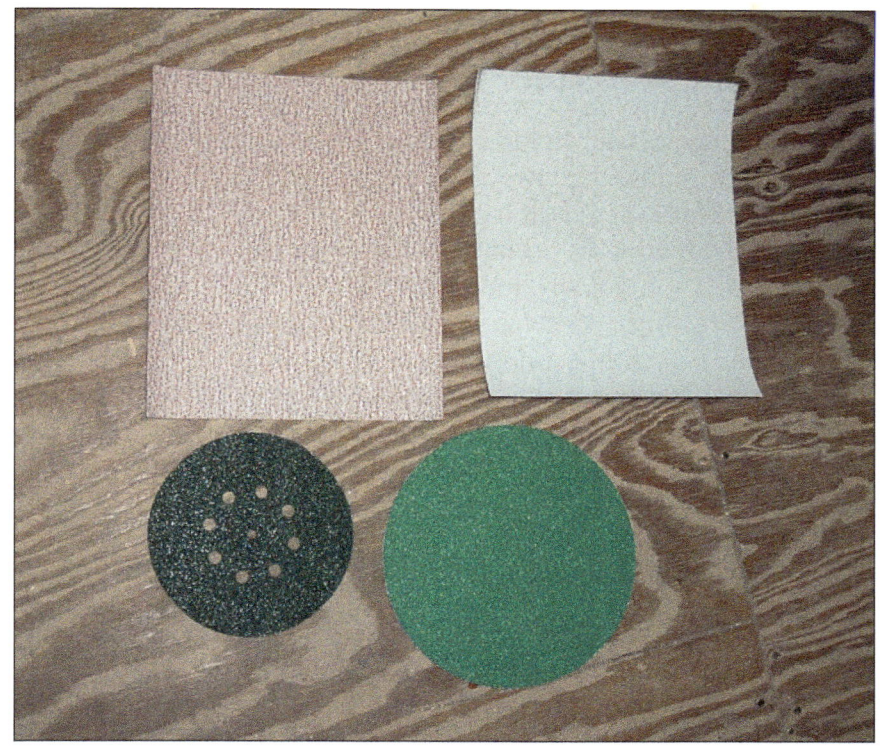

Various sanding discs and papers. The coarse-grit discs for orbital sanders are used for faster cutting but tend to leave swirl marks. Use finer papers (400 to 600) like those at top for final sanding when you want a very smooth racing finish.

Block sanding is a job for the entire family. Here my sons Michael and David are finish sanding the J/24.

out fairly quickly, which can make them cost-*ineffective* in the long run. A more expensive sander, such as the Bosch random orbit sander that I have been using for more than two years, provides good endurance even when used regularly.

Most professionals use air-powered sanders to complete a job quickly and efficiently, but the large compressor needed to operate an air-powered sander makes this option too costly for most do-it-yourselfers. (You need at least a 50-cubic-foot compressor; otherwise, the tool stops sanding until the compressor catches up.) If you do use one, remember that air-powered tools need to be lubricated, and you must be careful not to get lubricant on your sanding job.

A Few Sanding Tips

When using a power sander, try not to press down on the tool. Even though doing so removes a little more material, it also slows down the sander and makes it harder for the tool to work. If you press down too hard and too long, you will burn out the tool or break the connection between the armature and the random orbit disc. I learned this from experience.

Try to keep the sander flat on the surface, and move it in a figure eight rather than a circle. This makes it less likely that you will gouge the material or concentrate too much abrasion in one place.

Stay aware of how much material you have sanded off a surface. Suppose you are sanding a primer coat and get a little too aggressive in spots, leaving a few semi-bare patches. You may end up with slight ridges between the thicker paint layer and the thinner one. You probably can't see these ridges, but you can feel them with your fingertips if you pay close attention while running your hand across the surface. When you later apply the topcoat, these very slight ridges, which you may think wouldn't matter, will suddenly become quite visible. They therefore need to be sanded out. It's usually best to hand sand them using 400-grit paper on a sanding block or a longboard.

Painting • 165

If you plan to race your sailboat, getting the hull and keel extremely fair can be tricky and time-consuming. To do this work, you should acquire one or two longboards. Longboards are good for smoothing a surface over a large area, eliminating the inadvertent humps and hollows that can arise from other kinds of sanding. You can make your own longboard for just a few dollars, or you can purchase a good one for less than $100. (See page 62 for more on longboards.)

PAINTING

So you've sanded the topsides and think they are ready for primer. Not so fast! When the boat is coated with a glossy topcoat, the slightest imperfection will show up in the right light. Once you've completed the finish sanding with 220-grit paper, run your fingers gently over the hull, checking for any slight imperfections. Look for tiny ridges where filler went on a little thicker than the area next to it. Try to find every small scratch or ding and fill them with a thickened epoxy fairing compound. Wait 24 hours for the epoxy to dry and then sand these areas flush. Again check for any imperfections. If you find any, repeat the process. Finally, sand everything smooth. Only then are the topsides ready for primer, and only when you have sanded the primer coat (or the first layer of topcoat following the primer) smooth yet again with 320- to 400-grit will it be time to apply the final topcoat, either by spraying or rolling.

Masking Off

You will need to mask off the parts of the hull that you do not want painted. This is especially critical if you spray, because overspray travels everywhere. The usual approach when painting topsides is to mask off the deck edge and somewhere

(1) *The primed hull of the J/24 has been sanded and the boottop has been masked.* **(2)** *Here a rubrail is being masked off on a different boat.*

below the boottop so that the hull bottom does not get painted.

To mask off the deck edge, first go around it with a single strip of 1- to 2-inch-wide (25 to 50 mm) painter's masking tape (ordinary household or office masking tape is unsatisfactory for this job). Concentrate on getting the tape perfectly straight and covering the edges perfectly. The edge of the tape will define the edge of the new paint layer, so you do not want any wobbles or wavy edges. In most jobs you wind up masking twice, once for the primer coat and once for the topcoat, because the sanding you must do between coats is likely to burr the masking-tape edge. The masking tape for the topcoat needs to be about $1/16$ inch (2 mm) above the nominal paint edge to get a perfect seal. For example, where a topside meets a teak toerail, you would want a $1/32$- to $1/16$-inch (1 to 2 mm) width of wood showing. "If not," a professional painter told me, "you might see the white edge of the primer coat peeking out from beneath the topcoat." To get this width showing you may have to go around the edge of the toerail (or other abutting edge) and cut the tape with a razor blade. Don't begrudge the work, because the final result will justify it.

To prevent overspray from getting on the deck, it is wise to cover the deck with plastic or paper. Most marine paint outfitters sell 2- or 4-mil plastic for protecting against overspray.

With the first layer of tape in place, tape your plastic covering to the first masking tape layer. This allows you to make a slightly wavy edge with the plastic covering tape and still get a perfectly straight paint edge.

Make sure that your plastic or paper covering cannot be sucked down over the wet paint. Often a loose covering may be sucked toward the spray gun when it is spraying. If this were to happen, the loose covering could land on the new paint layer and make a mess. If you are protecting a trailer or the boat's bottom from overspray, tape the plastic at the boottop and to the trailer to make sure it cannot fly upward. Duct tape is sufficient to hold plastic to a trailer. Finally, check that there are no breaches that could permit overspray to get through, under, or around the cover. These include cockpit drain holes, gaps or holes in the plastic, the mast hole, and even tiny chainplate bolt holes. Mask them all.

Applying and Sanding a Primer

You can roll or spray on a primer coat of paint. Spraying makes it easier to get an even layer of paint. I usually use Interlux's Epoxy Primekote, a two-part paint, because I have gotten good results and am comfortable with it, but you can use any primer that is compatible with your choice of topcoat. After the primer is thoroughly dry, it should be sanded with 320- to 400-grit sandpaper to provide enough tooth for topcoat adherence (or with 220- to 320-grit if the next coat of paint will not be the final topcoat). This work can be done with a random orbit sander, a vibrating sander, or a hand-sanding block. As mentioned earlier, always be on the lookout for any tiny ridges, which may be thinner than a thin sheet of paper. These should be sanded away with a sanding board using 400-grit paper. If you leave the slightest edge between a heavier layer of paint and a thinner layer, it will show up in the finish coat.

You should do all sanding in a fore-and-aft direction so that any slight marks are in the horizontal rather than the vertical plane. This makes it harder to see the marks after the topcoat is applied. The ultimate goal is a perfectly smooth topside and a paint gloss that shows no ripples, "orange peel" (tiny bumps), or streaking. This can only be achieved with a lot of hard work and attention to detail.

After sanding the primer coat, as mentioned, you will need to apply a new layer of masking tape for the topcoat. Small nicks left in the masking tape by sanding can ruin the appearance of an otherwise perfect finish.

Blowing Off and Wiping Down

Before you can apply a topcoat, you should blow all the dust and dirt off the masked-off boat. Use a pressure air hose and literally "wash" the boat with air to get rid of dust. Pay particular attention to the hull and deck edges, where dust can lurk.

Painting • 167

We rolled and tipped the primer coat on my son's J/24 to save the expense of having it professionally sprayed. The unevenness of the rolled-on paint required a lot of sanding, however, so I would have sprayed it were I to do it again.

When the boat has been blown clean of dust, it will need to be wiped down with solvent. Use the solvent that is used to thin the paint or DuPont's Prep-Sol. Wear rubber kitchen gloves when applying solvent to keep it off your skin, and wear a respirator. Do not touch a surface after you have wiped it, as even the slight amount of oil on your skin will leave a mark in the finish coat.

(1) Sanding a primed hull and deck to prepare them for the topcoat. (2) A boat primed and ready for a topcoat.

Applying a Topcoat

There are two ways to apply a topcoat. You can roll and tip it on, or you can spray it. In the first method, one person rolls on the paint using a fine-nap foam roller and a second person "tips" the wet paint by lightly running the dry tip of a high-quality bristle brush over the job. Roll with vertical strokes, followed immediately by horizontal roller strokes, and then tip with vertical strokes from one masked edge to the other. Tipping removes the marks left

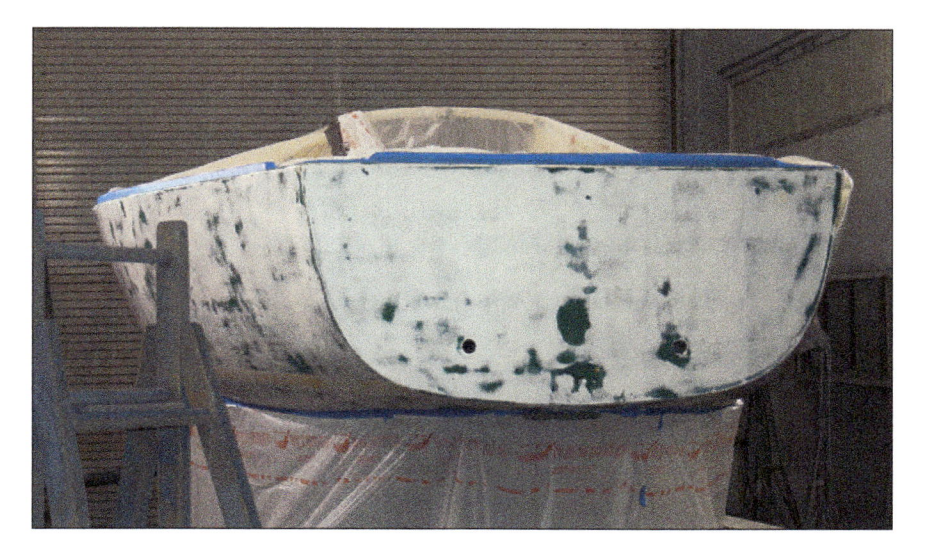

The J/24 hull has been blown off and wiped down with DuPont's Prep-Sol and is ready for spraying. At this point the cleaning crew should either leave the area or don respirators.

168 • FINISHING YOUR REPAIR WORK

Spraying a topcoat in a dedicated enclosed space called a spray booth. Even though the spray booth fans are running full tilt, there is still enough overspray to cloud the booth. The photographer was wearing a respirator when taking this picture, and you should not go into a spray booth without one.

by the roller and smoothes out the paint. (See below for greater detail.) When rolling and tipping is done properly, the paint layer is thicker and more consistent than a layer that is sprayed on. A professional-looking roll-and-tip job takes practice, however. When learning the technique, you should practice on a less obvious surface than your boat's topsides.

The second method of applying topside paint is spraying. You should thin the paint enough that it can be fired through a compressed-air spray gun. You should not spray a topside paint using a high-volume, low-density (HVLD) sprayer. Instead, you should use more conventional spraying equipment with a pot-type gun and a conventional air compressor.

Make sure you have more than enough paint on hand, and enough thinner not only to thin the paint but to clean up the spray gun and other tools. If you use up one can of paint and open another midway through

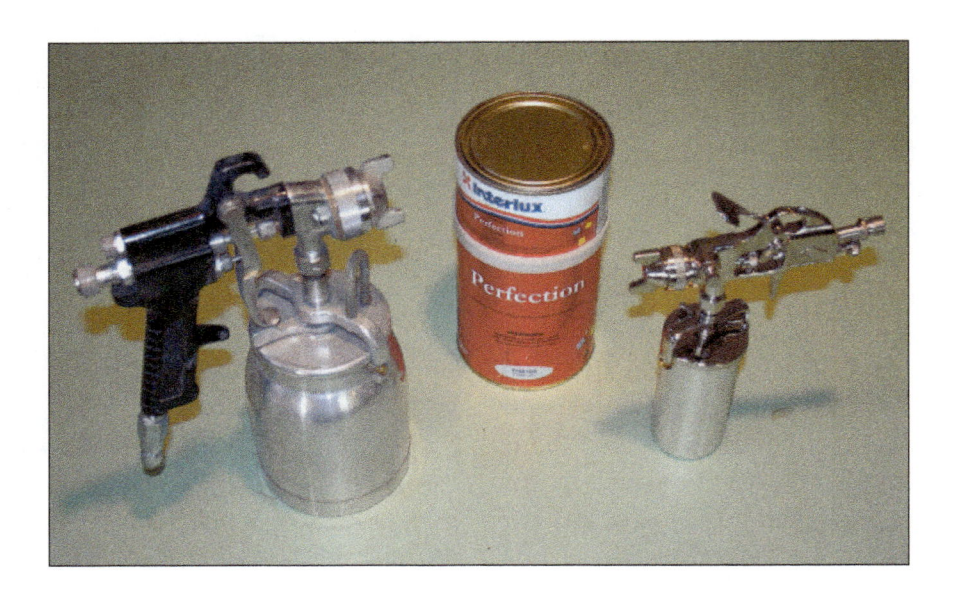

My spray guns almost ready for use. A regular gun on the left and a detail spray gun on the right. They still need to be connected to air hoses. The drop in pressure you experience through an air hose will depend on the length of the hose—use the shortest hose possible.

the job, you may end up with a small but still noticeable variation in the color of the finished topsides because the paints came from different batch lots. Professionals eliminate such differences by pouring all the cans of paint into one bucket and mixing them together to get a consistent color.

Rolling and Tipping Versus Spraying

Whether you can get a better finish with a roller and brush or with a spray gun is much debated. Long-time spray operators say the best paintwork is done with a spray gun. Expert brush painters say you can get a better, longer-lasting finish by applying the topcoat with a roller and brush. The truth of the matter is that a good spray operator and a good brush painter will both get a superb job.

According to Hans Devilee, head of the paint shop at De Vries Shipbuilding, preparation is what counts. "If you don't prepare the job properly, you will never get a good paint finish," he says. "You need to take special care that the hull is faired smooth, that it is clean, that the temperatures are correct, and that the painter knows how to do a good job." Devilee should know, because De Vries has worked with most major paint manufacturers and has a reputation for producing the best brush-painted hulls in the business.

A roller and brush, used well, can give you a thicker paint layer than you can obtain by spraying, and one without orange peel or other imperfections. A thicker paint layer lasts longer and maintains a better gloss than a sprayed-on layer does. Moreover, brush-painting reduces the need for masking and problems of overspray.

Brush-painting, however, is a learned art that requires practice. To get a good, smooth, high-gloss finish with no runs or streaks takes time and experience. You should apply the coat horizontally or vertically (often vertically with a fine foam roller, as noted above) and then smooth it with strokes at 90 degrees to the application strokes (i.e., using horizontal strokes if the paint was applied with vertical strokes). Then tip the wet paint using a dry badger-hair brush. Because lifting the brush off the paint surface will often leave a slight mark, most painters tip from one masked edge to the other—i.e., from sheer to boottop. Temperature also plays a large part in getting perfect results. If the hull is too cool, the paint takes a long time to dry and will sag or run. If the hull is too hot, the paint will set before the next area can be painted, leaving dry edges in the finish. The only cure for these problems is to sand the paint layer off and start over.

Details matter greatly. Brush type and size are critical, according to Devilee. "The brush should be no more than 10 cm (4 inches) wide," he says. He likes to use badger hair or similar high-quality brushes. If you elect to apply the paint with a foam roller and then tip it with a high-quality brush, be sure the roller doesn't leave bubbles in the paint—if it does, the result can be a surface that resembles orange peel. Some painters use good-quality foam brushes instead of rollers to apply the paint, but everyone agrees that the final tipping must be done with a quality bristle brush, and badger hair is often the preferred bristle.

I once saw Michael Herman, of Masterbrush, demonstrate the difference between a high-quality badger-hair brush and a less expensive brush. The badger-hair brush held a generous load of paint and had fine bristles that left a smooth finish. The less expensive brush did not have as thick a layer of bristles, could hold a good load of paint, and may tend to drop hairs into the paint layer. Herman showed me how brushes made by his company have the bristles secured in a layer of epoxy so that they cannot pull out of the brush handle.

Boero Yacht Paint (www.boeroyachtpaint.com) publishes a very good instruction manual on how to brush-paint a boat. It echoes the need to use high-quality brushes that are resistant to the solvents and thinners used in polyurethane products. Top-quality bristle brushes are recommended. Round and oval-shaped brushes are best used on difficult curved surfaces, with flat brushes doing well on flat areas. When applying Boero's Challenger topcoats with a brush, use Challenger HI-Tech catalyst in a ratio of 2:1 with the company's brush catalyzer. Catalyzed products last between 8 and 12 hours, depending on the ambient temperature, so mix only what you need for the day. Before adding the compatible thinner, wait about 15 minutes for the paint to mix properly and for the correct viscosity to be achieved. You need to brush on two coats, allowing 12 to 14 hours between coats. To apply the paint, make your strokes at 45 degrees to vertical (northeast to southwest) and then work in the other direction (northwest to southeast). Tip off vertically to minimize brush marks and make it easy to clean the paint surface. You'll need to repeat this procedure for each layer of paint. To obtain a smooth finish coat, Boero recommends that you sand between coats using 320- to 400-grit sandpaper.

Again, because paints vary slightly from batch to batch, a good painter will combine paint from different batches so that no variation shows up in the job. This mixed paint is not savable after the job is done, but you can save a quart from the original batch to touch up any problem areas later.

Paint Matters

The time to choose a topcoat is before you apply the primer coat, since the primer coat and topcoat must be compatible. To ensure compatibility, stick with one manufacturer's products from beginning to end.

I can see no reason to choose anything other than a two-part polyurethane for a topside topcoat. Yes, you can use a traditional marine alkyd enamel—developed in the days of wooden boats—on a fiberglass topside and obtain acceptable results, but the finished job will not have the gloss, durability, longevity, and outright beauty of a two-part polyurethane. You can also choose a single-part modified urethane—Brightside, from Interlux, is one example—and the result will be a step up from a marine alkyd enamel. But in my experience single-part urethanes are runny and leave sags and drips on the topsides. Once you're ready for the topcoat, you've done 90% of the work—so why not reward yourself by choosing the best possible paint?

Choose a two-part polyurethane that is readily available and formulated with do-it-yourself application in mind. For example, Awlgrip is the best-known two-part polyurethane topside paint but is meant to be sprayed by professionals who have been trained to use it. Other two-part polyurethanes, such as Perfection, from Interlux, can be used by do-it-yourselfers to obtain excellent results. I suggest that you go with the paint whose manufacturer gives you the best support and the least cleanup problems. Lest you think I am biased, I have had the most experience with Awlgrip

Various rollers used to apply topcoats. The foam rollers shown here are designed for marine paints and will not fall apart. The nylon rollers (pale green) are best used for nonskid.

This topcoat application is proceeding toward the camera. The paint is rolled on with a foam roller, then tipped with a good-quality brush. (Courtesy Interlux)

Mixing Perfection (two-part polyurethane paint) prior to spraying. The paint goes on easily but needs to be thinned for spraying. The painter is wearing heavy-duty kitchen gloves to mix the paint and is emptying several cans into one bucket to eliminate any slight variations in color from one can to the next.

Painting • 171

and Perfection and have better knowledge of them than other manufacturers' products. Both paints, I believe, yield a better finish when sprayed, even though Perfection is formulated with roller-and-brush application in mind. I have often chosen to do the prep work myself and then have had the finish coat sprayed by a professional.

Painting with Perfection

Perfection is Interlux's two-part polyurethane topside paint that is specially formulated for brush-painting a boat. This makes it ideally suited for the do-it-yourselfer who lacks spray-painting equipment. Perfection, however, is not just for brush work. It can also be sprayed. I have sprayed it and brushed it and the finish was excellent either way, with terrific depth of shine and a very high gloss.

Spraying on Perfection

Having faired, primed, and sanded the topsides of a 22-foot sailboat of my design, I decided to investigate what it would look like if the topside topcoat was sprayed on by a professional. So I asked nearby Jamestown Boat Yard, in Rhode Island, to do the job using Perfection. "It goes on really easily, and the gloss is terrific," said Xavier Martinez after completing the job. "It reminds me of the old Interspray 900 in how it goes on, but the gloss is much better." Martinez also commented on Perfection's good flow and lack of sag. Left in a warm

(1) *The hull after being sprayed with its first coat of Perfection. Note the high-gloss finish and the shine of the Perfection paint.* **(2)** *The finished hull.*

paint shop, Perfection set up quickly—faster than Awlgrip, according to Martinez—and once the boat was moved outside, it became apparent that Perfection's depth of shine is unmatched by many other paints.

Brushing on Perfection

I have also used Perfection to brush-paint a sportfishing boat with the roll-and-tip method. I found it best to use a yellow foam roller with a fairly light load of paint, because a heavy load caused the roller to slide. I used a good-quality dry brush for the tipping, dragging it lightly across the paint in a fore-and-aft direction. I then made the final brushstrokes vertically from the masking tape at the deck down to the masking tape at the boottop. This took virtually all the brush marks out of the paint. Tipping can be done as the paint cures in order to eliminate any sags or runs, but beware of letting the paint get too dry before working on it. If working alone, you must work fast to maintain a wet paint edge.

The Perfection went on easily without thinning, and it initially looked very smooth. But the

HULL PAINTING CHECKLIST

1. Before you start painting a hull, make sure you have all the required paint, safety gear, and disposables at hand.
2. Check the ambient, surface, and dew point temperatures as well as the temperature of the paint. (Store the paint for 24 hours in the same environment as the boat you are painting to ensure that the temperatures do not differ greatly.) The hull temperature should be at least 3°C (about 5.5°F) above the dew point. If not, water may start to condense on the newly painted surface.
3. Check that the fairing compound has been applied properly. Any fillers should be faired and sanded until a smooth layer is achieved. The final sanding grit to prepare for the primer coat should be 150 to 220.
4. Clean the area with a suitable solvent. Some paint manufacturers do not recommend using acetone for this purpose. Acetone is a fast-drying solvent and may not remove all the impurities as well as a slower-drying solvent will. For example, Awlgrip users work with Surface Cleaner T340, not with acetone.
5. Apply at least two layers of undercoat. If Interlux's Perfection is being used as a topcoat, Interlux suggests that you use its two-part epoxy Primekote as the first undercoat. You can then use Perfection topcoat paint or Primekote for the second layer of undercoat. If the topcoat will be Awlgrip, the undercoat should be Awlquick or Awlgrip's 545 Epoxy Primer.
6. For the finish sanding before the final topcoat, you should use 320- to 400-grit sandpaper.
7. Again, wipe the hull with a solvent to ensure that it is perfectly clean. When applying the topcoat, suspend other work around the boat so that dust is not stirred up. Many yards damp down the paint shop floor to keep dust from becoming airborne.
8. Check the hull temperature again to ensure that it is still above the dew point. The best temperature for painting a hull is between 21°C and 30°C (70°F and 86°F). Awlgrip products, for example, cure slowly below 18°C (65°F) and should never be applied below 13°C (55°F).
9. When painting, it is critical to keep a wet edge to the paint layer so that the entire job meshes seamlessly.
10. Tipping with a dry brush is essential for paintwork that is not sprayed. This can be done in several ways:

    - If two people are working together, one of them can roll on the paint with a foam roller, applying it with vertical and then rerolling with horizontal strokes. The second person then uses a dry high-quality bristle brush to tip off the paint layer, stroking from bottom to top or from top to bottom. If the brush is lifted off the job on the masking tape, you can get a good finish when the tape is removed. Do not tip horizontally, or the mark where the brush is lifted will show.
    - If you are working alone, you can apply the paint vertically with a high-quality brush, followed by working across the surface horizontally with the same brush. Then tip off vertically with a dry badger-hair brush as explained above.
    - A third way to do the job is to apply the paint with a high-quality foam brush and then tip off with a dry badger-hair brush.

11. The final paint layer should be at least 45 to 60 microns thick. Awlgrip and other paint manufacturers recommend 50 to 75 microns. Since Awlgrip brushes on to a maximum of 40 microns per coat, two coats are recommended, with a minimum of 12 to 14 hours at 20°C (68°F) between coats. For sprayed finishes, the layers of which may be only 25 to 30 microns thick, it is recommended that two to three coats be applied over 1 to 4 hours at 20°C (68°F).

shop was cool, about 60°F, so the paint did not cure quickly and consequently some sags formed. These were not much of a problem, however. It was relatively easy to sand the sags out of the hardened paint and repaint the affected areas. Later I painted another boat with Perfection using the roll-and-tip method in a temperature of 80°F, and this time sagging was much less of a problem.

I have been very happy with the finish on all my Perfection-painted boats. My spray-painted boat looks better than my brush-painted ones, but the brush-painted results are nevertheless very attractive. The finish coat has a high gloss that is pleasing, and you can clean it by just wiping it down.

> ## DEW POINT
>
> The *dew point* is the temperature at which cooling air becomes saturated with moisture. At this point, water vapor condenses into liquid and dew begins to form. A general rule for painting is that the temperature of the surface being painted should be at least 3°C (about 5.5°F) above the dew point. If the temperature is lower than this, you risk having water condense on the freshly painted surface.
>
> At a relative humidity of 85%, the lowest acceptable hull temperature for brush-painting is equal to the ambient temperature. For this reason, you should not paint outdoors when the relative humidity is above 85%.

Painting a Previously Painted Surface

It is not difficult to apply paint over a previously painted surface that you have repaired. After fairing and sanding, cover the area to be repainted with a layer of primer. Then sand it fair with 320- to 400-grit sandpaper to give it a smooth, matte finish, and wipe down the surface with a solvent. I use Interlux's Reducing Solvent 2333N, which can also be used to thin paint and clean up messes after painting. Many painters use DuPont's Prep-Sol, which is specially formulated to clean topsides. If you wipe down the job with acetone instead, the acetone may evaporate and dry before you have a chance to wipe away the unwanted wax or grease. It also softens the existing paint surface. In any case, make sure that the entire surface is free of wax, grease, and oil before painting. If in doubt, spread a little water on the surface. If it beads up, you need to wipe it down again with a solvent.

Once you have a clean, sanded surface, the next step is to apply a first layer of topcoat. You can thin the paint a little if you wish. A thinner paint will go on easier and give you a smoother finish, but you will need to apply two or three layers. Sand before applying each layer of topcoat. Continue the process until you are happy that the repaired area matches the remainder of the hull. If you cannot obtain an acceptable match, you will have to repaint the entire side of the boat rather than just the repaired portion.

Painting a Boottop and Cove Stripe

Once the topsides are painted, the last job is often to paint the boottop and the cove stripe. The boottop is difficult to mask off without a very long batten. Before we started refinishing the J/24 topsides, we took measurements from the deck edge to the marked waterline at several points along the hull. Sanding, fairing, and painting the topsides removed the existing boottop, so we positioned a long, flexible batten on the waterline measurements we had recorded, then drew the waterline with a pencil.

We applied masking tape around the hull at the waterline, putting the bottom of the 1-inch (25 mm) tape on the line. We wanted a 2-inch-wide (50 mm) boottop stripe parallel to the waterline, so we cut a piece of card stock to 2 inches wide and carefully set it on the top edge of the masking tape, making marks every 6 to 12 inches (15 to 30 cm). Using the long batten, we then drew a line and applied tape around the top of the stripe.

The next job was to sand the beautiful, freshly

applied topsides paint in the boottop area (delineated by the two strips of masking tape) with 320- to 400-grit sandpaper. This roughed up the surface enough to provide good tooth for the boottop paint. We then wiped down the boottop area with a solvent and tack rag to remove all sanding residues.

Now we were ready for painting. I mixed Perfection and worked around the boottop painting the stripe with a good-quality brush. Because the paint was white and the hull blue, it took two coats to get a satisfactory finish. To avoid brush marks in the paint, I found that it was best to start under the transom where the paint edge would not be seen. Then I painted forward in 2-foot (61 cm) increments, finishing each section by stroking the brush from the leading edge toward the starting point. With this technique, the brush left no marks where it was applied to the surface. Perfection dries so fast that by the time I had painted around the entire hull, I could keep going and apply the second coat.

We decided not to paint a cove stripe on this boat, but if you do paint a cove stripe that is not molded into the hull, you will need to use a similar technique to that outlined above. First make your measurements, then stand back and take a look at them. If you are happy with what you see, mask off the area and check it again before painting. Sand, wipe with a solvent and tack rag, then paint with a good-quality brush.

Finishing a Deck

After you have repaired or modified a deck—whether you installed a new hatch, repaired rotten deck core, or made some other improvement—you will need to repaint it, and in places you'll need to replace the nonskid. It is best to remove all deck gear prior to painting, but you can work around hardware if you mask it off carefully.

The glossy parts of a deck—areas free of nonskid—can be finished in the same way as the topsides. Sand them down, undercoat them, and then paint them either with a brush (roll and tip) or by spraying. Paint the glossy sections first, and don't worry about cutting a sharp edge along the transitions to nonskid. I typically paint about an inch into the nonskid areas to ensure that there will be no gaps between the high-gloss and nonskid paints when the job is done.

When the paint in the glossy areas has hardened, mask off the nonskid sections. Use good-quality painter's masking tape, and do not leave it on the job for more than a day or it might stick permanently, especially if you are working under a hot sun. To mask a corner properly, lay tape over the corner and use a razor knife to cut the proper corner radius. Depending on the radius you want to use, you can cut against a quarter, a roll of tape, or some other round object to ensure that each corner is identical. After the deck has been masked off, wipe the areas to be painted with a solvent to ensure that they are free of grease and oil. Avoid walking in these areas prior to painting.

Nonskid Commercial Paints and Home Formulations

You have three options for nonskid paint. The first is to buy a paint such as Interlux's Interdeck, which contains a nonskid compound; the second is to mix nonskid compound into an ordi-

Painting a boottop with Brightside, a single-part modified urethane paint. Notice how the top and bottom of the stripe are masked off. Nothing beats a two-part polyurethane for a topside paint, but two-part paints are hard to mix properly in the small quantities required for jobs such as a boottop. Single-part paints are convenient for such jobs.

Interlux's Interdeck is easy to apply and offsets the look of the white deck edges. Mask off all edges with painter's masking tape (do not use ordinary household masking tape for this), wipe the deck with a solvent prior to painting, and paint from stern to bow. You do not want to trap yourself in the cockpit, surrounded by wet paint.

nary boat paint; and the third is to paint the deck, sprinkle a nonskid compound over the wet paint, and then apply a second layer.

Of the three options, using a commercial nonskid paint is by far the easiest, but not very many colors are available, and you might not be able to get exactly the shade you want. If that's an issue, you may have to buy a standard boat paint and add nonskid compound. Interlux offers Intergrip, a white powdery polymeric compound that can be added to any paint in the Interlux line to turn it into a nonskid paint. You can add Intergrip to the paint while it is still in the can, or punch holes in the top of the Intergrip can and sprinkle it onto the freshly painted deck. Let the paint dry overnight and vacuum up the loose polymeric compound before applying a second coat of paint. If you add Intergrip you should probably add a flattener to the paint, too, to remove the high-gloss component. You don't want your nonskid to be glossy and slippery, after all!

To make your own formulation, you can apply a one- or two-part polyurethane paint, sprinkle sand or ground walnut shells into the freshly applied paint, and then apply a second coat of paint. Do not use beach sand, which might contain salt that would degrade the paint. And remember that sand can work like sandpaper on your foul-weather gear and quickly wear it away. Furthermore, sand does not absorb paint and tends to break out of the paint layer after moderate use. Some yards use ground walnut shells, but these can give a brownish cast to the paint.

If you use Pettit's Easypoxy (a topside and deck enamel paint), you need to add Pettit Skidless Compound 9900 to the paint before applying it to get a nonskid finish, and you must stir the paint often to keep the nonskid compound in suspension. Pettit recommends two coats of paint when the nonskid compound is used.

An alternative to painting is to apply a layer of pigmented gelcoat with a high-nap roller. Use a 3/16-inch-nap (4 mm) nylon roller over carefully masked-off areas when applying gelcoat, as described in Chapter 4. The latest method of renewing gelcoated nonskid is to use Flex-Mold, again as explained in Chapter 4.

If you have only a small area to cover, you might not want to paint it. You can use strips of 3M Safety-Walk General Purpose Surfacing S-124,

176 • FINISHING YOUR REPAIR WORK

The deck of my son's J/24 freshly painted with Interlux's Interdeck gray nonskid and white Perfection. A good paint job can increase the appearance and value of your boat far beyond anything else you can do.

which comes in 60-foot (18 m) rolls and widths from ¾ inch (19 mm) to 6 inches (15 cm). This product has abrasive mineral particles bonded to a durable polymer film with a pressure-sensitive adhesive on the back. To use it, cut the desired length from the roll, peel off the protective liner, and press it into place. To improve the looks of the tape and to prevent its corners from peeling upward after a season or two of use, you should round off each corner before pressing the tape down. Safety-Walk is particularly useful on ladders, narrow steps, and Plexiglas or acrylic hatch covers that are likely to be walked on.

Another product is Treadmaster M, which has terrific nonskid properties even when submerged. It comes in sheets 47½ inches (1 m) long by 35½ inches (90 cm) wide and about ⅛ inch (3 mm) thick. You permanently glue it down where you would normally paint nonskid. Available colors are white sand, gray, teak, and sport white. The only caveat is that covering a full deck with Treadmaster M will add appreciable weight.

A professional deck finish requires careful attention to detail, the right choice of materials, and plenty of time. You can glue a nonskid strip virtually anywhere. You can do your own painting using paint from Interlux, U.S. Paint, or any other manufacturer. You can use sand, polymeric compound, or ground walnut shells, but to get a high-quality job that will enhance the value of your boat and last for many years, you need to pay attention to the details.

Appendix: Building a Shelter

Finding a place to work on a boat is a challenge since many boats are too large to fit into a garage. My Seacraft, for example, was exactly 2 inches too wide to go into my garage, so I had to build a temporary shed to house it while I worked on it. Over the years I have built several boat sheds and learned from the construction of each. The first was a simple hoop-house-style shed and, at 14 feet wide and 20 feet long, barely had enough headroom to work on the boat. That shed lasted exactly one season. Next was a larger shed covered with construction polyethylene. That one lasted one week until a 50-mph gale blew the polyethylene off the building. I recovered the polyethylene, and the shed lasted until the next gale blew the cover off again. I recovered it once more, only to have the whole affair collapse in a heavy snowfall.

The third shed was a more robust affair covered with shrink-wrap (www.dr-shrink.com). Once the shrink-wrap was heated and tensioned the entire shed became extremely sturdy and has lasted through an entire winter complete with three heavy gales and several feet of snow. When it snows, I bang the underside of the cover from inside the shed, forcing the snow to slide off the slippery surface. A drawback of a shrink-wrap shed is that it stays moist inside—installing a simple vent at each end removes the moisture. (It was so wet that when using a propane torch to shrink the covering, we generated a fog inside the shed!)

The first of the temporary boat sheds. Note that the shed has to be taken apart to get the boat out! We put the boat on the old garage foundation and built the boat shed afterward. This shed was constructed by driving 3-foot (about one meter) lengths of rebar into the ground outside the foundation and spaced 3 feet (about one meter) apart so that only 1 foot (0.3 m) of rebar was showing. On top of the rebar 10 foot (about three meter) lengths of hollow 1-inch (25 mm) plastic water pipe was bent over and linked with + fittings across the top. A centerline pipe was cut into 3-foot (0.3 m) sections and installed between the arches. At the bottom a 2 x 6 (50 mm x 15 cm) plank was clamped to the pipe to form a perimeter.

The framework was covered with construction polyethylene that was fastened to the bottom planking with strips of 1 x 2 (approximately 25 mm x 50 mm) scrap wood. The entire structure was not very strong and tended to wave around in the breeze. In high winds the cover flapped heavily and tended to rip, but duct tape fixed most rips. We finally ran heavy string from side to side over the plastic cover to stop it flapping around, which helped to prolong the life of the shed.

178 • Building a Shelter

The second shed, made of 2 x 4s (50 mm x 10 cm) and 10 feet (about 3 m) high at the sides. The ridge was 14 feet (4.2 m) off the ground. The first covering arch of plastic pipe was a dismal failure: as soon as it snowed, the pipe inverted, forming a well for the snow. To remove the snow we heated the shed, making a hole in the cover for melted snow to drain. In the next storm the cover promptly blew off anyway.

The final shrink-wrap boat shed. This one turned out to be very rigid, cost a few hundred dollars, and provided a good light working environment. It was made of 2 x 4s (50 mm x 10 cm), 12 feet (about 3.6 m) long at the side. The center arches were built on the ground and lifted into place. The ridge pole is 16 feet (4.9 m) high and was difficult to install without a large ladder. The entire structure was covered with shrink-wrap, which was then heated to shrink it. Once the skin was shrunk, the building became strong and tight and so far has lasted two winters. **(1)** *The wooden structure being built and braced.* **(2)** *The finished wooden structure before covering.* **(3, 4)** *Framing up the roof joists: in the middle of the joist we used a centerline vertical to support the ridge pole and two short lengths of wood*

Building a Shelter • 179

to hold the ridgepole in place as shown. **(5, 6)** Laying the shrink-wrap over the frame until it is completely over the building. **(7)** After heating, the covering became taut as shown. Our biggest problem was setting the rafters without an adequately tall ladder. **(8)** To make this easy we blocked the rafter as shown to hold the sides apart. Once the rafters were set up, they were nailed in place. Adding cross bracing helped strengthen the structure against the wind. The shed was built by one person in two days, plus another three hours to shrink the covering. Two people could easily do this project in one day.

(9) The interior of the boat shed with a 22-footer (6.7 m) to my own design being worked on and the Seacraft 18. The remains of the shrink-wrap roll can be seen in the middle of the shed; along the right wall we built a rack for a sailboat mast and various dinghy rigs.

Index

A

acetone, 50, 54, 56, 62, 77, 78, 172
Airex PXc, 19
AkzoNovel, 160–61
alligatoring, 43. *See also* crazing
aramid fibers and core, 13, 20, 93
autoclaving, 12–13, 15, 16, 17
Avid powerboat, 2–6, 22
Awlfair, 76, 79, 107
Awlgrip paints, 132, 170–71, 172

B

balsa-cored hulls and decks
    construction of, 5, 16, 19, 25
    core materials, 19, 20
    core replacement, 123–25
    damage, signs of, 29
    grounding damage repairs, 143–49
    hardware installation, 17–18, 94–97
Baltek, 19
barrier coats, 108, 110, 111, 151, 158
Bio-Solv, 56, 62, 63, 76, 77
blisters and osmosis
    barrier coats, 108, 110, 111, 151, 158
    causes of, 9, 40, 150
    DIY repairs, 40, 150–51
    liquid in, 40, 150
    peeling the hull, 40, 151, 153, 154, 157
    preventing, 48, 68, 151, 158
    professional repairs, 40, 151–56
    puncturing, 40, 150
    resin types and, 9, 14, 40, 48, 68, 157
    signs of, 40
    surveying hull, 150
Boero Yacht Paint, 169–70
boron fibers, 13
bottom paint, 79, 110–11
brushes, 54, 55, 169
buffer, electric, 72, 73
buffing (rubbing) compound, 67, 68, 70–72, 74, 75
bulkheads
    damage to, 44–45
    drains and limber holes, 100
    hard spots on hull from, 97, 98
    hull construction, 20–21, 24
    repairing or installing, 44–45, 97–100

C

Captain's Choice Deck Grip paint, 175–76
carbon fiber, 12–13, 15, 37, 46, 93, 101
ceiling, 25
centerboards, 79–80, 81
chopper gun, 9, 10
cockpits, 43
coffee-can joint, 27, 28
compression tubes, 96, 97, 121, 122
computer-controlled routers, 8
Conanicut Marine, 143–49
Corecell, 19
cored decks. *See also* balsa-cored hulls and decks; delamination; foam-cored hulls
    characteristics of, 86
    compression tubes, 96, 97
    core materials, 19–20, 93, 96, 97
    core replacement, 123–25
    damage to, 40–43
    filling holes in, 26–27
    hardware installation, 26, 42–43, 94–97
    removing core, 96, 97
    repairing and renovating, 27, 93–94
    sealing core edges, 94–95, 97
cored hulls. *See also* delamination
    construction methods, 16–18
    core materials, 18, 19–20, 93
    damage, signs of, 29, 30
    delamination repairs, 16
    hardware installation, 17–18

outer skin/inner skin ratio, 86
repairing, 93–94, 125–33, 143–49
through-hull installation, 17–18
corner-radius tool, 60–62
cracks, 29
crazing, 32, 43, 67, 78–79
CRC boat-care products, 69, 70, 73
custom boats, 2

D

DAP, 19
Davis boat-care products, 69–70
decks, 123–25. *See also* cored decks
construction of, 25–27
damage, 40–43
hull-to-deck joints, 27–28
nonskid surfaces, 46, 80, 82–84, 174–76
painting, 80, 84, 174–75
repairing, 46
delamination
impact damage, 31–32, 42
repairing, 16, 35, 38
signs of, 35, 36, 43
testing for, 36–37
Devilee, Hans, 169
De Vries Shipbuilding, 169
dew point, 172, 173
Diab Group, 19
dings and scrapes, 32, 34–54, 75–78, 81
Divinycell, 19
D. L. Blount Associates, 8
dock box, 105
Dremel tool, 59–60
DuPont, 13, 173
dust masks and respirators, 54, 56, 60, 61, 70, 159

E

Eagle One NanoWax, 73
E glass, 12, 46–47
engine-well guard, 117–19
Epiglass epoxy, 14, 50, 53, 63
epoxy
additives and thickeners, 50–53, 63, 64
benefits and limitations of, 48, 49, 50
blisters and osmosis, 68
cost of, 48, 49
fiberglass suitable for, 48
filling and fairing compounds, 80, 81, 107, 110, 113, 132, 165
gelcoat and, 9, 48, 50, 76
hull construction, 9, 13, 14, 48
mixing and working with, 63–64
pumps and measuring devices for, 58–59
repairs made with, 14, 48, 49–53, 76, 78, 89–90
rot prevention, 45
safety precautions, 49–50, 51, 63, 64
sanding, 160, 161–62
sunlight and, 45
Evercoat Marine, 19–20

F

fairing
benefits and importance of, 107, 108, 115
centerboards, 79–80, 81
hulls, 79, 91, 107–11, 165
keels, 79–80, 81, 112, 114–15, 148, 149, 165
rudders, 79–80, 81, 115, 149
fairing compounds, 76, 78, 79, 80, 81, 107, 110, 113, 132, 165
fiberglass
cutting, 47, 56, 58
ease of repairing fiberglass hulls, 85
grinding, 85, 87, 89, 90, 128
printing through, 9, 69
resin and, 1, 9, 46, 48
resin-to-reinforcement ratio, 10, 17, 48, 65, 66, 139
safety precautions, 47, 85
types for repairs, 48
weight calculations, 10, 89
wetting out and rolling, 64–65
fiberglass, types of
biaxial roving, 47–48, 89
chopped strand mat (CSM), 9–10, 11, 47, 86
cloth, 10–11, 48, 89
composite roving and CSM, 11, 47, 89
E glass, 12, 46–47
quadraxial roving, 47–48
S glass, 12, 13, 46–47
triaxial roving, 47–48
unidirectional roving, 11, 47–48
woven roving, 10, 11, 14, 47, 89
fillet joints, 20–21, 24, 98–99, 101
finishing resin, 48, 49
fire-retardant resin, 157
flat panels, 100, 102
Flex-Mold, 83–84, 176
floors, 20–21, 22, 101, 119–22
foam-cored hulls, 1, 17–18, 19–20, 93
foam-cored reinforcements, 21
frictional drag, 107
furniture, 23–25, 28, 44

G

gelcoat. *See also* blisters and osmosis
abraded, 74–75
chips, 41
cracks, 30–32, 34, 42, 68
crazed, 32, 43, 67, 78–79
deck construction, 25
deterioration of, 67–68
dings and scrapes, 32, 34–54, 75–78, 81
epoxy and, 9, 48, 50, 76
hull construction, 4, 5, 9, 67, 74–75
impact damage, 31–32, 42
nonskid surfaces, 46, 80, 83–84, 174–76
oxidized, 68, 71–72
pigment matching, 49, 63, 75, 77
polyester resin and, 9, 14, 48
polymer coatings, 69
repairing, 74–84
restoring, 68–74
thickness of, 67, 69, 74–75
vinylester resin and, 9, 14
gelcoat putty, 49, 76
gelcoat repair kit, 76
Gibco Flex-Mold Company, 83–84, 176
gloves, 47, 49, 53, 54, 56

Goetz Custom Boats, 99
graphite fiber, 12–13. *See also* carbon fiber
grinders, 59, 87
grinding fiberglass, 85, 87, 89, 90, 128
grounding damage, 29–30, 38–40, 45
    repairing, 134–37, 143–49

H

hand-laid laminate, 10, 14, 15, 35, 66, 85–86, 138, 155
hardware
    backing plates, 43, 97
    cored construction and installation of, 17–18, 26, 42–43, 94–97
hatches
    nonskid surfaces for covers, 82
    replacing, 27, 140–42
headliner (interior liner), 25, 26
heat lamps and heaters, 49, 59, 151, 154
Herman, Michael, 169
Hexcel core, 20, 93
holes
    backing materials, 89, 91–93
    cored hulls and decks, 93–94
    ease of repairing fiberglass hulls, 85
    fiberglass for, 86
    grounding damage repairs, 134–37, 143–49
    resin for repairing, 89–90
    single-skin laminate repairs, 87–93
    wet layup technique, 91
HotVac System, 151
hull construction
    autoclaving, 12–13, 15, 16, 17
    cored construction, 16–20
    ease of repairing fiberglass hulls, 85
    forming the hull, 6, 9–20
    hand-laid laminate, 10, 14, 15, 35, 66, 85–86
    hull-to-deck joints, 27–28
    interior layout changes and, 24–25, 28
    molds, building, 1–6, 7–8

prepregs, 14, 15
reinforcements, 2, 15, 20–22
resin-transfer molding (RTM), 15–16
single-skin laminate, 9–16
skin materials, 12–13
thickness of hull, 11
vacuum bagging, 12–13, 15, 16–17, 65–66, 85, 138–39, 155–56
hull damage. *See also* delamination
    crazing, 32, 43, 67, 78–79
    grounding, 29–30, 38–40, 45
    identifying, 29–30
    impact damage, 31–32, 33–34, 45
    infrared surveys and, 37
    scrapes, 32, 34–54, 75–78, 81
    signs of, 29–30, 45
    trailer damage, 32, 35
    transom core damage and rot, 30–31
hull friction, 107
hull liners, 1, 22–23, 24–25, 91–93

I

icebox, 104, 105
impeller installation, 29
infrared surveys, 35, 36–37
interior layout changes, 24–25, 28
interior liner (headliner), 25, 26
interior pan (hull liner), 1, 22–23, 24–25, 91–93
interior structural damage, 29, 30
Interlux boat-care products, 70, 71, 74, 158
Interlux Epiglass epoxy, 14, 50, 53, 63
Interlux paints
    barrier coats, 108, 153, 158
    bottom paint, 111
    nonskid paint, 80, 84, 174, 175
    primers, 78, 91, 132, 166, 172
    topcoat, 78, 91, 132, 170–73
Irvine, Mike, 143, 144, 146

J

J/24
    deck core replacement, 123–25

floors, 21, 119–22
gelcoat, 68
hatch replacement, 140–42
hull repairs, 90
paint and painting, 173–74, 176
Jamestown Boat Yard, 72, 134–37, 171
Jamestown Distributors, 19
Johnson, Bruce, 72

K

keel bolts, 121, 122
keels
    damage to, 29–30, 38–39, 143, 144
    ratios and measurements, 113–14
    repairing and fairing, 79–80, 81, 112, 114–15, 148, 149, 165
    sump filler, 119, 121, 122
Kevlar, 13, 46, 93
Klegecell, 19
Kwik Foam, 19

L

laminate
    carbon fiber, 12–13
    determining type of before starting repairs, 85–87
    hand-laid laminate, 10, 14, 15, 35, 66, 85–86, 138, 155
    repairing scrapes and gouges, 76, 78, 81
    single-skin laminate, 9–16, 86, 87–93, 134–37
    strength of different materials, 12
    voids in, 15, 17, 19–20, 36, 37, 66, 138, 155
laminating resins, 14, 48–49
Lewmar hatches, 140–42
lighting, 24, 25
limber holes, 100, 121
longboards, 62, 111, 162, 165

M

Mancini, Mo, 143, 144, 146
Martinez, Xavier, 171

Index

MAS Epoxies, 51, 56, 62, 64, 83, 158
masts, 15, 17
mast step, 38, 40
methyl ethyl ketone peroxide (MEKP), 14, 48, 62, 63
mixing sticks and cups, 53–54, 55
moisture
    dew point, 172, 173
    infrared surveys, 35, 36–37
    problems associated with, 35
    removing, 151, 154
    testing for, 35, 36, 150, 154
moisture meter, 35, 36, 150, 154
mold release wax, 4, 5, 6, 53, 102, 103
molds and plugs
    building, 1–6
    carving with five-axis router, 7–8
    complex molds, 106
    for repairs, 56, 102–6
    two-part molds, 4, 105–6
Mundy, Jan, 70

N

nonskid surfaces, 46, 80, 82–84, 174–76

O

oilcanning, 86
one-off boats, 2
osmosis. *See* blisters and osmosis
outboard installation, 31

P

paint and painting
    barrier coats, 108, 110, 111, 151, 158
    boottop, 173–74
    bottom paint, 79, 110–11
    checklist, 172
    choosing paint, 170–71
    compatibility between primers and topcoats, 78, 170
    consistent color, 168–69, 170
    cove strip, 174
    decks, 84, 174–75
    masking off, 165–66, 173, 174
    nonskid paint, 80, 174–76
    perfect finishes, 159
    polymer coatings and, 74
    primers, 78, 91, 165, 166, 167, 172
    repainting, 173
    roller and brush application, 91, 167–68, 169–70, 171–73
    safety precautions, 60, 61, 159
    spray application, 91, 168, 169, 171, 172, 173
    surface preparation, 160–65, 166–67, 172
    temperature and humidity and, 172, 173
    topcoat, 78, 91, 167–73
    types of paints, 132
peeling the hull, 40, 151, 153, 154, 157
Peel Ply release fabric, 17, 65, 138, 139
Penske board, 19
Pettit paints and barrier coats, 80, 158, 175
plastic sheeting, 53, 56, 85, 86, 165
plugs. *See* molds and plugs
polishing machines, 73–74
polyester putty, 49, 76
polyester resin
    additives and thickeners, 64
    blisters and osmosis, 9, 14, 40, 48
    filling and fairing compounds, 107, 110
    gelcoat and, 9, 14, 48
    hull construction, 13, 14, 48
    limitations of, 9
    mixing and working with, 62–63, 64
    pumps and measuring devices for, 58–59
    repairs made with, 48–49, 76, 89–90
    rot and, 19
    safety precautions, 62–63
    sanding, 160, 161–62
    types of, 48–49
polyethylene sheeting, 53, 56, 85, 86, 165
polymer coatings, 69, 74
prepregs, 14, 15
Prep-Sol, 76, 100, 167, 173
ProBalsa core, 19
projects. *See* repairs and projects
protective and safety gear, 47, 49, 53, 54, 56, 60, 61, 70, 72, 85, 128, 159

R

Rapid Cure epoxy, 51
repairs and projects. *See also* structural repairs
    guideline for organizing, 117
    skills for, 116–17
    time estimates, 116, 117
repairs and projects, instructions for
    deck core replacement, 123–25
    engine-well guard, 117–19
    floors, replacing, 119–22
    grounding damage repairs, 134–37, 143–49
    hatch replacement, 140–42
    transom, repairing, 125–33
    wakeboard repair, 138–39
resin. *See also* epoxy; polyester resin; vinylester resin
    fiberglass and, 1, 9, 46
    repairs made with, 46, 48–53
    resin-to-reinforcement ratio, 10, 17, 48, 65, 66, 139
resin pumps and measuring devices, 58–59
resin-transfer molding (RTM), 15–16
respirators and dust masks, 54, 56, 60, 61, 70, 159
rollers and roller tray, 54, 57, 58, 170
rot
    balsa core, 19, 25, 29
    conditions for, 45
    floors, replacing, 119–22
    hardware installation and, 17
    parts affected by, 45
    prevention of, 45
    transoms, repairing, 125–33
routers, 7–8
rubbing (buffing) compound, 67, 68, 70–72, 74, 75
rudders
    construction of, 43
    damage to, 43–44, 144
    repairing and fairing, 79–80, 81, 115, 149

S

safety precautions
- epoxy, 49–50, 51, 63, 64
- fiberglass, 47, 85
- paint and painting, 60, 61, 159
- polyester resin, 62–63
- protective and safety gear, 47, 49, 53, 54, 56, 60, 61, 70, 72, 85, 128, 159

sanders, 111, 162–64
sanding, 160–65
sandpaper, 62, 160–61, 163
scarfs, 87, 92, 93, 94, 128, 135
scrapes and dings, 32, 34–54, 75–78, 81
SCRIMP (Seemann Composites Resin Infusion Molding Process), 15
Seacast foam, 126, 132–33
Seacraft transom repair, 125–32, 177
Seapower Products, 71
Seemann Composites Resin Infusion Molding Process (SCRIMP), 15
S glass, 12, 13, 46–47
sheds and shelters, 177–79
Shurhold buffing compound, 71
silicone sealer, 27
single-skin laminate
- hull construction, 9–16, 86
- laminate schedule, 89
- repairing, 87–93, 134–37
- wet layup technique, 91

skin materials, 12–13
SMI Group, 25
soaps, 69
SP (Gruit), 19
splash for missing parts, 102–4
spreaders, 54
stain removers, 69–71
stanchion bases, 41, 42–43
Star brite boat-care products, 69, 71, 74
stiffeners, 100, 102, 103
stringers, 20–22
structural repairs
- activities before starting, 85–87
- bulkheads, 97–100, 101
- cored laminate, 93–94
- missing parts, 102–6
- single-skin laminate, 87–93
- strength of, 86
- wet layup technique, 91

surveys, 35, 36–37, 150
syringes, 55
System Three epoxy and barrier coats, 51, 53, 55, 58, 158

T

tabbing, 20–21, 24, 98, 99, 101
tack-free additive (TFA), 49
teak decks, 41
thermosetting resins, 14, 48, 97
3M boat-care products, 69, 70–71, 72–73
3M nonskid materials, 82, 176
through-hulls, 17–18
tools
- disposable tools, 53–56
- nondisposable tools, 56–60
- professional tools, 60–62

trailer damage, 32, 35
trampolining, 86
transoms
- core damage and rot, 30–31
- engine-well guard, 117–19
- outboard installation, 31
- repairing, 125–33

Treadmaster M, 176
Tyvek bunny suit, 53, 72, 128, 159

U

Uniflite Corporation, 157

V

vacuum bagging, 12–13, 15, 16–17, 65–66, 85, 138–39, 149, 155–56
Valiant sailboats, 157
Valiant Yachts, 157
varnish, 45
vermiculite, 119
Vertglas, 69, 72, 74
vinegar, 49–50, 56
vinylester resin
- benefits and limitations of, 48
- blisters and osmosis, 9, 14, 48, 68
- gelcoat and, 9, 14
- hull construction, 9, 13, 14

voids, 15, 17, 19–20, 36, 37, 66, 138, 155
volatile organic carbons (VOCs), 9, 15, 16

W

wakeboard repair, 138–39
wax, boat, 71, 73–74
wax, mold release, 4, 5, 6, 53, 102, 103
WEST System epoxy and barrier coats, 14, 50, 52, 55, 63, 108, 158
WEST System resin measuring scale, 58
WEST System vacuum bagging kit, 66, 138–39
wet layup technique, 91
window replacement, 27
wiring, 24, 25, 26